Bloom's Modern Critical Views

African-American
 Poets: Volume I
African-American
 Poets: Volume II
Aldous Huxley
Alfred, Lord Tennyson
Alice Munro
Alice Walker
American Women
 Poets: 1650–1950
Amy Tan
Anton Chekhov
Arthur Miller
Asian-American
 Writers
August Wilson
The Bible
The Brontës
Carson McCullers
Charles Dickens
Christopher Marlowe
Contemporary Poets
Cormac McCarthy
C.S. Lewis
Dante Aligheri
David Mamet
Derek Walcott
Don DeLillo
Doris Lessing
Edgar Allan Poe
Émile Zola
Emily Dickinson
Ernest Hemingway
Eudora Welty
Eugene O'Neill
F. Scott Fitzgerald
Flannery O'Connor
Franz Kafka
Gabriel García
 Márquez

Geoffrey Chaucer
George Orwell
G.K. Chesterton
Gwendolyn Brooks
Hans Christian
 Andersen
Henry David Thoreau
Herman Melville
Hermann Hesse
H.G. Wells
Hispanic-American
 Writers
Homer
Honoré de Balzac
Jamaica Kincaid
James Joyce
Jane Austen
Jay Wright
J.D. Salinger
Jean-Paul Sartre
John Irving
John Keats
John Milton
John Steinbeck
José Saramago
J.R.R. Tolkien
Julio Cortázar
Kate Chopin
Kurt Vonnegut
Langston Hughes
Leo Tolstoy
Marcel Proust
Margaret Atwood
Mark Twain
Mary Wollstonecraft
 Shelley
Maya Angelou
Miguel de Cervantes
Milan Kundera
Nathaniel Hawthorne

Norman Mailer
Octavio Paz
Paul Auster
Philip Roth
Ralph Ellison
Ralph Waldo
 Emerson
Ray Bradbury
Richard Wright
Robert Browning
Robert Frost
Robert Hayden
Robert Louis
 Stevenson
Salman Rushdie
Stephen Crane
Stephen King
Sylvia Plath
Tennessee Williams
Thomas Hardy
Thomas Pynchon
Tom Wolfe
Toni Morrison
Tony Kushner
Truman Capote
Walt Whitman
W.E.B. Du Bois
William Blake
William Faulkner
William Gaddis
William Shakespeare:
 Comedies
William Shakespeare:
 Histories
William Shakespeare:
 Tragedies
William Wordsworth
Zora Neale Hurston

Bloom's Modern Critical Views

WILLIAM SHAKESPEARE:
HISTORIES
New Edition

Edited and with an introduction by
Harold Bloom
Sterling Professor of the Humanities
Yale University

BLOOM'S
LITERARY CRITICISM
An imprint of Infobase Publishing

Bloom's Modern Critical Views:
William Shakespeare: Histories—New Edition

Copyright © 2009 by Infobase Publishing
Introduction © 2009 by Harold Bloom

Bloom's Literary Criticism
An imprint of Infobase Publishing
132 West 31st Street
New York NY 10001

Library of Congress Cataloging-in-Publication Data
  William Shakespeare. Histories / edited and with an introduction by Harold Bloom. — New ed.
    p. cm. — (Bloom's modern critical views)
  Includes bibliographical references and index.
  ISBN 978-1-60413-638-8 (hardcover)
  1. Shakespeare, William, 1564–1616—Histories. 2. Historical drama, English—History and criticism. I. Bloom, Harold. II. Title. III. Series.
  PR2982.W478 2009
  822.3'3—dc22

                                        2009022859

Bloom's Literary Criticism books are available at special discounts when purchased in bulk quantities for businesses, associations, institutions, or sales promotions. Please call our Special Sales Department in New York at (212) 967-8800 or (800) 322-8755.

You can find Bloom's Literary Criticism on the World Wide Web at http://www.chelseahouse.com.

Contributing editor: Pamela Loos
Cover designed by Takeshi Takahashi

Printed in the United States of America
IBT IBT 10 9 8 7 6 5 4 3 2 1

This book is printed on acid-free paper.

All links and Web addresses were checked and verified to be correct at the time of publication. Because of the dynamic nature of the Web, some addresses and links may have changed since publication and may no longer be valid.

Contents

Editor's Note   vii

Introduction   1
    Harold Bloom

The Bolingbroke Plays (*Richard II, Henry IV*)   17
    Northrop Frye

Prophetic Behavior in Shakespeare's Histories   43
    Kirby Farrell

Structural Pattern in Shakespeare's Histories   67
    Sherman Hawkins

King John   93
    Maurice Charney

Sitting upon the Ground (*Richard II*, IV, i)   103
    Harry Levin

The Death of John Talbot   123
    Alexander Leggatt

Food for Words: Hotspur and the Discourse of Honor   141
    Harry Berger Jr.

The Major Histories   181
    A.D. Nuttall

Chronology   215

Contributors   217

Bibliography   219

Acknowledgments   223

Index   225

Editor's Note

My introduction centers on Sir John Falstaff, whose greatness and instant popularity constituted Shakespeare's breakthrough into complete independence of Christopher Marlowe.

After the Falstaffiad (*Henry IV, Parts 1* and *2*), I go on to *Richard III* and *Richard II*, the first still Marlovian but the second merely playing with Marlowe.

Northrop Frye, somewhat deficient in his regard for the sublime Falstaff, provides a doubtless more measured account than I give, due to my love for the greatest wit in all literature.

Proleptic design in the Histories is subtly expounded by Kirby Farrell, while Sherman Hawkins extends his Spenserian numerology to Shakespeare.

King John, dominated by the marvelous Falconbridge, is studied by Maurice Charney, after which the mandarin Harry Levin sits us down on the ground to hear the sad story of the death of Richard II.

Heroic warrior Talbot of the *Henry VI* plays is admired by Alexander Leggatt, while the always brilliant Harry Berger Jr. accords dazzling justice to the flamboyant Hotspur.

This volume concludes strongly with the late A.D. Nuttall, who does well by *Henry V*, a play toward which my Falstaffian symphathies cause me to entertain considerable ironic ambivalence, which however I partly assign to Shakespeare himself.

HAROLD BLOOM

Introduction

Shakespeare's greatest history play is the ten-act drama constituted by *King Henry IV, Parts 1* and *2*. Judged as a single work, this vast Falstaffiad is one of Shakespeare's major achievements, akin to *Antony and Cleopatra, As You Like It, Twelfth Night, Measure for Measure*, and *The Winter's Tale*. The four high tragedies—*Hamlet, Othello, King Lear*, and *Macbeth*—stand a little apart, in their own cosmos, as does *The Tempest*. The Falstaffiad is at the center of Shakespeare's work, and its superb protagonist, Sir John Falstaff, rivals Shakespeare's other triumphs in the invention of the human: Hamlet, Rosalind, Iago, Lear, Macbeth, Cleopatra. Criticism, particularly in our century, is frequently both inaccurate and unkind about Falstaff. That is because the brilliant and uncanny wit outfaces and outrages his undertakers. He also buries them. Falstaff is so large a form of life and thought that all of us have trouble catching up with him. He confounds our expectations and calls our compromises into question.

Falstaff's vitality, his battle-cry being—"Give me life"—is the most crucial of his attributes, but his intelligence is endless and matches his exuberance. Nearly everything he says rewards much pondering, for he beholds reality and not the shams that mock it. Sir John long since has seen through the "honor" for which Hotspur and Prince Hal compete. Falstaff may be an outrageous Socrates but so was Socrates. Sir John's other affinities are with Cervantes's Sancho Panza and with Rabelais's Panurge and most closely with Chaucer's Wife of Bath. Heroic vitalists all, these abide as images of gusto in its highest form, allied to wisdom and to laughter.

1

Aligned against Falstaff are the state and time, and the state, in the guise of the newly crowned Henry V, will destroy him. Though legions of scholars have acclaimed this destruction, their sentiments are not Shakespeare's. Shakespeare carefully excluded Falstaff from *Henry V*, except for Mistress Quickly's poignant description of Sir John's deathbed scene. Can we imagine King Henry V eloquently saluting his "happy few" if Falstaff were among them, bottle of sack in his holster?

In his darker moments, Falstaff is haunted by the parable of Lazarus the leper and a purple-clad glutton who refuses him food and water (Luke 16: 19–26). This is a parable of rejection, first of Lazarus by the wealthy glutton, and then of the glutton by Abraham, who takes Lazarus into his bosom while refusing to aid the stingy rich man, who burns in hell. Falstaff's three allusions to this parable reveal his own fear of rejection by Hal, an apprehension that is realized when Falstaff kneels to the purple-clad newly crowned Henry V and is denounced and exiled. Shakespeare's answer comes in Mistress Quickly's declaration that the deceased Falstaff is "in Arthur's bosom," a clear displacement of Abraham's bosom.

A.C. Bradley, nearly a century ago, made the definitive comment on the sublime Falstaff:

> And, therefore, we praise him, we laud him, for he offends none but the virtuous, and denies that life is real or life is earnest, and delivers us from the apprehension of such nightmares, and lifts us into the atmosphere of perfect freedom.

Henry IV, Parts 1 and *2*

Falstaff is to the world of the histories what Shylock is to the comedies and Hamlet to the tragedies: *the* problematical representation. Falstaff, Shylock, Hamlet put to us the question: precisely how does Shakespearean representation differ from anything before it, and how has it overdetermined our expectations of representation ever since?

The fortunes of Falstaff in scholarship and criticism have been endlessly dismal, and I will not resume them here. I prefer Harold Goddard on Falstaff to any other commentator, and yet I am aware that Goddard appears to have sentimentalized and even idealized Falstaff. I would say better that than the endless litany absurdly patronizing Falstaff as Vice, Parasite, Fool, Braggart Soldier, Corrupt Glutton, Seducer of Youth, Cowardly Liar, and everything else that would not earn the greatest wit in all literature an honorary degree at Yale or a place on the board of the Ford Foundation.

Falstaff, I will venture, in Shakespeare rather than in Verdi, is precisely what Nietzsche tragically attempted yet failed to represent in his Zarathustra:

a person without a superego, or should I say, Socrates without the *daimon*. Perhaps even better, Falstaff is not the Sancho Panza of Cervantes, but the exemplary figure of Kafka's parable "The Truth about Sancho Panza." Kafka's Sancho Panza, a free man, has diverted his *daimon* from him by many nightly feedings of chivalric romances (it would be science fiction nowadays). Diverted from Sancho, his true object, the *daimon* becomes the harmless Don Quixote, whose mishaps prove edifying entertainment for the "philosophic" Sancho, who proceeds to follow his errant *daimon*, out of a sense of responsibility. Falstaff's "failure," if it can be termed that, is that he fell in love, not with his own *daimon* but with his bad son, Hal, who all too truly is Bolingbroke's son. The witty knight should have diverted his own *daimon* with Shakespearean comedies and philosophically have followed the *daimon* off to the forest of Arden.

Falstaff is neither good enough nor bad enough to flourish in the world of the histories. But then he is necessarily beyond, not only good and evil but cause and effect as well. A greater monist than the young Milton, Falstaff plays at dualism partly in order to mock all dualisms, whether Christian, Platonic, or even the Freudian dualism that he both anticipates and in some sense refutes.

Falstaff provoked the best of all critics, Dr. Johnson, into the judgment that "he has nothing in him that can be esteemed." George Bernard Shaw, perhaps out of envy, called Falstaff "a besotted and disgusting old wretch." Yet Falstaff's sole rival in Shakespeare is Hamlet; no one else, as Oscar Wilde noted, has so comprehensive a consciousness. Representation itself changed permanently because of Hamlet and Falstaff. I begin with my personal favorite among all of Falstaff's remarks, if only because I plagiarize it daily:

> O, thou has damnable iteration, and art indeed able to corrupt a saint. Thou hast done much harm upon me, Hal, God forgive thee for it! Before I knew thee, Hal, I knew nothing, and now am I, if a man should speak truly, little better than one of the wicked.

W.H. Auden, whose Falstaff essentially was Verdi's, believed the knight to be "a comic symbol for the supernatural order of charity" and thus a displacement of Christ into the world of wit. The charm of this reading, though considerable, neglects Falstaff's grandest quality, his immanence. He is as immanent a representation as Hamlet is transcendent. Better than any formulation of Freud's, Falstaff perpetually shows us that the ego indeed is always a bodily ego. And the bodily ego is always vulnerable, and Hal indeed has done much harm upon it and will do far worse and will need forgiveness, though no sensitive audience ever will forgive him. Falstaff, like Hamlet, and like Lear's Fool, does speak truly, and Falstaff remains, despite Hal, rather better than one of the wicked or the good.

For what is supreme immanence in what might be called the order of representation? This is another way of asking: Is not Falstaff, like Hamlet, so original a representation that he originates much of what we know or expect about representation? We cannot see how original Falstaff is because Falstaff *contains* us; we do not contain him. And though we love Falstaff, he does not need our love any more than Hamlet does. His sorrow is that he loves Hal rather more than Hamlet loves Ophelia or even Gertrude. The Hamlet of act 5 is past loving anyone, but that is a gift (if it is a gift) resulting from transcendence. If you dwell wholly in this world, and if you are, as Falstaff is, a *pervasive* entity, or as Freud would say, "a strong egoism," then you must begin to love, as Freud also says, in order that you may not fall ill. But what if your strong egoism is not afflicted by any ego-ideal, what if you are never watched or watched over by what is above the ego? Falstaff is *not* subject to a power that watches, discovers, and criticizes all his intentions. Falstaff, except for his single and misplaced love, is free, is freedom itself, because he seems free of the superego.

Why does Falstaff (and not his parody in *The Merry Wives of Windsor*) pervade histories rather than comedies? To begin is to be free, and you cannot begin freshly in comedy any more than you can in tragedy. Both genres are family romances, at least in Shakespeare. History in Shakespeare is hardly the genre of freedom for kings and nobles, but it is for Falstaff. How and why? Falstaff is of course his own mother and his own father, begotten out of wit by caprice. Ideally he wants nothing except the audience, which he always has; who could watch anyone else on stage when Ralph Richardson was playing Falstaff? Not so ideally, he evidently wants the love of a son, and invests in Hal, the impossible object. But primarily he has what he must have, the audience's fascination with the ultimate image of freedom. His precursor in Shakespeare is not Puck or Bottom, but Faulconbridge the Bastard in *The Life and Death of King John.* Each has a way of providing a daemonic chorus that renders silly all royal and noble squabbles and intrigues. The Bastard in *John*, forthright like his father Richard the Lion Heart, is not a wicked wit, but his truth telling brutally prophesies Falstaff's function.

There are very nearly as many Falstaffs as there are critics, which probably is as it should be. These proliferating Falstaffs tend either to be degraded or idealized, again perhaps inevitably. One of the most ambiguous Falstaffs was created by the late Sir William Empson: "He is the scandalous upper-class man whose behavior embarrasses his class and thereby pleases the lower class in the audience, as an 'exposure.'" To Empson, Falstaff also was both nationalist and Machiavel, "and he had a dangerous amount of power." Empson shared the hint of Wyndham Lewis that Falstaff was homosexual and so presumably lusted (doubtless in vain) after Hal. To complete this portrait, Empson added that Falstaff, being both an aristocrat and a mob leader, was "a familiar dangerous type," a sort of Alcibiades, one presumes.

Confronted by so ambiguous a Falstaff, I return to the sublime knight's rhetoric, which I read very differently, since Falstaff's power seems to me not at all a matter of class, sexuality, politics, or nationalism. Power it is: sublime pathos, *potentia*, the drive for life, more life, at every and any cost. I will propose that Falstaff is neither a noble synecdoche nor a grand hyperbole but rather a metalepsis or far-fetcher, to use Puttenham's term. To exist without a super ego is to be a solar trajectory, an ever-early brightness, which Nietzsche's Zarathustra, in his bathos, failed to be. "Try to live as though it were morning," Nietzsche advises. Falstaff does not need the advice, as we discover when we first encounter him:

> FALSTAFF: Now, Hal, what time of day is it, lad?
> PRINCE: Thou art so fat-witted with drinking of old sack, and unbuttoning thee after supper, and sleeping upon benches after noon, that thou hast forgotten to demand that truly which thou wouldst truly know. What a devil hast thou to do with the time of the day? unless hours were cups of sack, and minutes capons, and clocks the tongues of bawds, and dials the signs of leaping-houses, and the blessed sun himself a fair hot wench in flame-color'd taffata; I see no reason why thou shouldst be so superfluous to demand the time of the day.

I take it that wit here remains with Falstaff, who is not only witty in himself but the cause of wit in his ephebe, Prince Hal, who mocks his teacher but in the teacher's own exuberant manner and mode. Perhaps there is a double meaning when Falstaff opens his reply with: "Indeed, you come near me now, Hal," since near is as close as the Prince is capable of, when he imitates the master. Master of what? is the crucial question, generally answered so badly. To take up the stance of most Shakespeare scholars is to associate Falstaff with "such inordinate and low desires, / Such poor, such bare, such lewd, such mean attempts, / Such barren pleasures, rude society." I quote King Henry the Fourth, aggrieved usurper, whose description of Falstaff's aura is hardly recognizable to the audience. We recognize rather: "Counterfeit? I lie, I am no counterfeit. To die is to be a counterfeit, for he is but the counterfeit of a man who hath not the life of a man; but to counterfeit dying, when a man thereby liveth, is to be no counterfeit, but the true and perfect image of life indeed." As Falstaff rightly says, he has saved his life by counterfeiting death, and presumably the moralizing critics would be delighted had the unrespectable knight been butchered by Douglas, "that hot termagant Scot."

The true and perfect image of life, Falstaff, confirms his truth and per-
fection by counterfeiting dying and so evading death. Though he is given
to parodying Puritan preachers, Falstaff has an authentic obsession with the
dreadful parable of the rich man and Lazarus in Luke 16:19ff. A certain
rich man, a purple-clad glutton, is contrasted with the beggar Lazarus, who
desired "to be fed with the crumbs which fell from the rich man's table; moreover the dogs came and licked his sores." Both glutton and beggar die, but
Lazarus is carried into Abraham's bosom, and the purple glutton into hell,
from which he cries vainly for Lazarus to come and cool his tongue. Falstaff
stares at Bardolph, his Knight of the Burning Lamp, and affirms, "I never see
thy face but I think upon hell-fire and Dives that liv'd in purple; for there he
is in his robes, burning, burning." Confronting his hundred and fifty tattered
prodigals, as he marches them off to be food for powder, Falstaff calls them
"slaves as ragged as Lazarus in the painted cloth, where the glutton's dogs
lick'd his sores." In *Henry IV, Part 2*, Falstaff 's first speech again returns to
this fearful text, as he cries out against one who denies him credit: "Let him
be damn'd like the glutton! Pray God his tongue be hotter!" Despite the ironies abounding in Falstaff the glutton invoking Dives, Shakespeare reverses
the New Testament, and Falstaff ends, like Lazarus, in Abraham's bosom,
according to the convincing testimony of Mistress Quickly in *Henry V*, where
Arthur Britishly replaces Abraham:

> BARDOLPH: Would I were with him, wheresome'er he is, either in
> heaven or in hell!
> HOSTESS: Nay sure, he's not in hell; he's in Arthur's bosom, if ever
> man went to Arthur's bosom. 'A made a finer end, and went away
> and it had been any christom child.

In dying, Falstaff is a newly baptized child, innocent of all stain. The
pattern of allusions to Luke suggests a crossing over, with the rejected Falstaff a poor Lazarus on his knees in front of Dives wearing the royal purple
of Henry V. To a moralizing critic this is outrageous, but Shakespeare does
stranger tricks with biblical texts. Juxtapose the two moments:

> FALSTAFF: My King, my Jove! I speak to thee, my heart!
> KING: I know thee not, old man, fall to thy prayers.
> How ill white hairs become a fool and jester!
> I have long dreamt of such a kind of man,
> So surfeit-swell'd, so old, and so profane;
> But being awak'd, I do despise my dream.

And here is Abraham, refusing to let Lazarus come to comfort the "clothed in purple" Dives:

And beside all this, between us and you there is a great gulf fixed: so that they which would pass from hence to you cannot; neither can they pass to us, that would come from thence.

Wherever Henry V is, he is not in Arthur's bosom, with the rejected Falstaff.

* * *

I suggest that Shakespearean representation in the histories indeed demands our understanding of what Shakespeare did to history, in contrast to what his contemporaries did. Standard scholarly views of literary history, and all Marxist reductions of literature and history alike, have the curious allied trait of working very well for, say, Thomas Dekker but being absurdly irrelevant for Shakespeare. Falstaff and the Tudor theory of kingship? Falstaff and surplus value? I would prefer Falstaff and Nietzsche's vision of the use and abuse of history for life, if it were not that Falstaff triumphs precisely where the Overman fails. One can read Freud on our discomfort in culture backwards and get somewhere close to Falstaff, but the problem again is that Falstaff triumphs precisely where Freud denies that triumph is possible. With Falstaff as with Hamlet (and, perhaps, with Cleopatra) Shakespearean representation is so self-begotten and so influential that we can apprehend it only by seeing that it originates us. We cannot judge a mode of representation that has overdetermined our ideas of representation. Like only a few other authors—the Yahwist, Chaucer, Cervantes, Tolstoy—Shakespeare calls recent critiques of literary representation severely into doubt. Jacob, the Pardoner, Sancho Panza, Hadji Murad: it seems absurd to call them figures of rhetoric, let alone to see Falstaff, Hamlet, Shylock, and Cleopatra as tropes of ethos and/or of pathos. Falstaff is not language but diction, the product of Shakespeare's will over language, a will that changes characters through and by what they say. Most simply, Falstaff is not how meaning is renewed but rather how meaning gets started.

Falstaff is so profoundly original a representation because most truly he represents the essence of invention, which is the essence of poetry. He is a perpetual catastrophe, a continuous transference, a universal family romance. If Hamlet is beyond us and beyond our need of him, so that we require our introjection of Horatio so as to identify ourselves with Horatio's love for Hamlet, then Falstaff, too, is beyond us. But in the Falstaffian beyonding, as it were, in what I think we must call the Falstaffian sublimity, we are never permitted by Shakespeare to identify ourselves with the Prince's ambivalent affection for Falstaff. Future monarchs have no friends, only followers, and Falstaff, the man without a superego, is no one's follower. Freud never speculated as to what a person without a superego would be like, perhaps because that had been the dangerous prophecy of Nietzsche's Zarathustra. Is there not some sense in which Falstaff's whole being implicitly says to us, "The wisest among you is also merely a conflict and a hybrid between plant and phantom. But do I bid you become phantoms or plants?" Historical critics who call Falstaff a phantom, and moral critics who judge Falstaff to be a plant, can be left to be answered by Sir John himself. Even in his debased form, in *The Merry Wives of Windsor*, he crushes them thus:

> Have I liv'd to stand at the taunt of one that makes fritters of English? This is enough to be the decay of lust and late-walking through the realm.

But most of all Falstaff is a reproach to all critics who seek to demystify mimesis, whether by Marxist or deconstructionist dialectics. Like Hamlet, Falstaff is a supermimesis and so compels us to see aspects of reality we otherwise could never apprehend. Marx would teach us what he calls "the appropriation of human reality" and so the appropriation also of human suffering. Nietzsche and his deconstructionist descendants would teach us the necessary irony of failure in every attempt to represent human reality. Falstaff, being more of an original, teaches us himself. "No, that's certain, I am not a double man; but if I be not Jack Falstaff, then am I a Jack." A double man is either a phantom or two men, and a man who is two men might as well be a plant. Sir John is Jack Falstaff; it is the Prince who is a Jack or rascal, and so are Falstaff's moralizing critics. We are in no position then to judge Falstaff or to assess him as a representation of reality. Hamlet is too dispassionate even to want to contain us. Falstaff is passionate and challenges us not to bore him, if he is to deign to represent us.

Richard III

Why, I, in this weak piping time of peace,
Have no delight to pass away the time,
Unless to see my shadow in the sun
And descant on mine own deformity.
And therefore, since I cannot prove a lover
To entertain these fair well-spoken days,
I am determined to prove a villain

And hate the idle pleasures of these days.
  (1.1.24–31)

The opening ferocity of Richard, still duke of Gloucester, in *The Tragedy of Richard the Third* is hardly more than a fresh starting point for the development of the Elizabethan and Jacobean hero-villain after Marlowe, and yet it seems to transform Tamburlaine and Barabas utterly. Richard's peculiarly self-conscious pleasure in his own audacity is crossed by the sense of what it means to see one's own deformed shadow in the sun. We are closer already not only to Edmund and Iago than to Barabas but especially closer to Webster's Lodovico who so sublimely says: "I limn'd this nightpiece and it was my best." Except for Iago, nothing seems farther advanced in this desperate mode than Webster's Bosola:

O direful misprision!
I will not imitate things glorious
No more than base: I'll be mine own example.—
On, on, and look thou represent, for silence,
The thing thou bear'st.
  (5.4.87–91)

Iago is beyond even this denial of representation, because he does will silence:

Demand me nothing; what you know, you know:
From this time forth I never will speak word.
  (5.2.303–4)

Iago is no hero-villain, and no shift of perspective will make him into one. Pragmatically, the authentic hero-villain in Shakespeare might be judged to be Hamlet, but no audience would agree. Macbeth could justify the description, except that the cosmos of his drama is too estranged from any normative representation for the term *hero-villain* to have its oxymoronic coherence. Richard and Edmund would appear to be the models, beyond Marlowe, that could have inspired Webster and his fellows, but Edmund is too uncanny and superb a representation to provoke emulation. That returns us to Richard:

Was ever woman in this humor woo'd?
Was ever woman in this humor won?
I'll have her, but I will not keep her long.

What? I, that kill'd her husband and his father,
To take her in her heart's extremest hate,
With curses in her mouth, tears in her eyes,
The bleeding witness of my hatred by,
Having God, her conscience, and these bars against me,
And I no friends to back my suit [at all]
But the plain devil and dissembling looks?
And yet to win her! All the world to nothing!
Hah!
Hath she forgot already that brave prince,
Edward, her lord, whom I, some three months since,
Stabb'd in my angry mood at Tewksbury?
A sweeter and a lovelier gentleman,
Fram'd in the prodigality of nature—
Young, valiant, wise, and (no doubt) right royal—
The spacious world cannot again afford.
And will she yet abase her eyes on me,
That cropp'd the golden prime of this sweet prince
And made her widow to a woeful bed?
On me, whose all not equals Edward's moi'ty?
On me, that halts and am misshapen thus?
My dukedom to a beggarly denier,
I do mistake my person all this while!
Upon my life, she finds (although I cannot)
Myself to be a marv'llous proper man.
I'll be at charges for a looking-glass,
And entertain a score or two of tailors
To study fashions to adorn my body:
Since I am crept in favor with myself,
I will maintain it with some little cost.
But first I'll turn yon fellow in his grave,
And then return lamenting to my love.
Shine out, fair sun, till I have bought a glass,
That I may see my shadow as I pass.
        (1.2.227–63)

Richard's only earlier delight was "to see my shadow in the sun / And descant on mine own deformity." His savage delight in the success of his own manipulative rhetoric now transforms his earlier trope into the exultant command: "Shine out, fair sun, till I have bought a glass, / That I may see my shadow as I pass." That transformation is the formula for interpreting the Jacobean hero-villain and his varied progeny: Milton's Satan, the Poet in Shelley's *Alastor*, Wordsworth's Oswald in *The Borderers*, Byron's Manfred and Cain, Browning's Childe Roland, Tennyson's Ulysses, Melville's Captain Ahab, Hawthorne's Chillingworth, down to Nathanael West's Shrike in *Miss Lonelyhearts*, who perhaps ends the tradition. The manipulative, highly self-conscious, obsessed hero-villain, whether Machiavellian plotter or hater, idealistic quester, ruined or not, moves himself from being the passive sufferer of his own moral and/or physical deformity to becoming a highly active melodramatist. Instead of standing in the light of nature to observe his own shadow and then have to take his own deformity as subject, he rather commands nature to throw its light upon his own glass of representation, so that his own shadow will be visible only for an instant as he passes on to the triumph of his will over others.

Richard II

There is a general agreement that Shakespeare represents Richard II as a kind of spoiled adolescent (in our terms, not Shakespeare's, since adolescence is a later invention sometimes ascribed to Rousseau). I suspect it might be better to term Shakespeare's Richard II an almost perfect solipsist. He is certainly, as everyone sees, an astonishing poet and a very bad king. The puzzle of the play, to me, is why Richard II is so sympathetic. I do not mean dramatic sympathy, such as we extend to Macbeth, overwhelmed as we are by his intense inwardness. Macbeth is anything but humanly sympathetic. Richard II is, despite his self-pity, his petulance, and a veritable hoard of other bad qualities.

Northrop Frye eloquently calls Richard's "overreacting imagination that sketches the whole course of a future development before anyone else has had time to figure out the present one" a weakness. Pragmatically this is a weakness because it makes Richard doom-eager, but it also renders him curiously attractive, particularly in contrast to the usurper, Bolingbroke. Harold Goddard, whose readings of Shakespeare never leave me, termed Richard "a man of unusual, though perverted, gifts," the principal perversions being sentimentalism and narcissism. Since Shakespeare's most original quality, in my judgment, was the representation of change through a character's self-overhearing, I would call Richard II the first major manifestation of that originality, and I suspect that is why he moves us to a very troubled sympathy. He is indeed a mimesis that compels more of reality to divulge itself than we could have seen without him.

A.D. Nuttall, in his remarkable *A New Mimesis*, the best study of Shakespeare's representation of reality, also emphasizes Richard II's proleptic stance toward his own catastrophe:

Richard II is plagued not so much by Bolingbroke as by his own capacity for conceptual anticipation: Bolingbroke does not force Richard from the throne, he moves into spaces successively vacated, with elaborately conscious art, by Richard.

A Freudian reading would find Richard an instance of "moral masochism," the collapse of the ego before the superego, sometimes related to strongly manifested bisexuality. But Freud seems to me a codification of Shakespeare, so that a Shakespearean reading of Freud is more enlightening and shows us that moral masochism is a theatrical tendency in which the ego dramatizes its doom-eagerness in order to achieve a priority in self-destructiveness, so as to anticipate the severity of the shadows of early and abandoned object-affections. Richard II assists at his own crucifixion because he desires a firstness in the exposure of a reality that he knows he cannot master. His perverse, final trace of the royal is to be strong only in his own overthrow.

Since Richard is the anointed king as well as much the most interesting personage in his drama, we are compelled to take his poetry very seriously indeed. There is no one else in Shakespeare's dramas up through 1595 who is anything like his imaginative equal. Had Shakespeare died in 1595, then Richard would have been his principal study in a dramatic consciousness, with Shylock, Falstaff, Rosalind, and Hamlet still to come in the five years subsequent. Until the advent of Hamlet, there is nothing like Richard's eloquence in Shakespearean verse. The edge of that eloquence first troubles us when Richard first despairs:

> No matter where—of comfort no man speak:
> Let's talk of graves, of worms, and epitaphs,
> Make dust our paper, and with rainy eyes
> Write sorrow on the bosom of the earth.
> Let's choose executors and talk of wills;
> And yet not so, for what can we bequeath
> Save our deposed bodies to the ground?
> Our lands, our lives, and all are Bullingbrook's,
> And nothing can we call our own but death,
> And that small model of the barren earth
> Which serves as paste and cover to our bones.
> For God's sake let us sit upon the ground
> And tell sad stories of the death of kings:
> How some have been depos'd, some slain in war,
> Some haunted by the ghosts they have deposed,
> Some poisoned by their wives, some sleeping kill'd,

All murthered—for within the hollow crown
That rounds the mortal temples of a king
Keeps Death his court, and there the antic sits,
Scoffing his state and grinning at his pomp,
Allowing him a breath, a little scene,
To monarchize, be fear'd, and kill with looks,
Infusing him with self and vain conceit,
As if this flesh which walls about our life
Were brass impregnable; and humor'd thus,
Comes at the last and with a little pin
Bores through his castle wall, and farewell king!
Cover your heads, and mock not flesh and blood
With solemn reverence, throw away respect,
Tradition, form, and ceremonious duty,
For you have but mistook me all this while.
I live with bread like you, feel want,
Taste grief, need friends: subjected thus,
How can you say to me I am a king?

It is an astonishing outburst, and Richard is crucially changed by it. We may not like him any the better for it, but he is highly conscious of the gap between his royal legitimacy and the luxuriance of his despair. His sense of "the king's two bodies" is more dialectical than that doctrine should allow. Shakespeare's sense of it is very clear; you can celebrate England and its soil if the rightful king is in power, however inadequate he is, but the celebration turns sour if a usurper, however capable, reigns. Richard is both his own victim, or rather the victim of his own imagination, and the sacrifice that becomes inevitable when the distance between the king as he should be and the actual legitimate monarch becomes too great. The shock of his own increasing consciousness of that distance is what changes Richard from a rapacious and blustering weakling into a self-parodying ritual victim. In this change, Richard does not acquire any human dignity, but he does begin to incarnate an extraordinary aesthetic dignity, both lyrical and dramatic. I think he becomes Shakespeare's first implicit experiment in representation, which is to risk identifying poetry and a national ritual sacrifice. The risk is not that Richard will fail to be persuasive, but that he will put poetry and its powers of representation into question.

His rhetoric of pleasurable despair is more than oxymoronic and enforces the lesson that Nietzsche learned from the poets; what makes representation memorable is pleasurable pain, rather than painful plea sure. I know of many readers and students who agree with Dr. Samuel Johnson in his judgment that *Richard II* "is not finished at last with the happy force of some other of his tragedies, nor can be said much to affect the passions, or enlarge the understanding." Yet even these recalcitrants thrill to the justly famous cadences of "For God's sake let us sit upon the ground / And tell sad stories of the death of kings." I think of Hart Crane's marvelous variation upon this in *Voyages* VI:

> Waiting, afire, what name, unspoke,
> I cannot claim: let thy waves rear
> More savage than the death of kings,
> Some splintered garland for the seer.

Crane shrewdly interprets Shakespeare as associating the death of kings and the splintering of poetic wreaths. Dr. Johnson, best of critics, was too unmoved by *Richard II* to achieve an accurate sense of the king's transformation:

> It seems to be the design of the poet to raise Richard to esteem in his fall, and consequently to interest the reader in his favour. He gives him only passive fortitude, the virtue of a confessor rather than of a king. In his prosperity we saw him imperious and oppressive, but in his distress he is wise, patient, and pious.

In his fall, Richard is not wise but eloquent, not patient but driving toward death, not pious but a kind of Christ parody. His wounded narcissism is augmented by the turning of his aggressivity against himself, and he overgoes Marlowe's Edward II as a rhetorician of self-pity:

> They shall be satisfied. I'll read enough,
> When I do see the very book indeed
> Where all my sins are writ, and that's myself.
> Give me that glass, and therein will I read.
> No deeper wrinkles yet? Hath sorrow struck
> So many blows upon this face of mine,
> And made no deeper wounds? O flatt'ring glass,
> Like to my followers in prosperity,
> Thou dost beguile me! Was this face the face
> That every day under his household roof
> Did keep ten thousand men? Was this the face
> That like the sun, did make beholders wink?
> Is this the face which fac'd so many follies,

That was at last out-fac'd by Bullingbrook?
A brittle glory shineth in this face,
As brittle as the glory is the face,
[*Dashes the glass against the ground.*]
For there it is, crack'd in an hundred shivers.
Mark, silent king, the moral of this sport,
How soon my sorrow hath destroy'd my face.

The outrageous parody of Marlowe's Faustus celebrating Helen is scarcely an accident in a play that subsumes Marlowe's *Edward II*. By associating Richard with two of Marlowe's antiheroes, Shakespeare suggests a likeness between his Richard and the self-destructive, narcissistic great poet who was Shakespeare's closest precursor. It may seem fantastic to suggest that the aura of Christopher Marlowe seeps into the rhetoric and psychology of Richard II, but this was a complex trick that Shakespeare was to play again. The fine symbolic gesture of dashing the mirror to pieces is wholly appropriate for the Marlovian protagonists and for Christopher Marlowe's own fate. Here as elsewhere Shakespeare is warning himself (and us) that Marlowe's way was not to be taken up.

Formally, *Richard II* is a tragedy, as Johnson took it to be, but it is the tragedy of a self-indulgent poet rather than the fall of a great king. The dashing of the glass is also the destruction of the legitimate royal countenance, yet when Richard is murdered we do not experience the shock of a monarch dying. Hamlet, who never ascends a throne, dies more than royally, but Richard's apparent courage when he kills the attendants is precisely what Goddard called it: "the reflex action of a man without self-control in the presence of death." There is aesthetic dignity in Richard's rhetoric of decline and fall but not in the actual way that he dies. It is the death of the poet who has not matured into the possession and representation of wisdom.

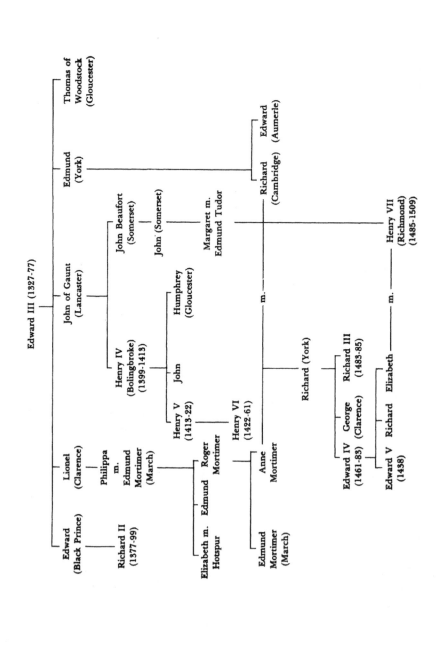

The Bolingbroke Plays
(Richard II, Henry IV)

I've mentioned the sequence of plays, four in all, that Shakespeare produced early in his career, on the period of the War of the Roses between Lancaster and York (so called because the emblem of Lancaster was a red rose and that of York a white one). With *Richard II* we begin another sequence of four plays, continuing through the two parts of *Henry IV* and ending with *Henry V*. The two central characters of the whole sequence are Bolingbroke, later Henry IV, who appears in the first three, and his son, later Henry V, who appears in the second, third and fourth. Although there are ominous forebodings of later events in *Richard II*, the audience would pick up the allusions, and we don't need to assume that Shakespeare began *Richard II* with the ambition of producing another "tetralogy" or group of four plays. The second part of *Henry IV* looks as though it were written mainly to meet a demand for more Falstaff. Still, each play does look back to its predecessors, so there is a unity to the sequence, whether planned in advance or not. And, as the Epilogue to *Henry V* tells us, the story ends at the point where the earlier sequence began.

I've provided a table of the intermarriages of English royalty between the reigns of Edward III and Henry VII, the period that covers the eight history plays. If you add Henry VIII, Henry VII's son, all the histories are covered that Shakespeare wrote except *King John*. In order to show the important

---

From *Northrop Frye on Shakespeare*, edited by Robert Sandler, pp. 51–81. © 1986 by Northrop Frye.

marriages, I haven't always listed sons and daughters in order of age, from the left. We can see that there were not many Romeo and Juliet situations: in the aristocracy at that time you simply married the man or woman who would do most for the fortunes of your family.

We start with Edward III's five sons. Shakespeare speaks of seven sons: the other two, both called William, died early on. Edward's eldest son and heir, Edward the "Black Prince," who would normally have succeeded his father, died the year before his father did, and the rules of succession brought his son, Richard, to the throne when he was still a boy. As some of his contemporaries remarked, "Woe to the land that's governed by a child!", and yet Richard lasted for twenty-two years, as long as Henry IV and Henry V together, Shakespeare's play covering only the last year or so of his reign.

The daughter of the second son, Lionel, married into the family of Mortimers; her daughter in turn married Hotspur of the Percy family. When Richard II's life ended in 1399, his heir, by the rules of succession, should have been the third Edmund Mortimer, Earl of March, who was also nominated, according to the conspirators in *Henry IV*, by Richard II as his successor. That was the issue that the revolt against Henry IV, which involved Hotspur so deeply, depended on. Bolingbroke was the son of John of Gaunt, Edward III's third son, and so not the next in line to the crown. However, he succeeded in establishing the Lancastrian house as the royal family, and was followed by his son and grandson. Apart from what the conspirators say, the fact that Bolingbroke seized the crown from Edmund as well as Richard is played down in this sequence, but there is a grimly eloquent speech from this Edmund, dying in prison, in *1 Henry VI* (although Shakespeare, if he wrote the scene, has confused him with someone else).

The Yorkist line came from the fourth son, Edmund, Duke of York, whose dramatic switch of loyalties from Richard to Bolingbroke, and the resulting conflict with his son Edward, called Aumerle, is the real narrative turning point of *Richard II*. The Yorkist line was not consolidated until the marriage of Aumerle's brother, Richard, to a descendant of Lionel produced Richard, Duke of York, who began the War of the Roses. The Yorkists got the upper hand in the war, and the Yorkist heir succeeded as Edward IV. Edward's two young sons, Edward (called Edward V because he had a theoretical reign of two months, although never crowned) and Richard, were supposed to have been murdered in the Tower by their wicked uncle, who became Richard III. Whether Richard III did this, or whether the story came from the Tudor propaganda machine, is still disputed: in any case Shakespeare bought it. Richard III, after a reign of about two years, was defeated and killed in battle by the Duke of Richmond, a descendant of John of Gaunt through a later wife. (She was not his wife when their son was born, and the line had to be legitimized by a special act of Richard II.) The Duke of Richmond then ascended the throne as Henry VII and founded what is called the House of Tudor, from the name of his father. Because of his descent from John of Gaunt, his victory technically restored the House of Lancaster, but one of the first things he did was to marry the Yorkist heiress Elizabeth, and the marriage put a symbolic end to the war by uniting the red and white roses. References to this could easily be turned into a compliment to Queen Elizabeth's complexion: a sonnet by the poet Fulke Greville begins:

Upon a throne I saw a virgin sit,
The red and white rose quartered in her face.

The fifth son, Thomas of Woodstock, Duke of Gloucester, had been murdered just before the action of *Richard II* begins, and the duel that Bolingbroke and Mowbray are about to fight in the opening scene of the play results from Mowbray's being implicated in the murder. There was another well-known contemporary play on this subject, *Thomas of Woodstock* (anonymous). This play is probably a source for Shakespeare, as it seems to be earlier, although it loads the case against Richard more heavily than Shakespeare does. According to this play Woodstock lost his life because he was too persistent in giving Richard II advice, and Richard was as much involved with his death as Mowbray.

Shakespeare's play seems to have made a deep impression on his public, and there were six Quartos of it, five of them within his lifetime. The first three omitted the deposing scene at the end of Act IV; the fourth, the first one that had it, appeared five years after Queen Elizabeth's death. The cutting out of the deposing scene could have happened anyway, because of the official nervousness about showing or printing such things, but there is evidence that the play was revived during the conspiracy of Essex against Elizabeth, perhaps for the very purpose the censors worried about, that of accustoming the public to the thought of deposing a monarch. The queen herself made the connection, and is reported, to have said: "I am Richard II, know ye not that? This tragedy was played forty times in open streets and houses." We may perhaps take "forty" to be (literally) Elizabethan rhetoric for "at least once," but even the commission of inquiry must have realized that there was no relation between the reckless and extravagant Richard and the cautious and stingy Elizabeth. It is perhaps a measure of her sense of insecurity, even at this period of her reign, that she thought there was.

As for Shakespeare's own dramatic vision, we have that curious garden scene (III.iv), for which scholars have never located a source, and which is two things that Shakespeare's writing practically never is, allegorical and sentimental. Considering the early date of the play (mid-1590s, probably), it is most unlikely that there was any contemporary allusion, but if the Essex group did revive the play for propaganda, this scene would have backfired on them, as it says that a capable ruler ought to cut ambitious nobles down to size before they get dangerous.

In *Richard II* Shakespeare had to make a marriage of convenience between the facts of medieval society, so far as they filtered down to him from his sources, and the Tudor mystique of royalty. That mystique regarded government by a central sovereign to be the form of government most in accord with both human nature and the will of God. It is true that no English sovereign except Henry VIII ever had the unlimited power that was very common on the Continent then and for many centuries thereafter. But still the reigning king or queen was the "Lord's anointed," his or her person was sacred, and rebellion against the sovereign was blasphemy and sacrilege as well as treason. The phrase "Lord's anointed" comes ultimately from the Bible. The Hebrew word Messiah, meaning "the anointed one," is applied in the Old Testament to a lawfully consecrated king, including even the rejected King Saul. The Greek equivalent of Messiah is Christ, and Jesus Christ was regarded as the king of the spiritual world, lawful kings in the physical world being his regents. If a lawful king happened to be a vicious tyrant, that was ultimately the fault of his subjects rather than of him, and they were being punished through him for their sins.

So when Richard II, during the abdication scene particularly, draws so many parallels between his trial and the trial of Christ, he is not comparing himself directly to Christ, but saying that the same situation, of the world rejecting the Lord's anointed, is being enacted once again. Of these echoes from the Passion in the Gospels, perhaps the most striking is that of Pilate's washing of his hands in a futile effort to make himself innocent of the death of Christ. Bolingbroke uses this image when he is making his first act as the next king, in ordering the execution of Bushy and Green; it is repeated in a contrasting context by Richard:

> Not all the water in the rough rude sea
> Can wash the balm off from an anointed king
>   (III.ii. 54–55)

and explicitly linked with Pilate by Richard in the abdication scene. The closing lines of the play are spoken by Bolingbroke, and express his purpose of going on a crusade "To wash this blood off from my guilty hand."

One awkward question might be raised in connection with this doctrine of the sacredness of the royal person. Suppose you're second in line from the throne, and murder the one who's first in line, do you thereby acquire all the sanctity of the next Lord's anointed? Well, in some circumstances you do. Shakespeare's King John becomes king when his nephew, Prince Arthur, is really in line for the succession, and although the prince technically commits suicide by jumping out of a window, John is certainly not innocent of his murder. John thereby becomes by default the lawful king, and when he dies his son Prince Henry becomes his legitimate heir. The strongest man in the country at the time is Falconbridge, bastard son of Richard I, who would have been king if he were legitimate, and could probably seize power quite easily in any case. But he holds back in favour of Prince Henry, and the play comes to a resounding patriotic conclusion to the effect that nothing can happen "If England to itself do rest but true," which in the context means partly keeping the line of succession intact. You may not find this particular issue personally very involving, but the general principle is that all ideologies sooner or later get to be circumvented by cynicism and defended by hysteria, and that principle will meet you everywhere you turn in a world driven crazy by ideologies, like ours.

A lawful king, as Shakespeare presents the situation, can be ruthless and unscrupulous and still remain a king, but if he's weak or incompetent he creates a power vacuum in society, because the order of nature and the will of God both demand a strong central ruler. So a terrible dilemma arises between a weak king de jure and a de facto power that's certain to grow up somewhere else. This is the central theme of *Richard II*. Richard was known to his contemporaries as "Richard the Redeless," i.e., a king who wouldn't take good advice, and Shakespeare shows him ignoring the advice of John of Gaunt and York. His twenty-year reign had a large backlog of mistakes and oppressions that Shakespeare doesn't need to exhibit in detail. In the scene where his uncle John of Gaunt is dying, John concentrates mainly on the worst of Richard's administrative sins: he has sold, for ready cash, the right of collecting taxes to individuals who are not restrained in their rapacity by the central authority. This forms part of what begins as a superbly patriotic speech: Shakespeare's reason for making the old ruffian John of Gaunt a wise and saintly prophet was doubtless that he was the ancestor of the House of Tudor. We also learn that Richard had a very undesirable lot of court favourites, spent far too much money on his own pleasures, and at the time of the play was involved in a war in Ireland that had brought his finances into a crisis. As we'll see later, getting into a foreign war is normally by far the best way of distracting a disaffected people, but Ireland roused no one's enthusiasm.

In the Middle Ages the effective power was held by the great baronial houses, which drew their income from their own land and tenants, many of them serfs; they could raise private armies, and in a crisis could barricade themselves into some very strong castles. In such a situation a medieval king had a theoretical supremacy, but not always an actual one, and, as his power base was often narrower than that of a landed noble, he was perpetually hard up for money. So if he were stuck with a sudden crisis, as Richard II is with the Irish war, he would often have to behave like a brigand in his own country and find pretexts for seizing and confiscating estates. What kind of law does a lawful king represent who resorts to illegal means of getting money? Or, who resorts to means that are technically legal, but violate a moral right?

Depends on what the moral right is. If it's abstract justice, protection of the poor, the representation of taxpayers in government, the right of the individual to a fair trial or the like, forget it. Shakespeare's *King John* never mentions Magna Carta, and *Richard II* never mentions the most important event of the reign, the Peasants' Revolt (twenty years earlier, but the social issues were still there). But if you take private property away from a noble house that's powerful enough to fight back, you're in deep trouble. The Duke of York tries to explain to Richard that his own position as king depends on hereditary succession, and that the same principle applies to a nobleman's right to inherit the property of his father. When Richard seizes John of Gaunt's property, he's doing something that will make every noble family in England say "Who next?" So John's son Henry Bolingbroke gets a good deal of support when he defies Richard's edict of banishment and returns to claim his own. We don't know much about what is going on in Bolingbroke's mind at any one time, and that's largely because he doesn't let himself become aware of the full implications of what he's doing. When he says at first that he merely wants his rights, it's possible that he means that. But this is the point at which Richard's spectacular incompetence as an administrator begins to operate. In the demoralized state of the nation a de facto power begins to gather around Bolingbroke, and he simply follows where it leads, neither a puppet of circumstances nor a deliberately unscrupulous usurper.

The rest of the play is the working out of this de jure and de facto dilemma. Some, like the Duke of York, come over to Henry's side and transfer the loyalty owed the Lord's anointed to him. So, when York's son Aumerle conspires in favour of Richard, York accuses his son of the same treason and sacrilege he'd previously accused Bolingbroke of before he changed sides. In the scene, where York insists on the king's prosecuting his son for treason and his duchess pleads for pardon, Bolingbroke is at his best, because he realizes the significance of what's happening. He's made the transition from being the de facto king to being the de jure king as well, and after that all he needs to do is get rid of Richard.

There are others, like the Bishop of Carlisle, who take the orthodox Tudor line, and denounce Bolingbroke for what he is doing to the Lord's anointed. As Shakespeare presents the issue, both sides are right. Henry becomes king, and makes a better king, as such things go, than Richard. When his nobles start quarrelling among themselves in a scene that reads almost like a reprise of his own challenge to Mowbray, he puts all the challenges "under gage," postpones all action, and squashes instantly what could become a dangerous brawl. But the way he came to the throne leaves a curse over the House of Lancaster that starts working out after Henry V's death twenty years or so later. Perhaps the only thing that would really resolve the situation is for Henry IV to go on the crusade he keeps talking about, because killing Moslems is so meritorious an act that it wipes out all previous sins, however grievous. John of Gaunt introduces the theme of crusade, as one of the things England was devoted to in its prime: he was doubtless thinking of the contrast between Richard and his namesake, Richard I, who spent so much of his ten-year reign fighting in the Third Crusade. But Henry's plans to go on a crusade are interrupted by revolts against him, and that again is inevitable: one revolt begets another. He carries on as best he can, and the comforting prophecy that he will die in Jerusalem turns out to apply to the name of a room in the palace of Westminster. It is a particularly savage irony, from Bolingbroke's point of view, that his enemy Mowbray, who, unlike him, was banished for life, should have died fighting in a crusade.

It should be clear by now that Shakespeare is not interested in what we would normally think of as history. What is really happening in history is extremely difficult to dramatize. Shakespeare is interested in chronicle, the personal actions and interactions of the people at the top of the social order. And the centre of his interest is in the kind of dramatic performance involved in being a leader in society, more particularly a king. All social relationships are in a sense theatrical ones: as soon as someone we know appears, we throw ourselves into the dramatic situation that our knowledge of him makes appropriate, and act it out accordingly. If we're alone, like Hamlet or like Richard in prison, we soliloquize; that is, we dramatize ourselves to ourselves. And what we all do, the prince makes history, or chronicle, by doing. In his vision of leadership, Shakespeare often comes curiously close to Machiavelli's *The Prince*. Curiously, because it is practically impossible that Shakespeare could have known Machiavelli's writings, and because Shakespeare's social vision is a deeply conservative one, whereas Machiavelli's was realistic enough to make the horrified idealists of his time give him a reputation in England and elsewhere as the voice of the devil himself. He comes in, for example, to emit cynical sentiments as the prologue speaker of Marlowe's *Jew of Malta*. But the theorist and the dramatist converge on two points: the dramatic nature of leadership and the fact that the qualities of the born leader are not moral qualities.

In ancient times stage actors usually wore masks, and the metaphor of the masked actor has given two words to the language. One is "hypocrite," which is Greek in origin and refers to the actor looking through the mask; the other is "person," which is Latin and refers to his speaking through it. Today we also use the word "persona" to mean the social aspect of an individual, the way he encounters other people. To some extent it's a misleading term, because it implies a real somebody underneath the masks, and, as the soliloquy reminds us, there's never anything under a persona except another persona. What there is is a consistency that limits the variety of social relations to a certain repertoire: that is, Hamlet always sounds like Hamlet, and Falstaff like Falstaff, whatever their roles at the moment. But for Shakespeare, as we'll see further later on, the question of identity is connected with social function and behaviour; in other words with the dramatic self, not with some hidden inner essence.

Well, "hypocrite" is a moral term and "person" is not: we accept that everyone has a personality, but it's supposed to be wrong for people to be hypocrites. Hypocrisy has been called the tribute that vice pays to virtue, but to know that you're saying one thing and thinking another requires a self-discipline that's practically a virtue in itself. Certainly it's often an essential virtue for a public figure. Situations change, and the good leader does what the new situation calls for, not what is consistent with what he did before. When Bolingbroke orders the execution of the king's favourites, one of his gravest charges against them is the way that they have separated the king from the queen, but an act or so later he himself is ordering a much more drastic separation of them. A successful leader doesn't get hung up on moral principles: the place for moral principles is in what we'd call now the pr job. The reputation of being virtuous or liberal or gracious is more important for the prince than the reality of these things, or rather, as in staging a play, the illusion is the reality.

Bolingbroke begins and ends the play, and the beginning and ending are in a most symmetrical relationship. At the beginning there is to be a public duel, or trial by battle, between Bolingbroke and Mowbray, over the murder of Thomas of Woodstock. Although Mowbray belongs to the house of Norfolk, not York, here is in embryo the theme of the eight historical plays: two noblemen quarrelling among themselves, with the king driven to stratagems to maintain his ascendancy. Perhaps a shrewder monarch would have left them to fight it out, on the ground that a duel to the death would get rid of at least one dangerous nobleman, but Richard stops the duel and banishes both, Mowbray for life, Bolingbroke for ten years, later reduced to six. The duellists talk so much that we suspect they're both lying, but it's Bolingbroke who drops the key image of civil war, Cain's murder of his brother Abel:

That he did plot the Duke of Gloucester's death . . .
Which blood, like sacrificing Abel's, cries
Even from the tongueless caverns of the earth.
    (I.i. 100–105)

At the end of the play, Bolingbroke, now Henry IV, hints that the death of the imprisoned Richard would be most convenient to him, and his follower Exton carries out the murder, and returns expecting a reward for faithful service. He forgot that leaders have to dissociate themselves immediately from such acts, whether they ordered them or not, and the play closes with Exton banished and Henry saying, "With Cain go wander thorough shades of night," echoing Mowbray's line about his banishment: "To dwell in solemn shades of endless night."

The play is thus enclosed by the image of the first human crime, Cain's murder of his brother, the archetype of all civil wars that follow. In the middle comes the scene of the queen and the gardener. The gardener is addressed as "old Adam's likeness," which, means that this is not a garden like Eden, where nothing was "unruly" and there were no weeds, but a garden made from the soil that Adam was forced to cultivate after his fall. Another phrase, of the queen's, "To make a second fall of cursed man," is repeated in a very curious context in *Henry V*. Every fall of every consecrated ruler repeats the original fall of man. Since then, history has proceeded in a series of cycles: Shakespeare's audience was thoroughly familiar with the image he uses constantly in his plays, the wheel of fortune, and would see the entire action of this play, from the murder of Woodstock to the murder of Richard, as a single turn of that wheel. Richard's image for this is that of two buckets, one going up and the other down, "The emptier ever dancing in the air," a most sardonic comment on the sort of person who succeeds in the way that Bolingbroke has succeeded. One corollary from this conception of a wheel of fortune is that in history it is only the past that can be idealized or thought of as heroic or peaceful. The *Henry VI* plays look back to the great and victorious Henry V; the play of *Henry V* looks back to the time of Richard as a time when there was no curse of usurpation on the royal house; and in this play we have John of Gaunt idealizing an earlier time, apparently the reign of Edward III, the reign that saw the Black Death and the beginning of the Hundred Years' War with France.

What keeps the wheel turning is the fact that people are conditioned to a certain reflex about it: whenever there's a change in personnel in the state, the assumption is normally that somehow or other an old age is going to be renewed. As the Duchess of York says to Aumerle after the king has pardoned him, "Come, my old son: I pray God make thee new." The joyful expectation on the part of the people that a new king will give a new life to the nation is put by York into its proper context:

> As in a theatre the eyes of men,
> After a well-graced actor leaves the stage,
> Are idly bent on him that enters next.
>   (V.ii. 23–25)

The illusion of movement in history corresponds to the processional aspect of a drama, the series of events that holds the interest. We have to listen on a deeper level, picking up such things as the Cain imagery, to realize that the beginning and the end are much the same point.

We feel this circularity of movement from the very beginning, the ordeal by battle that opens the play. Such ordeals, in medieval times, were surrounded by the most detailed ritual and punctilio. The combatants appeared before the king and formally stated their cases; the king would try to reconcile them; he would fail; he would then allow a trial by battle at a time and place duly stated. As the play goes on, the duel modulates to one between Bolingbroke and King Richard, but the same ritual formality continues, except that there is no longer any question of a fair fight. That is one reason why *Richard II* is written, contrary to Shakespeare's usual practice, entirely in verse: no contrasting force from outside the duelling ritual breaks in to interrupt the action.

Bolingbroke realizes that one of the qualities of the leader is inscrutability, giving the impression that there are great reserves of power of decision not being expressed. Of course many people look inscrutable who are merely stupid: Bolingbroke is not stupid, but he understands that the leaders who attract the greatest loyalty and confidence are those who can suggest in their manner that they have no need of it. Later, in *1 Henry IV*, Bolingbroke is telling his son Prince Hal that, in the dramatic show a leader puts on, the one essential is aloofness. He says that he appeared publicly very seldom, and always with calculation:

> By being seldom seen, I could not stir
> But like a comet I was wond'red at
>   (*1 Henry IV*, III.ii. 46–47)

and contrasts his own skilful performance with Prince Hal's wasting time with low company in Eastcheap, which he says is repeating the mistake of "the skipping king" Richard, who lost his crown mainly because he was seen too often and not with the right people. What Henry says may be true as a general political principle, though whether it was true of his own behaviour at the time or not is another question: certainly the communique from Richard's headquarters about Bolingbroke is very different from what Bolingbroke remembers of it:

> Off goes his bonnet to an oyster-wench;
> A brace of draymen bid God speed him well
> And had the tribute of his supple knee
>   (*Richard II*, I.iv. 31–33)

One aspect of this question of leadership has been studied in a fine piece of scholarship, a book called *The King's Two Bodies*, by E.H. Kantorowicz. Oversimplifying a bit, the king's two bodies, as distinguished in medieval and Renaissance theory, are his individual body as a man and his symbolic aspect as the body of his nation in an individual form. To extend this in the direction of *Richard II*, if the individual man is A, and the symbol of the nation as a single body is B, then the real king is B, the consecrated and sacrosanct figure, the king de jure. But the stronger the king is as an individual, and the more de facto ability he has, the more nearly A will equal B, and the better off both the king and his society will be. In any case, whether A equals B or not, it is clear that A minus B equals nothing, and that equation is echoed in the words "all" and "nothing" that run through the abdication scene, and in fact are continuing as late as *King Lear*.

Richard has been brought up to believe in the sanctity of his office, and unfortunately that has not made him more responsible but less so. Hence he turns to magic and fantasy as soon as he is even momentarily frustrated. When he goes to see the dying John of Gaunt, thinking of how soon he can get his money, he soliloquizes:

> Now put it, God, into the physician's mind
> To help him to his grave immediately!
>   (I.iv. 59–60)

This is not the voice of a strong-willed and powerful king, but of a spoiled child, and those who talk in such accents can never get away with what they do for long. John of Gaunt tells him his flatterers have got inside his individual castle, and have cut him off from that identification with his society that every genuine king must have. Nobody could express the doctrine of the two bodies more clearly than John of Gaunt does:

> A thousand flatterers sit within thy crown,
> Whose compass is no bigger than thy head;

And yet, incaged in so small a verge,
The waste is no whit lesser than thy land.
    (II.i. 100–103)

After his return from Ireland, Richard refuses for a time to believe that anything can affect an anointed king adversely. But after the roll call of disasters has been recited to him he suddenly reverses his perspective, fascinated by the paradox that an individual, as vulnerable and subject to accident as anyone else, could also be the body of his whole kingdom. In short, he turns introvert, and that is a dangerous thing for a ruler to be who expects to go on being a ruler.

It is obvious, long before his final murder, that Richard is no coward, but his growing introversion gives him some of the weaknesses that make other men cowards. One of them is an overreacting imagination that sketches the whole course of a future development before anyone else has had time to figure out the present one. Sometimes these flashes of the future are unconscious: at the beginning he tells Mowbray that he is not favouring Bolingbroke and would not "Were he my brother, nay, my kingdom's heir." That could pass as the straight thematic anticipation that we've met before in Shakespeare. So, more doubtfully, could his complaint about John of Gaunt's "frozen admonition":

        chasing the royal blood
With fury from his native residence.
    (II.i. 118–19)

But when disaster becomes objective he instantly begins to see himself as the central figure of a secular Passion. When Northumberland reports Bolingbroke's wish for Richard to come down and parley with him in the "base court" (the *basse cour* or lower courtyard of Flint Castle), the symbolism of the whole operation flashes at once through his mind:

Down, down I come, like glist'ring Phaeton . . .
In the base court? Base court, where kings grow base . . .
In the base court? Come down? Down, court! Down, king!
    (III.iii. 178–82)

So active an imagination makes Richard a remarkable poet, but cripples him as a practical man, because his mental schedule is so different from those of people who advance one step at a time, like Bolingbroke. We are reminded here, as so often in Shakespeare, that successful action and successful timing are much the same thing. His being a day late in returning from Ireland has resulted in twelve thousand Welshmen, on a rumour that he was dead, deserting to Bolingbroke. Very little is said about fortune or fate or the stars here, because Richard has made so many mistakes in timing that something like this was bound to hit him sooner or later.

Eventually Richard comes to understand, if not consciously at first, that he is programming himself as a loser, and has thrown himself into the elegiac role of one who has lost his throne before he has actually lost it. This in its turn is a kind of self-indulgent retreat from the confronting situation: "that sweet way I was in to despair," as he calls it. In the abdication scene he makes what could look like a last throw of the dice:

> And if my word be sterling yet in England,
> Let it command a mirror hither straight
>   (IV.i. 264–65)

It is Bolingbroke who gives the order to bring a looking glass: there is nothing sterling about Richard's word anymore. As far as history is concerned, Richard has had it: nothing remains but to find some device for murdering him. But as far as drama is concerned, Richard is and remains the unforgettable central figure, and Bolingbroke is a supporting actor. How does this come about? How does Richard manage to steal the show from Bolingbroke at the very moment when Bolingbroke is stealing his crown?

The reason goes back to the distinction we made earlier between the two forms of mask: the hypocrite and the person. We all have to be persons, and that involves our being hypocrites at times too: there's no way out of that. But Richard is surrounded with nobles solidly encased in hypocrisy of various kinds: many of them, as we'll discover more fully in the next play, are just gangsters glorified by titles and blank verse, and all of them, including Bolingbroke, are engaged in pretending that a bad king is being deposed for a good one. Some truth in it, of course; there's always a lot of truth in hypocrisy.

When Richard says he sees traitors before him, that is only what a loser would be expected to say. But when he goes on:

> Nay, if I turn mine eyes upon myself,
> I find myself a traitor with the rest.
>   (IV.i. 247–48)

he may sound as though he were saying what Northumberland is trying to bully him into saying, or signing: that he is justly deposed as a criminal. But in fact something else is happening: in that solid mass of rebels ritually carrying out a power takeover, Richard is emerging as a stark-naked personality, and the others can do nothing but stare at it.

There follows the inspired mirror scene, in which he dramatizes his phrase "turn mine eyes upon myself." He's still putting on an act, certainly; but it's a totally different act from what he was expected to put on. In one of his two aspects, the king is a human being: by forcing everyone to concentrate on him as a human being, while he stares in the mirror, a kind of royalty becomes visible from that humanity that Bolingbroke will never in this world find the secret of. We see a principle that we see later on in *King Lear*: that in some circumstances the real royalty is in the individual person, not in the symbolic one. Bolingbroke lives in a world of substance and shadow: power is substantial to him, and Richard with his mirror has retreated to a world of shadows. But a nagging doubt remains, of a kind related to the close of *A Midsummer Night's Dream*: which has the more effective power, the Duke of Athens or the king of shadows in the wood? In the context of a history the issue is clearer cut than in a fantastic comedy, of course, except for the audience's response. The audience takes Richard out of the theatre, and groups everyone else around him.

The contrast between what Bolingbroke has become and what Richard has been all along comes out in the two final episodes of the play. The first episode is the one we've glanced at already: Bolingbroke's pardoning of Aumerle, who conspired against him, in response to the impassioned pleas of the Duchess of York. In this episode there are two themes or verbal phrases to be noticed: the theme of the beggar and the king, and the theme of setting the word against the word. Bolingbroke is now king, and everyone else becomes in a sense a beggar: if a subject does anything that puts his life in danger, he must sue to the king for his life as a beggar would do. The "word" being discussed is the word of royal command, specifically the word "pardon." The Duke of York, as hot for prosecuting his son as ever, urges Bolingbroke to say pardon in French, where *pardonnez-moi* would have the general sense of "sorry, nothing doing." But Bolingbroke knows that he is now in a position where he is the source of the word of command, and must make all such words as unambiguous as possible, even when he does what he is soon to do to Exton.

This scene is immediately followed by Richard's great prison speech, which in many respects sums up the play, and repeats these two themes of the beggar and the king and of setting the word against the word. The prison is the final actualizing of the individual world dramatized by the mirror earlier, and Richard is fascinated by the number of personae he can invoke. His soul and brain become an Adam and an Eve, and they germinate between them a whole new world of thoughts. Some of the thoughts are ambitious, wanting only to get out; some are resigned (perhaps Boethius, writing *The Consolation of Philosophy* while awaiting execution in prison, is in the background here), but all of them are discontented. Not because of the prison: they'd be discontented anywhere. Here, setting "the word against the word" refers to the words of Scripture, the commands that come from the spiritual world and so often seem ambiguous; and the king and beggar are the same identity, different only in mask and context. He concludes:

> Nor I, nor any man that but man is,
> With nothing shall be pleased till be he eased
> With being nothing.
>   (V.v. 39–41)

Ever since the beginning of language, probably, "nothing" has meant two things: "not anything" and "something called nothing." Richard is saying here (not very grammatically) that every human being, including himself, is discontented, not pleased with anything, until he becomes that something we call nothing, i.e., in this context, dead. This double meaning becomes very central in *King Lear* later.

In *A Midsummer Night's Dream* the two worlds of the play, Theseus's court and Oberon's wood, represent two aspects of the mind, the conscious, rational, daylight aspect and the dreaming and fantasizing aspect. One dwells in a world of things and the other in a world of shadows; the shadow mind may live partly in the imaginary, in what is simply not there, but it may live partly also in the genuinely creative, bringing into existence a "transfigured" entity, to use Hippolyta's word, which is neither substantial nor shadowy, neither illusory nor real, but both at once. In *Romeo and Juliet* we got one tantalizing glimpse of this world in Mercutio's Queen Mab speech, but what we see of it mostly is the world created out of the love of the two young people, a world inevitably destroyed as the daylight world rolls over it, but possessing a reality that its destruction does not disprove.

Richard II is in a more complex social position, and has been caught in the paradox of the king, who, we remember, possesses both an individual and a sacramental body. The latter includes all the subjects in his kingdom; the former, only himself. In the prison, however, an entire world leaps into life within his own mind: the other world he was looking for in the mirror. He has as many thoughts as he has subjects, and, like his subjects, his thoughts are discontented, rebellious and conflicting. But the king's two bodies are also God's two realities, linked by the anointing of they king.

The imagery changes as music sounds in the background: Richard comments on the need for keeping time in music, and applies the word to his own life: "I wasted time, and time doth now waste me." From there two conceptions of time unfold: time as rhythm and proportion, the inner grace of life itself that we hear in music, and time as the mechanical progress of the clock, the time that Bolingbroke has kept so accurately until the clock brought him to power. Near the beginning of the play, John of Gaunt refuses to take active vengeance for Woodstock's death on the Lord's anointed. He leaves vengeance to heaven, which will release its vengeance "when they see the hours ripe on earth." The word "they" has no antecedent: John must mean something like "the gods," but the image of ripening, and of acting when the time is "ripe," brings in a third dimension of time, one that we don't see in this play, or perhaps fully anywhere else, although there are unconscious commitments to it like Edgar's "ripeness is all." There is a power in time, with its own rhythm and form: if we can't see it in action, perhaps it sees us, and touches the most sensitive people, such as Hamlet, with the feeling that it shapes our ends. If we did see it, perhaps the world of history would burst like an eggshell and a new kind of life would come forth.

Richard II was, we said, written entirely in verse, the reason being that the action is centred on what is practically a ritual, or inverted ritual: the deposing of a lawful king and the crowning of the successor who has forced him out. At the beginning of Henry IV, the hangover has set in. Bolingbroke, realizing that there is nothing worse for a country than a civil war, has determined at the outset to get started on a crusade. The idea, we said, was partly that God would forgive anyone anything, even deposing an anointed king, if he went on a crusade. But even more, an external enemy unites a country instead of dividing it. Shortly before his death, Henry IV tells Prince Henry that when he becomes king he should make every effort to get a foreign war started, so that the nobles will be interested in killing foreigners instead of intriguing against each other and the king—advice Prince Henry is not slow to act on. But at this point the new king's authority is not well enough established for a foreign war, much less a crusade. Henry finds that there are revolts against him in Scotland and Wales, and that many of the lords who backed him against Richard II are conspiring against him now. So Henry IV contains a great deal of prose, because this play is taking a much broader survey of English society, and showing the general slump in morale of a country whose chain of command has so many weak links. Falstaff speaks very early of "old father antic the law," and both the Eastcheap group and the carriers and ostlers in the curious scene at the beginning of the second act illustrate that conspiracy, at all levels, is now in fashion.

In the opening scenes two issues make their way into the foreground. One is the fact that medieval warfare was in large part a ransom racket: you took noblemen prisoner in battle, and then their tenants had to put up enough money to buy them back. That's why there's so much said about the denying of prisoners: they were a perquisite of the king's. The other is the fact that Edmund Mortimer, Earl of March, has in some respects a better claim to the throne than Henry IV has, and though he is at first theoretically on Henry's side, he marries the daughter of the Welsh rebel Owen Glendower, and forms a rallying point of sorts for a plot against the House of Lancaster.

The conspirators are not an attractive lot: Northumberland, for example, the father of Hotspur, was a bully in *Richard II* and is a coward in this play: he was a traitor to Richard, then a traitor to Bolingbroke, and ends by betraying his own son. Worcester is sulky and insolent: Henry is compelled to assert his royal authority and send him offstage, and Worcester realizes that once he is distrusted by the king there is no turning back. The only attractive figure is Hotspur, who's already a legendary fighter and a logical leader of the conspirators—if only they can get him to shut up. But they don't trust him either, because Hotspur, however foolish in many respects, is at least ready to fight in good faith: he doesn't have a conspiratorial mind, and doesn't really understand what his colleagues are after, which is their own interests. Before long they have produced what for a Tudor audience would be one of the most terrifying of symbols, later to appear at the beginning of *King Lear*: a map, with proposals to divide the country into parts.

Prince Henry is mentioned in contrast to Hotspur in the first scene, and is said to be the same age as Hotspur, though historically Hotspur was twenty years older. In the second scene the Prince appears, with Falstaff. The Prince is the central figure of this and the next two plays, and it's a very careful planning that shows him from the beginning flanked with these two characters. Hotspur is a kind of parody brother and Falstaff a parody father: later in the play Falstaff actually puts on a dramatic subscene in which he plays the role of Prince Henry's father, and this scene displaces one that the Prince had already proposed, in which he would take the part of Hotspur and Falstaff that of Hotspur's wife. In this scene, too, the Prince represents Hotspur as answering, when his wife asks him how many he has killed today, "some fourteen," and before long we have Falstaff's story about his fighting with two men in buckram who expand eventually into fourteen. The comic symmetry has a serious side to it. The central and essential virtue for a king who's eventually going to win the battle of Agincourt is courage. According to an ethical system that goes back ultimately to Aristotle, a virtue is a mean between extremes, and the virtue of courage is a mean between cowardice at one extreme and rashness or foolhardiness at the other. Falstaff represents one extreme and Hotspur the other, little as that statement does justice to the complexity of either.

Shakespeare's treatment of Hotspur's rhetoric is, even for him, an extraordinary technical tour de force. To paraphrase a remark of Worcester's, Hotspur says everything except the point of what he wants to say. "I profess not talking," he says calmly later in the play, but he is certainly an enthusiastic enough amateur. But he can't seem to give form or direction to what he says, and as you listen to him—and of course you have to listen to someone who hardly ever stops—a conviction begins to settle in your mind: whatever his courage or other good qualities, this man will never be a king. No one else in Shakespeare, not even the much later Coriolanus, who resembles him in some respects, shows such energy in breaking away from people. In the opening scene he gives us his brilliant portrait of the dandy who professes to regret the invention of gunpowder: no great point in it, except that it shows us how Hotspur divides people into the men who fight and the anthropoids who don't. Later he comes on the stage reading aloud from a letter—we never learn who wrote it. We learn only that the letter urges caution, and Hotspur gets claustrophobia when anyone urges caution.

Then there is the hilarious scene in which Hotspur ridicules Owen Glendower and his fantasies about the omens surrounding his birth. The failure of Glendower to come to his aid at the battle of Shrewsbury clearly has some connection with this. Again, Hotspur has no taste for music or poetry—always a bad sign in Shakespeare—because he can't sit still long enough to listen to them. We couldn't imagine him carousing in Eastcheap with Falstaff and Poins: he'd be bored out of his mind in five minutes. His obviously adoring wife addresses an eloquent and pathetic speech to him about his neglect of her, but he's engaged in men's work and won't listen. In the last act, brushing aside some letters for him, he complains:

> the time of life is short!
> To spend that shortness basely were too long
> (V.ii. 81–82)

Fighting is the one thing that does not bore him, and nothing that does not lead to fighting is worth bothering with. His wife's name, incidentally, is Kate: the historical Lady Percy was named Elizabeth, and Shakespeare's main source calls her Eleanor. I don't for a moment think there's any particular significance in Kate, but it would be highly characteristic of Hotspur if in fact he were not quite sure what his wife's name was.

In contrast to Falstaff, who is all realism, Hotspur is a quixotic figure, as much in love with honour as Falstaff is detached from it. With many of his supporters abandoning him, and thinking that his glory will be all the greater with the odds against him, he goes into battle and is struck down by Prince

Henry. His dying speech is the reverse of all the rest of his rhetoric, and says exactly and very economically what he means:

O Harry, thou hast robbed me of my youth! ...
But thought's the slave of life, and life time's fool;
And time, that takes survey of all the world,
Must have a stop.
  (V.iv. 76–82)

Most editors now follow the First Quarto for the second line, which gives a simpler reading: "But thoughts, the slaves of life, and life, time's fool." I don't question their editorial judgment, but if I were directing the play I'd insist on the Folio reading above. Going back to the ethic of the golden mean, of virtue as a middle way between extremes, we notice that the extremes have a good deal in common, and are less opposed than they look. Rashness or foolhardiness can be a form of cowardice, as any psychologist will tell you. And however absurd it sounds to associate Hotspur with cowardice, this speech indicates that all his life he has been running away from something, something that has a great deal to do with time and the way that time ticks away the moments of his youth, that all too brief interval when he can be still a first-class fighting man. We notice also the word "fool," apparently meaning victim, in the sense in which Romeo calls himself fortune's fool; a sense that will become very important in *King Lear*. The theme of time we must leave and pick up later.

Falstaff is so complex a character that it's hardly possible to make an unqualified statement about him, even that his name is Falstaff. His name was originally Oldcastle: when this gave offence, Shakespeare reverted to a very minor character introduced into what may well have been his first play, *Henry VI*. There a Sir John Falstaff comes running across the stage away from a battle; when asked with contempt if he will desert his great commander Talbot, he says: "All the Talbots in the world, to save my life." We note that this Falstaff is in a panic, something the Falstaff we know never is, apart from some very unreliable reports about him. The "cowardice" of Falstaff comes from a cool and reasonable approach to a situation full of hypocritical ideal-ism: as is said of him by another character, he will fight no longer than he sees reason. As a result his cowardice is full of humour—something a mere panicky deserter never could have—and also very disturbing, because it calls into question a lot of clichés about honour and glory. His soliloquy on honour on the field of Shrewsbury must have seemed to many in the original audi-ence about as funny a speech as had ever been spoken on a stage, because they accepted more of the idealism about honour, and for them the speech would probably have had far greater psychological release than for us. In one of the plays in Shaw's *Back to Methusaleh*, set in the future, a monument has been erected to Falstaff. It is explained that after a few experiences of warfare (even though this is early twentieth century, and before the atom bomb), it had been realized that cowardice was a major social virtue, and so a monument had been set up to the sage who discovered the fact. We're closer to that state of mind today than we are to the Elizabethan attitude, to say nothing of the medieval one.

To the kernel of the stage coward have been added a large number of other stage types. Falstaff is also a *miles gloriosus* or bragging soldier, who claims to have killed Hotspur; he is a parasite, a type deriving from Classical comedy, with the bottomless capacity for drink appropriate to a parasite (the point is made very early that his bills are paid by Prince Henry); he is a comic butt, someone to be played tricks on in order to see how he can wriggle out of them; he is a vice, a central figure of the old morality plays who acted as a tempter and stirred up complications, later someone with the role of starting a comic action going. Above all, he is a jester, whose outrageous boasts are his way of keeping the party lively: his two men in buckram grow into an astonishing number, but he is not a schizophrenic, as he would have to be to expect to be believed. In part two, after he meets Shallow, he soliloquizes: "I will devise matter enough out of this Shallow to keep Prince Harry in continual laughter the wearing out of six fashions."

Characters in comedy normally do not have enough scope to become counterparts of the great tragic heroes: Falstaff is the only comic character in Shakespeare who does, because his setting is a history play. The Falstaff of the comedy, *The Merry Wives of Windsor*, is a much smaller figure. But the Falstaff of the histories ranks with Don Quixote as an inexhaustible comic study, though for opposite reasons. Don Quixote clings to his idealistic and romantic hallucinations about the age of chivalry in a society which ignores them; Falstaff clings to a self-serving rationality and a prose rhythm, while all the noblemen bumbling in blank verse are, if equally self-serving, better at disguising the fact.

As long as Prince Henry's interest in him holds out, he seems invulnerable, but there are two weak spots in his armour. In the first place, he is Sir John Falstaff, knight, well enough known to have a rebel officer surrender to him because of his name alone. Consequently he is involved in the war game whether he wants to be or not, and is empowered to recruit soldiers for the war against the conspirators. Being a vice, he takes bribes to let the good recruits off and conscript only worthless ones: our sympathy for him goes down a good deal when he tells us complacently what he's done, but again his realism gives us a side to such warfare that the blank-verse history makers give little hint of. He speaks of the men he's collected as "the cankers of a calm world and a long peace," and defends their lean and beggarly appearance with the phrase "food for powder." What difference does it make whether a soldier has been a good or a bad soldier if he's dead? At the battle of Shrewsbury he tells us that of his hundred and fifty men about three are left alive, "and they are for the town's end, to beg through life." And while his exploits on the field of Shrewsbury are absurd enough, we may also remember that he is far too old to be on a battlefield at all, and is not, to put it mildly, in top physical condition. He's isolated also in a different and subtle way. I've spoken of elements in the action of a Shakespeare play that we don't see but know are there, like the sun in *Romeo and Juliet* and the moon in *A Midsummer Night's Dream*. In the histories we don't, except in film productions, see any horses, though we realize that horses are constantly carrying all the important people over the country and into battle. But we can't imagine Falstaff on top of a horse.

His other weakness is his very real fondness for Prince Hal, who is, as he tells us early on, merely using Falstaff and the others as stooges for putting on an act of his own. In his opening scene he says to the Prince: "Thou hast the most unsavoury similes, and art indeed the most comparative, rascalliest, sweet young prince." There is no mistaking the genuineness of the affection in that tone: even the frigid Prince feels it occasionally, though never deeply. Falstaff is aware that his hold on Prince Henry is by no means secure, and this awareness increases as the two plays go on, driving him in the second part to make the very foolish move of writing the Prince a letter warning him against Poins, who, as the best of the Eastcheap lot, is the normal object of his jealousy. But even so we are told quite explicitly in *Henry V* that his public rejection by Henry has destroyed his will to live.

One of the sources for *Henry IV* and *Henry V* is an older play called *The Famous Victories of Henry the Fifth*, a messy dog's breakfast of a play that still helped to give Shakespeare a central idea for his own plays: that the popular appeal of a great king who conquered France would be immensely enhanced if he were presented first as a "madcap" Prince, associating with ordinary or low social types, getting into trouble with the law, and displaying the kind of undirected energy for which his later career provided an outlet. In this play Prince Hal tells us at the start that he is putting on a show very carefully designed for maximum effect, in which a reputation for being idle or even profligate will be suddenly reversed when he enters on his responsibilities. Throughout the play he seems utterly confident of his eventual success and his ability to take care of Hotspur as well: we may wonder what his confidence is based on, as whatever else he may be doing in Eastcheap, he is not getting much practice in fencing. Perhaps he already feels what comes out clearly in the imagery of *Henry V*: that he is on the rising side of the wheel of fortune, and so nothing can stop him. In this soliloquy, at the end of the second scene, two images are used that are important. One is the sun, which Henry will imitate when he rises from prince to king after having been sunk in the darker elements of his kingdom. Falstaff speaks of his group as "Diana's foresters, gentlemen of the shade, minions of the moon," which sounds like a parody of Oberon's wood in *A Midsummer Night's Dream*, and he urges the Prince, with unconscious irony, to make a place for the activities of the night when he becomes king. The other image is that of time, which emerges in the last line of the soliloquy: "Redeeming time when men least think I will."

As we'll be seeing at intervals all through, the role of time is always centrally important in Shakespeare. The tragic action normally cuts into time, and anyone who, like Hamlet, feels that there is no right time for him, and that the whole time of his activity is out of joint, can meet nothing but disaster. Macbeth often reproaches himself for acting a second too late, allowing someone crucial to escape his massacres by not seizing the exact moment. In comedy, time is usually a little more leisurely, sometimes taking a generation or so to work out its designs, as in *The Winter's Tale*. Prospero in *The Tempest*, in contrast, has studied astrology and knows when the right moment comes for him. For a king to be successful, a sense of timing is perhaps the most important ability he can have: in *Henry V* it is said of the new king, when he is about to invade France:

> Now he weighs time
> Even to the utmost grain.

The first remark Falstaff makes in this play is to ask Prince Hal what time it is, and he is told that such people as Falstaff, who sleep all day and drink all night, don't need to know the time. Falstaff is a time-blocking figure, someone who gets in the way of the movement of history. Hotspur's hair-trigger reactions also indicate that he has no sense of time, though for opposite reasons: he tends to jump his fences before they are there, and only in the enlightenment of his dying speech does he realize that life is time's fool, the plaything and often the victim of time.

Prince Henry himself is rather helpless when his father upbraids him for the manner of his life and tells him that he is simply being Richard II all over again. His plan of action is based on the crucial difference between the reputation of a prince, who is still technically a private citizen, and a king, a difference Richard did not take account of. Henry IV tells his son that when he was making his way to the throne he appeared very seldom in public and always with the maximum effect (this, we noted, is the opposite of what Richard II said about him, but something no doubt has to be allowed for selective memory). And clearly the Prince can't say: "Yes, but I'm going to be in a much stronger position than you—thanks I admit largely to you—and I'm putting on a far better act than you ever thought of." When this scene is parodied in the Eastcheap tavern, with Falstaff taking the role of the Prince's father and ending, naturally, with a plug for himself as the Prince's companion ("Banish plump Jack, and banish all the world"), the Prince answers, "I do; I will," and we realize that he means precisely what he says.

Prince Henry fits the general pattern of the play in that he is looking out primarily for his own interests: his companions are people to use and manipulate, and, as his father has already discovered, a king cannot afford real friends. The long scene in the Eastcheap tavern, Act II, Scene iv, begins with an episode I still find puzzling, but I think it has something to do with the same principle. The Prince enters laughing and perhaps drunk, telling Poins that he has become very popular with the drawers and servants of the tavern, who regard him as a good fellow and not proud like Falstaff, and one of them, named Francis, has offered him a gift of a pennyworth of sugar. There follows an elaborate practical joke on Francis, solely with the object of making him look a fool. After this has gone on for quite a while, Poins says: "What cunning match have you made with this jest of the drawer: come, what's the issue?" In other words: "What's so funny?" Francis has done nothing but try to express some affection for the Prince: his gift is not worth much, but it's the first rule of chivalry never to devalue a gift from a social inferior for that reason. The Prince does not answer Poins's question at all; he says:

> I am now of all humours that have showed themselves humours
> since the old days of goodman Adam to the pupil age of this
> present twelve o'clock at midnight.
>
> (II.iv. 89–91)

The surface meaning of this is that he feels like indulging any fancy that has ever entered the mind of the human race. I think there may be something more being said: something to the effect that Prince Henry is very close to completing his "madcap prince" act, and that what he has got from putting it on is a sense of having soaked himself in every social aspect of the kingdom he is going to rule. He is becoming his entire nation in an individual form, which is symbolically what a king is. It is interesting though that this statement, a very important one if I've got it anywhere near right, comes in a scene that shows him pulling away from someone who is trying to appreciate him as a person.

It is true that the battle of Shrewsbury shows him in a much more sympathetic role: he gives what he thinks is the dead Falstaff an obituary speech that one might make about a dog that has been run over, but still there are traces of affection in it, and when Falstaff revives, with his preposterous claim of having killed Hotspur himself, he allows him to get away with it. Considering what Hotspur's opinion of Falstaff would have been, Henry's generosity comes close to a desecrating of Hotspur's body. The First Part of *Henry IV* is, in one of its aspects, the tragedy of Hotspur, and it ends with the triumphant survival of Falstaff. It is possible that Shakespeare had planned the rejection of Falstaff in a second play by this time. The historical material in the second part is thin enough to make it likely that a demand for more Falstaff was the main reason for the second part's existence, and Shakespeare must have known that his audience would find the scene of his public rejection a bit hard to take. Nonetheless, as the first part includes the tragedy of Hotspur, so the second part includes the tragedy of Falstaff, so far as Falstaff is capable of a tragic role.

2 Henry IV follows the same general outline as the first part; but it soon becomes clear that the Eastcheap group is heading for rapid disintegration. The first scene with Falstaff begins with Falstaff asking his page for the doctor's report on his urine; the third includes Falstaff's order "Empty the jordan." We feel that we are being physically pushed closer to Falstaff than we really want to get. Mistress Quickly is not so amiably chuckle-headed as before: Falstaff is still sponging off her, as he was in the first part, but her reluctance to pawn her plate to fill his clamorous belly has a genuine pathos, and the abortive lawsuit she brings has a kind of desperation. One gets the impression that Falstaff's supplies from the Prince are being cut down, and that it is much harder for him to support all his vices in the style to which they are accustomed.

Other characters indicate that the setting is not all good fun, clean or dirty. We meet Pistol, who is a familiar type of braggart soldier, but he is neither witty, nor, in Falstaff's phrase, a cause of wit in other men. Doll Tearsheet is fairly typical of the stage whores of the drama of the time, very tough-talking and belligerent and generally drunk. Even she is somewhat taken aback by Falstaff's lifestyle. When at the end of the play she is arrested and the beadle remarks "there hath been a man or two lately killed about her," we get a glimpse of underworld activities that no prince, however much of a "madcap" act he puts on, can afford to get mixed up with.

Similarly with others Falstaff meets. He is accustomed to feel that it doesn't matter what he does if his evasions afterward are sufficiently amusing, but such techniques do not work with the Chief Justice, nor with Prince Henry's younger brother John, who has about as much humour as the horse he rides on. Falstaff, in short, is beginning to feel the strain of a professional jester whose jokes no longer go over, apart from the fact that he does not stop with jokes. He spends time with Justice Shallow, the one fully realized character peculiar to this play, and the time extends, because each of them thinks he has something to gain from the other. But nostalgic reminiscences reminding him how old he is and how long it was since he was young are hardly what Falstaff wants to hear at this point.

In this play Henry IV is near his death: he is perpetually exhausted and he can't sleep. His great strength has always been in his ability to take short views, to do what has to be done at the time and not worry about the remoter perspectives. But in this play a long and desolate speech breaks out of him about how any youth, if he could see the entire pattern of time stretching out ahead of him, would simply lie down and die and refuse to go through with it. The nemesis of usurpation is working itself out: a good deal of the discussion between the king's party and the rebels consists of rehashing feuds and grudges that go back to the beginning of *Richard II*, or even earlier. The implication is partly that rebellion is, among other things, caused by a sterile brooding on history with the object, not of building up a future, but of reshaping the past. Meanwhile Prince Henry is very near the point at which he is to take over as king, and the wish for his father to die and change the scene is very close to his consciousness, as a conversation with Poins shows. In the meantime he is in a state of doldrums, anxious to break away from his madcap act, but still having to wait for his cue. His guideline is still "in everything the purpose must weigh with the folly," but the folly and the idleness are beginning to chafe. Eventually there comes the scene in which he is caught trying on his sick father's crown: one of the traditional episodes of the madcap prince saga that had to be included. His excuses when discovered sound lame—he has learned something from Falstaff but not enough—but then King Henry is dying and starved for affection, and he accepts the excuses with a certain wry amusement, mingled with hope.

Falstaff, though he has had many warnings that he will not be in as much favour with the new king as he thinks, pushes all the slights he has had out of his mind, and just as the impetuous Hotspur realizes at the moment of death that he has been running away from something, so the leisurely and heavily moving Falstaff plunges into a frenetic energy to get to the coronation of the new king and become the second-greatest man in the kingdom. Well, we know what happened to that dream. At the end of part one, on the battlefield of Shrewsbury, there is the greatest possible contrast between all the ferocious fighting and the absurd antics of Falstaff with his bottle of sack. But in the second part there seems a closer connection between the rejection of Falstaff and the main historical action of the play, in which Prince John gets the rebel army to disarm by a rather shabby and obvious trick. The Archbishop of York, on the rebel side, remarks:

> we are all diseased,
> And with our surfeiting and wanton hours
> Have brought ourselves into a burning fever,
> And we must bleed for it.
>   (IV.i. 54–57)

Bloodletting was so standard a medical practice at the time that the analogy carries on into the social body. But there is a crucial distinction, which the Archbishop misses, between the bloodletting of civil war and of foreign war, and this tough, gritty, cynical play ends with the expectation of very soon invading France.

KIRBY FARRELL

Prophetic Behavior in Shakespeare's Histories

I

Let me begin this exploration of history and prophetic behavior in Shakespeare by recounting an episode from 1532 in which prophecy played a
central role. In that year William Neville, one of fifteen younger brothers of
the third Lord Latimer, fell under the influence of a motley group of wizards—by trade an astrologer, a caulker, and an Oxford scholar who special-
ized in alchemy and sorcery. Sizing up their new client, the wizards began
forecasting that his inconvenient older brother would soon die, whereupon
William Neville would become the powerful lord. To keep their dupe's
imagination fired up, the seers staged omens, revealed wondrously auspicious dreams, and portentously discussed politics and magic. Eventually
the talk became dangerous. Neville began speculating about, then openly
predicting, the deaths of his brother and Henry VIII as well. As G. R. Elton
puts it, "Neville was talking like a man planning to overthrow the state in
his search for what he had come to regard as his proper rights."[1] At least
one of the wizards fueled Neville's delusions by foreseeing that he would
inherit the earldom of Warwick, as if Neville were a long-lost changeling
child related to the legendary Guy of Warwick. Obsequiously the wizard
addressed his client as earl of Warwick, although later he claimed he had
only been making sport of Neville, "who was a laughing stock around the
neighborhood," a disclaimer, Elton judges, which "carries hardly any convic-

From *Shakespeare Studies* 19 (1987): 17–40. © 1987 by Associated University Presses.

tion" (p. 53). Eventually several of these inspired characters ended up in the Tower suspected of treason, although in the end none suffered the ghastly death executed on many another prophet of the time.

On the surface, Neville's experience is a tale of cynical deception reminiscent of Jonson's *The Alchemist*.[2] And yet all involved, even the rogues, seem to have been radically equivocal in their attitudes toward the occult. The Oxford wizard, for example, promised to make the King's fortune if they would only release him from the Tower so he could finish mastering the philosopher's stone. Neville himself had "an unhealthy interest in magic," and had even tried to make a cloak of invisibility for himself out of certain magical parts of a dead horse.[3] Pricked by prophecies to ever more perilous ambition, he built a gallery in his house whose secret doors could admit a troop of armed men to help him seize his glorious future by force. In his flirtation with catastrophe Neville seems like a burlesque of the ambitious Macbeth. Yet under interrogation he claimed that he had always loyally contradicted or pooh-poohed the wizards' predictions.

To our disenchanted eyes, Neville's prophecies reveal more about his character and his world than about destiny. Through the sycophantic wizards he presumably sought to fashion a new identity for himself which otherwise would have been unthinkable. In effect, the prophecies were collaborative acts of storytelling which tried to counter paralyzing cultural taboos against self-aggrandizement and make history itself obey the power of wishes. Not surprisingly, Neville's prophetic "plots" were as ambivalent as they were equivocal. Even as they dispatched his brother and the King to happy deaths, the stories validated Neville's own apotheosis as "a great man of the realm" who would lead a force to subdue vague enemies whom "the King had made of low blood" (pp. 53, 54). Identifying with a dangerous oppressor, he imagines himself destroying base upstarts and hence preserving the King who, in reality, represents the powers that make Neville himself a nonentity of "low blood." The transparent reversal in this fantasy richly confuses love and rage, expansiveness and dread. In his heart, that is, Neville was at once a murderous usurper, a potentially tragic overreacher, and yet also a faithful kinsman like Prince Hal or *As You Like It*'s Orlando, a comic hero destined to save the day. In his actual life Neville remained immobilized between these comic and tragic possibilities. After all, he operated with mild deviousness in his conquest of fate until credulity made him brash. The cloak of invisibility he sought perfectly expresses the desperate doubleness in his mind insofar as it promised his boundless self-aggrandizement even as it would have made him a totally secure nonentity as well.

However silly the man himself, Neville's adventures provide a useful contemporary context in which to consider how prophetic imagination shapes the destinies of two of Shakespeare's most important historical figures, Richard III and Prince Hal. In *Richard III*, predictions intimately structure history. In a way the play is a verbal struggle to control the future. Richard himself initiates the action by using "drunken prophecies . . . To set my brother Clarence and the King / In deadly hate the one against the other" (I.i.33–35).[4] He murders not so much to satisfy any personal hatred as to seize the future from his victims. In turn Queen Margaret and his other victims retaliate by invoking a world to come which will confound and subsume Richard, making him God's avenging angel—in A. P. Rossiter's words, an "angel with horns."[5]

In a sense prophetic behavior is natural, even fundamental. As psychologist George Kelly has shown, personality itself can be understood as a process of anticipating events.[6] Where Freud emphasizes the shaping influence of the past, Kelly's theory sees the individual living toward the future, creating a vision of the world which seeks to predict and control the course of events. Some kinds of prophecy might be said to reduce the processes of identity to concrete, manipulable form. The forecasts of his hired wizards, for instance, clearly enabled Neville to formulate a wishful new identity as a lord, supplying him ready-made roles and scenarios.

In *Richard III*, Crookback's victims repeatedly use prophecy in an effort to substantiate themselves in the face of crushing oppression and death. "Say poor Margaret was a prophetess!" cries the bereft Queen, damning her enemies to a punishing future and casting herself as the triumphal agent of God's wrath (I.iii.300–02). Trying to nullify her "frantic curse," Hastings explicitly repudiates her "false-boding" or falsely prophetic role (246). As for Richard, the deepest source of his power is his ability to anticipate the behavior of others in his plots and "inductions dangerous" (I.i.32). To manipulate others he has to predict their responses to him, shaping himself to meet their expectations. His hair-raising seduction of Lady Anne, say, depends on his intuition that the "poor Anne" who weeps "helpless balm" over Henry's coffin (I.ii.9,13) unconsciously wishes to be an exalted Cleopatra whose apocalyptic beauty, as Richard vows, "did haunt me in my sleep / To undertake the death of all the world" (122–23). Similarly, he senses that King Edward's latent fears will enable a mere "drunken prophecy" to turn him against his brother Clarence. Again and again Shakespeare allows his villain to preempt adversaries with thrilling prescience. Richard ambiguously shares the dramatist's privileged insights into the plot, especially at the outset, where if anything he triumphs a little too mechanically. Shakespeare plainly expects his audience to marvel at Crookback's apparently uncanny grasp of the future and therefore of destiny itself.

To be sure, prophetic behavior need not always be conscious. Time and again characters in the play unwittingly foresee events in self-revealing ways. Richard's treacherous formula that "G / Of Edward's heirs the murtherer shall be" (I.i.39–40) betrays not only King Edward but himself also. For ironically the false prophecy proves to be true when "G"—not George (Clarence) but himself, Gloucester—comes to murder the young princes. While Richard's words dramatize the ancient belief that murder will out, they also suggest that Shakespeare understood prophecy as imaginative behavior: in this instance as the vehicle of violent thoughts and the compulsion to confess.

In a similar fashion Hastings ignorantly predicts his own execution. Feigning loyalty to Richard, eager to have Crookback slaughter his enemies for him, Hastings nevertheless impulsively vows to "have this crown of mine cut from my shoulders Before I'll see the crown so foul misplac'd" on Richard's head (III.ii.43–44). We are meant to feel a preternatural shiver as the man blindly decrees his own death. At the same time the double meaning (amphibole) affords striking insight into his character. Consciously, Hastings' vow defiantly asserts his own power. Unconsciously, he expresses guilt and fear that in using Richard's cruelty against his own enemies he exposes himself to the headsman's ax. And sure enough, once condemned, he pours out pity for his enemies and loathing for Richard with the apocalyptic relief of a man finally coming to face a truth long hidden from himself. "I, too fond, might have prevented this," he laments (III.iv.81). He rues his "too triumphing" hatred of "butcher'd" enemies who could have been his natural allies, and his identification "in grace and favor" with Richard (89–91).[7] Finally he predicts "The fearfull'st time ... That ever wretched age hath look'd upon," calling down death on the persecutors who now "smile at me" (104–07). As self-discovery, Hastings' speech resembles Stanley's monitory dream that "the boar had rased off his helm" to kill him (III.ii.11), Lady Anne's blind forecast of her torment as Richard's wife—"If ever he have wife, let her be made ... miserable" (I.ii.26–27)—and Clarence's unwittingly clairvoyant dream of drowning (I.iv.9–63).[8] In each instance characters intuit a future they cannot consciously accept. When truth can no longer be contained, characters surrender to it with expedient fatalism. In the end the skeptical Hastings (III.iv.82–93), Anne (IV.i.80), Buckingham (V.i.27), and even Richard himself (IV.ii.96, 107; V.iii.204–06) come to believe destiny shaped by prophetic powers beyond their control.

Like individuals, governments also may be seen to define themselves into the future. Laws—the king's objectified will—imply the character of the state even as they act to regulate and thereby form the future. As William Neville's imagination vividly illustrates, where power is steeply hierarchical and absolute, personified in one figure, rebellion is apt to be symmetrical, invoking absolute, supernatural authority to justify itself. As Keith Thomas points out, "prophecies ... were employed in virtually every rebellion or popular uprising which disturbed the Tudor state."[9] Paradoxically and ambivalently, ancient predictions "had the effect of disguising any essentially revolutionary step by concealing it under the sanction of past approval" (p. 423). For in a society like Tudor England which justified its existence by claiming unbroken links to a remote, legitimizing origin, "the facts of change are rapidly reinterpreted to sustain the illusion of a static society.... A pretender to the throne must demonstrate genealogical continuity. Hence the great cult of prophecies during the fifteenth century," when York and Lancaster murderously struggled for legitimacy (p. 426).

In Shakespeare usurpers from Crookback to Glendower and Macbeth use supernatural forecasts to sanction their ambitions.[10] But likewise, however expediently, the plays invoke predictions to validate the Tudors. Shakespeare has Crookback remember that "Henry the Sixt / Did prophesy that Richmond should be king" (IV.ii.95–96). And years afterward (1613) *Henry VIII* directly connected the sanctioned Richmond with the living Jacobean audience in the Globe Theater by producing a rhapsodic Cranmer to foretell the apotheosis of Richmond's granddaughter Elizabeth and her "star-like" heir James, whose progenitive honor and name "Shall ... make new nations," thereby securing a blessed future (V.iv.51–52).

Strictly speaking, as Keith Thomas observes, prophecy had a conservative function insofar as its use "disguised the break with the past. Contemporaries were therefore mistaken when they declared that it was the circulation of prophecies which fomented rebellion. Essentially it was the existence of rebellious feelings which led to the circulation of prophecies" (p. 425). Considered as behavior, that is, prophecy is a form of disguising or play which gives concrete shape to hopes and fears otherwise inadmissible. Like theater, which allows a common actor to rule the world as Tamburlaine or a king of fairies, prophetic behavior tacitly dramatizes the power of imagination. Covertly it makes the creation of identity and personal power a problem anyone might come to think about. An individual may use prophecy, but also, reciprocally, prophecy may promise to recreate the individual inasmuch as it can supplant conventional authorities in validating a new identity—witness the experience of William Neville.

Hence the principle that governs Shakespeare's judgment of prophetic behavior: the deep taboo in the plays against attempts to seize the future by force. Like Macbeth's "dagger of the mind, a false creation" (II.i.38), prophecy may objectify desires to coerce the world into a new shape, even as it appears to dissolve personal responsibility, "marshalling" a deceptively passive self "the way that [it] was going" (42). Not the least of these deceptions is the way prophecy appears to keep history static or predestinate even though it cannot help but imply the possibility of change and in turn ambition. In contemporary political ideology as in theology, to strive to control time was ultimately to usurp the autonomy of king and God, and thereby spawn hellish chaos. In this context prophecy threatens to produce madness even as it promises exaltation. Touched by the witches' forecast of his kingship, for instance, Macbeth's identity begins to disintegrate with terrifying ease. The prospect of seizing supreme power unfixes his hair, unseats his heart, and raises "horrible imaginings" (I.iii.135–38):

> My thought, whose murther yet is but fantastical,
> Shakes so my single state of man that function
> Is smother'd in surmise, and nothing is
> But what is not.
>   (139–42)

Like the consciousness the serpent offered Eve, the witches' forecast cannot actually confer the godlike autonomy it seems to promise (you shall be king: ye shall be as gods) and yet, fearfully, it cannot be forgotten either. Such "soliciting / Cannot be ill, cannot be good" (130–31). Macbeth cannot go ahead without ruinous violence; yet he can't go back either. The result is the struggle against madness and dissolution that makes Macbeth tragic and not merely evil.

Conversely, prophecy proves benevolent for selfless figures. Banquo will accept honor, he tells Macbeth, provided that "I lose none / In seeking to augment it" (II.i.26–27).[11] Vicariously, asking nothing for himself, Banquo will become king through his posterity as the witches predicted. *Richard III* likewise makes Richmond self-effacing toward destiny, and accordingly Richmond fulfills Henry VI's prophecy that "he should be king." Although Crookback and the ghosts at Bosworth Field attribute Richmond's success to predestination, Shakespeare takes pains to show Richmond humbly beseeching divine aid (V.iii.108–17). In prayer he makes his own will transparent: the vehicle of divine purpose.

Where prophetic behavior reinforces the established order outside the theater, playing out a vision of community, it is apt to take the form of a blessing, as at the close of *Henry VIII*. After slaying Crookback, for example, Richmond invokes a benign future to be based on marriage. In ritually charged language, sanctifying prediction as prayer, he vows:

> O now let Richmond and Elizabeth,
> The true succeeders of each royal house,
> By God's fair ordinance conjoin together!
> And let their heirs (God, if thy will be so)

Enrich the time to come with smooth-fac'd peace,
With smiling plenty, and fair prosperous days!
(V.v.29–34)

By contrast, where prophetic behavior expresses the helpless righteousness of victims, it takes the form of curses. For Queen Margaret and the ghosts who haunt Richard, victims who have lost everything and are literally selfless, curses turn the future against their powerful tormentors. As Keith Thomas reminds us, "although post-Reformation Protestants usually denied both the propriety and the efficacy of ritual cursing, they frequently believed that, if the injury which provoked the curse were heinous enough, the Almighty would lend his endorsement. . . . It was a moral necessity that the poor and the injured should be believed to have this power of retaliation when all else failed" (p. 507). To suffer injury from another is to suffer effacement, while the aggressor appropriates the victim's personal force, magnifying himself and his own strength. And so the victim's curse serves to restore a static, just relationship in the time to come, forcing destiny and yet not violating the taboo against self-aggrandizement. One by one, for instance, Margaret's tormentors go to their deaths acknowledging, as Grey says, that her "curse is fall'n upon our heads" (III.iii.15). The doomed Buckingham makes the prophetic behavior explicit: "Margaret's curse falls heavy on my neck: 'When [Richard],' quoth she, 'shall split thy heart with sorrow, / Remember Margaret was a prophetess'" (V.i.25–27).

Few characters could coerce destiny more violently than Crookback. Consider Richard's famous command: "Shine out, fair sun, till I have bought a glass / That I may see my shadow as I pass" (I.ii.262–63). His words command not only the sun but the future also. Like Hastings' unwitting clairvoyance, his language is crucially ambiguous. Seeking to celebrate his progress toward the apotheosis of kingship, Richard ironically foretells his end at Bosworth Field, where he becomes a shadow passing through illusion into annihilation.[12] Grasping at figments of identity, his future now decreed by ghosts commanding him to "Despair and die!" he cries out in his nightmare: "I am I," "No. Yes, I am," "I love myself," "I rather hate myself," and so on. Groping repetition calls attention to the riddling emptiness of the self in words: "I myself / Find no pity to myself" (V.iii.183–204). On a sunless morrow he "enacts more wonders than a man" in battle (V.iv.2); yet he dies slashing wildly at six illusory Richmonds (11), nullified, in a negative apotheosis.

Ultimately Richard is shadowy because he lives not for any immediate self-interest, but for an endlessly empowering future. His power comes from his ability to keep himself invisible while pretending to mold himself to the expectations—the futures—of others. His sole delight, he swears, is to "spy my shadow in the sun / And descant on mine own deformity" (I.i.26–27).[13] "Spy" suggests that this self-awareness is accidental and even unnatural to him. Celebrating his deformity, he repudiates himself with heroic contempt, speaking as if from outside himself, with a disembodied and inhuman idealism. To "descant" on deformity is to make an art of hate, gaining a sense of power by rejecting an imperfect creature and an imperfect present time as a god might.[14]

One way to understand this synergistic self-hate and self-inflation is to recognize that Richard's ugly "unfinish'd" body (I.i.20) objectifies the elemental terror of death and meaninglessness that haunts mankind.[15] Insofar as prophetic behavior enables Richard to live endlessly in an imminent future, it promises him undying potency. To be "sent before my time / Into this breathing world, scarce half made up" (20–21) is to be cheated of an ideal destiny. As long as he can "feel now / The future in the instant," as Lady Macbeth puts it, he can act out an illusion of self-transcendence.

The paradigm for this self-transcending behavior comes at the close of *3 Henry VI*, where the King predicts Richard's career and Richard kills him, equivocally justifying himself by prophecy as one "ordain'd" to kill the King. Stabbing his victim, Richard exclaims: "die, prophet, in thy speech: / For this, amongst the rest, was I ordain'd" (V.vi.57–58). In Richard's words Muriel Bradbrook finds "a direct recollection of the role of the Prophet" in the old craft cycles in which a "providential pattern linked events."[16] More complexly, Moody E. Prior contends that Richard's claim to be "ordain'd" in his action "carries a fleer at the prophetic pretensions of Henry, yet in context the line becomes a part of Henry's inspired projection of the future and suggests that Henry is indeed the mouthpiece of an ordaining power."[17] In this clash of prophets, each strives to subsume the other and identify himself with superhuman necessity.

The confrontation, then, dramatizes a symbolic struggle for being. The King decrees Richard "less than a mother's hope / ... an indigested and deformed lump" at birth (50–51). Born incomplete yet with full teeth (53) to "bite the world" (54), Richard is to the King all appetite: a sort of cannibal or vampire homicidally hungry for life. Henry's prophecy would dehumanize or more exactly decreate Richard into parts: teeth, a scarcely existent lump. Richard reacts to this threat of nightmarish unbeing by stabbing Henry in an act of violent self-assertion, acting out the superiority of "living" force to "dying" words which his own language tacitly vows: "die, prophet, in thy speech: / For this, amongst the rest, was I ordain'd" (57–58).

As an apotheosis, England himself, embodying God's will and alone in society truly autonomous, the King possesses superhuman potentiality and potency. By title and execution he makes and unmakes men. In a vicious parody of the King's supremacy, Richard slays him appealing to his own "ordain'd" authority. The murder, that is, enacts a fantastic project of self-creation whose ultimate object will be Richard's apotheosis as king. In biting the world, consuming the vitality of others, he pursues chimerical supremacy trying to overcome the unbearable nullity which man, God, and "dissembling nature" pronounce on him through the King. "Counting myself but bad till I be best" (91), Crookback undertakes feats of superhuman destruction striving to establish that "I am myself alone" (83).

Such a project is of course as evil as it is futile. In theory Henry subsumes the identities of all his subjects, and even the lowliest partake of cosmic power and life through him as through Christ. In this respect his role is sacrificial: he is all and nothing. Assaulting him, Richard acts to aggrandize all power to himself with demonic selfishness. In this sense he "bites" or devours the world, finally consuming himself as well. In his opening soliloquy in *Richard III*, for example, the terms of Henry's prophetic judgment recur as if Richard has taken his words as well as his life. Descanting on his own deformity and insubstantiality, he is still trying to escape the King's judgment. Internalized, Henry's prediction virtually comes to haunt his murderer. Proclaimed an "indigested and deformed lump" in *3 Henry VI* (V.vi.51), Richard now compulsively expands upon the epithet as if to co-opt the King and thereby remove the painful sting. In his own words he is

> curtail'd of this fair proportion,
> Cheated of feature by dissembling nature,
> Deform'd, unfinish'd, sent before my time
> Into this breathing world, scarce half made up.
> (I.i.18–21)

Although he vows that "I am determined to prove a villain" (30), his word "determined" signifies not only his resolute will but also helpless fatality.[18] The King's haunting prediction, that is, witnesses the futility of his murder even as it looks forward to the slaughtered yet triumphant ghosts at Bosworth Field and Richard's dying assault on the six illusory impersonators of Richmond.

Prophetic behavior, then, reveals the fetishistic nature of the crown, the life-giving apotheosis. Like Macbeth, Richard grasps at power to no earthly end, not for policy or any quotidian pleasure. Rather, he appears compelled by the crown's promise of vitality. Overtly desacralized, even mocked, kingship nevertheless retains a power for him that can only be called superhuman, and Richard devotes himself to it with a fanaticism reminiscent of the terrifying genocidal struggles for religious supremacy which Shakespeare's world knew all too well. It could be argued that Richard's behavior parodies the bloodthirsty absolutism of Henry VIII, Mary Tudor, and—in ideology if not in actual practice—the early Elizabeth. In this perspective Shakespeare's Richard appears to express an unconscious resentment against royalty's overwhelming appropriation of power and autonomy to itself in the Tudor period. He caricatures the providential Richmond and his inheritors even as the viciously fascinating Satan does the Christian God.[19] In psychological terms, as the plays' imagery insists, Richard is also an enraged, "biting" child capable of ferocious and yet exhilarating independence. Rather than suffer himself to be subsumed in the identity of the father-king and to share in a vicarious transcendence, as doctrine prescribed, he threatens to devour the patriarch himself. Rather than internalize the repressive values of the father-king, he acts out repression with homicidal fury on others, and with transcendent self-hatred on himself.

For all his strategic clarity, in short, Richard dramatizes the same profoundly human desperation which surfaced more transparently in the "small army of pseudo-Messiahs" which the reign of Elizabeth produced. Among them was one William Hacket,

> an illiterate and bankrupt ex-serving man, who had persuaded himself that he was the Messiah and had come to judge the world on God's behalf. He laid claim to gifts of prophecy and miracle-working; and he threatened a series of plagues upon England unless immediate reformation took place. He was a fierce man, who was said to have once bitten off and eaten an antagonist's nose; "his manner of praying" was observed to be "as it were speaking to God face to face."
>
> (Thomas, pp. 133–34)

To his associates Hacket "was both King of Europe and the Angel who would come before the Last Judgment to separate the sheep from the goats" (p. 134). Truly an angel with horns, Hacket attacked the authority of the Queen and cried annihilation against the world while advertising himself to be personally indestructible up to the moment in 1591, in the streets of London, when his monarch had him put to death.

From this standpoint history itself threatens to stand revealed as an awesome struggle for apotheosis. When kings and heroes fail—when vicarious transcendence fails for whatever reason—civil slaughter is apt to follow. It is a measure of Shakespeare's insight that at one point or another nearly every one of Richard's victims betrays a compulsion toward power. Just such a compulsion is comically at the center of William Neville's escapades with wizards, and tragically latent in his fantasies about commanding an armed uprising. And just this sort of awareness, it seems to me, underlies the dying Henry IV's fear of a future England "peopled with wolves" (*2H4*, IV.v.137). He foresees mankind consuming one another in a wolfish rage for survival, destroyed by the monstrous compulsion to "bite the world" as Richard would.[20] Even as the failing King Henry couches his horror in a controlling prophecy, so *Richard III* controls its vision of universal savagery by a network of prophetic projections which appears to secure at last Richard's accursed extermination and Richmond's triumphant airy benediction.

II

Let me balance this dark example of prophetic behavior with a happier one, the destiny of Prince Hal. As Henry V, Hal himself was credited with powers of prognostication in the Tudor period. In *A Defensative against the Poyson of Supposed Prophecies* (1583), for example, Henry Howard, Earl of Northampton, anxiously catalogs the evils of prophecy: and with good reason since he had lost two kinsmen—the poet Earl of Surrey and the Duke of Norfolk—to the headsman thanks to incited ambition. Unexpectedly the Earl interrupts his supererogatory catalog of follies to endorse Hal's prescience: "Henry the fifth, [sayth maister Haule] prognosticated, that the young Earle of Richmonde, who was then his page, should one day stint the strife betweene Yorke & Lancaster: which secret coulde not have beene revealed, as some thinke, without deeper insighte into future things, then common sense or reason can attaine or reach unto."[21] Following Hall, the Earl connects the idealized Henry V with the founder of the Tudor dynasty, Crookback's nemesis, and justifies the ascendancy of Richmond by appealing to the uncanny prescience of Henry V.

Like Richard III, Hal too has a crucial soliloquy which functions as a self-validating prophecy. But where Richard blindly foretells his own shadowy dissolution (I.ii.262–63), Hal's sense of the future is never confuted. Where Richard would force the future to his will, violating taboo and thereby confounding himself, Hal would "imitate the sun" by effacing himself behind base clouds while his father commands England's awe (I.ii.197). "By so much shall I falsify men's hopes," he vows, for "My reformation, glitt'ring o'er my faults, / Shall show more goodly and attract men's eyes" (211, 214–17). While he imparts his intentions in the soliloquy, on another level his words also foretell the play's action. It would be a mistake, I think, merely to construe the speech as the personal revelation of a Machiavellian scheme. At the least the soliloquy has the justificatory cast so often associated with prophecy. The voice projects a Prodigal Son scenario with the atavistic detachment of a chorus or prologue in an old play. Although it appears colloquial, in the end Hal's language has an apothegmatic and ritualistic quality. Echoing Ephesians 5:7, itself a vision of "the ages to come," Hal predicts: "I'll so offend, to make offense a skill, / Redeeming time when men least think I will" (216–17).

In the course of the play Hal defines himself partly by countering the "hopes" or predictions of others, especially his father. "The hope and expectation of thy time / Is ruin'd," the King laments, "and the soul of every man / Prophetically do forethink thy fall" (III.ii.36–38). From his early forecast that "thou art only mark'd / For the hot vengeance, and the rod of heaven" (III. ii.9–10) to his deathbed foreboding that his dissolute son will rule an England peopled with wolves, Henry forcefully works to reshape Hal's character. In effect, he invokes various appalling futures for his son in an effort to fore-close them. The Prince counters at last, in the crisis before Shrewsbury, with a "promise" to "redeem" the time "in the name of God" (III.ii.132–59). At some moments his language is charged with echoes of the New Testament:

> I will redeem all this on Percy's head,
> And in the closing of some glorious day
> Be bold to tell you that I am your son,
> When I will wear a garment all of blood,
> And stain my favors in a bloody mask,
> Which wash'd away shall scour my shame with it.
>   (132–37)

It is tempting to regard this speech as the valorous trumpeting of youth and nothing more. Apt to be overlooked is the subliminal pattern of salvationist eschatology in Hal's vision of his atonement with his father. By suffering a bloody purgation, he vows, he will "wash away" his shame or sin, and "redeem all this." He "will tear the reckoning" from his adversary Hotspur's heart (152), and by his victory heal his father's wounds, "the long-grown wounds of my intemperance" (156). Magnifying himself and his struggle, the Prince concludes on an apocalyptic note. Rather than fail, he swears, he "will die a hundred thousand deaths" (158). Catching the spirit of righteous annihilation, the King retorts: "A hundred thousand rebels die in this." Whereupon he identifies his will with his son's: "Thou shalt have charge and sovereign trust herein" (160–61).

In Hal's peroration, it seems to me, we can hear echoes of the medieval Christian worldview in which "life tends to be seen as a mortal struggle waged by good fathers and good children against bad fathers and bad children."[22] Coexistent in Hal's vision with chivalric "favors" and "honor," that is, is a vocabulary of messianic struggle. In its most crudely extravagant form the medieval version of this struggle pitted the Christ of the Parousia or the Christ-like Emperor of the Last Days against Antichrist. The son of God personally confronted the "son of perdition" in an apocalyptic clash. In that final resolution a host of demonic fathers and sons would oppose the armies of the saints, the opposing hosts "each the negative of the other" and "held together in a strange symmetrical pattern" (p. 71). At Shrewsbury the disposition of forces is similarly symmetrical, and the Prince explicitly sees himself in a cosmic collision with Hotspur since "Two stars keep not their motion in one sphere" (V.iv.65). Hal's image dramatizes the completeness of the annihilation threatened by his symmetry with Percy. It is important to keep in mind that "gallant" Percy represents not merely defiance but personalized death to Prince, King, and kingdom alike. He would not simply eliminate Hal; he would take his place.

Let me consider the dynamics of the apocalyptic fantasy more closely:

> As in the eschatalogical Messiah, so in the eschatalogical Enemy, Antichrist, the images of the son and the father are fused—only here of course the images are those of the bad son and the bad father. . . . In his relation to God the Father Antichrist appears as a defiant and rebellious child . . . even daring to usurp the fathers place and ape his authority. In his relation to human beings, on the other hand, Antichrist is a father scarcely to be distinguished from Satan himself: a protecting father to his devilish brood, but to the Saints an atrocious father . . . a cunning tyrant who when crossed becomes a cruel and murderous persecutor.
>
> (p. 71)

Not to be distracted, we need to focus on the dynamics of the roles in the fantasy. Toward his surrogate fathers, Glendower (who can reckon up "the several devils' names / That were his lackeys" [III.i.155–56]), the treacherous Worcester, and the King, Hotspur is of course compulsively rebellious.[23] Toward ordinary human beings, however, he can act the "atrocious father." At least in Hal's fantasy Percy is a cannibalistic ogre who "kills me some six or seven dozen of Scots at a breakfast, washes his hands, and says to his wife, 'Fie upon this quiet life! I want work'" (II.iv.102–05). For his part, the Prince is both obedient son and, at Shrewsbury, the powerful symbolic father who personally saves the King. As King (witness his disguised debate with Williams on the night before Agincourt), Hal self-consciously defines himself as the burdened father to his people.

As in the apocalyptic fantasy, where Antichrist acts out rebellion which would be unthinkable in the militantly idealized Christ, so in the Henriad, as

Ernst Kris and others have noticed, Hotspur plays out the defiant aggression which Hal repudiates in himself."[24] What's more, the destruction of the evil alter ego leads not merely to renewed obedience but to a glorious apotheosis. After all, Hal's atonement speech foresees not meek submission to his father but superhuman—or if need be, suicidal—heroism. And the magnitude of the Prince's struggle against the rebel in himself can be seen in the shocking meaning latent in the King's equation of the hundred thousand deaths Hal vows to die with the deaths of "a hundred thousand rebels" (160). The King's equation can be taken to express a complex psychological state in which he tacitly and yet unconsciously acknowledges that in choosing fidelity to the crown, Hal is choosing to destroy the rebel in himself.

The tremendous attraction and horror of rebellion may be measured in the price of its atonement, the sacrifice of a hundred thousand other people. In 1600 Thomas Wilson estimated the total population of nobles, bishops, knights, esquires, and yeomen—that is, anyone who was anyone in England—to number only a hundred thousand.[25] This context helps to suggest the intensity of the psychic violence at the heart of the Henriad. Even in this relatively early speech we can make out motivation plausible for the Henry V who will later strive to subdue France. At the same time we can see that the psychic conflicts in Hal's speech relate it, however indirectly, to the fantasies of William Neville, the literal-mindedly messianic William Hacket, and the horned angel Richard III. In each instance prophetic behavior would mediate between irreconcilable visions of the self and its destiny.

In *2 Henry IV* the Prince once again has to justify himself to his father. Imagining that his son has "taken away" his crown (IV.v.88), the dying King utters a long, harrowing prophecy which projects a shameful character for the future Henry V (119–37). The Prince in turn appeals to a benevolent future in order to overcome his father's ominous forecast. "If I do feign, O, let me in my present wildness die," he prays, and "Let God for ever keep the crown from my head" (151–52, 174). Hal pledges himself by invoking a competing future, but without resorting to self-aggrandizing prophecy. The moment might be seen to replay the confrontation between Henry VI and Richard insofar as it presents a failing king who attempts to control a would-be successor through prophecy, fearing death at his hands (Hal's trial of the crown, his father complains, "helps to end me" [64]). In Hal's hands the crown is an object, momentarily demystified and impotent. Sensing kingship in jeopardy, both rulers fantasize about mankind as wolves. Left alone with Richard by the Lieutenant, Henry VI sighs, "So flies the reakless shepherd from the wolf, / So first the harmless sheep doth yield his fleece, / And next his throat unto the butcher's knife" (*3H6*, V.vi.7–9). Under Henry V, Bolingbroke foresees the butchery of civil war in an England peopled with wolves (IV.v.137).

Where Henry VI recoils from the Richard who "cam'st to bite the world" (54), Bolingbroke dreads that "the wild dog / Shall flesh his tooth on every innocent" (131–32). But where Richard mockingly justifies his assassination as "ordain d," all the while ignorantly subsumed in a larger prophetic pattern that dooms him, Hal conspicuously submits to God's future.

Humbled before his father, Hal deflects Henry's horror of devouring aggression from himself to the crown. Not a usurper but the crown itself and therefore all who live through the King have "fed upon the body of my father" (159). In effect, Hal recreates the King's own image of wolfish cannibalism as the urge underlying all human striving for power and survival. As in the Mass, he implies, where sacrifice of Christ's body promises immortal life, the metonymic crown "hast eat thy bearer up" (164). In construing his father's approaching death as a willed dispensation of self, a martyr's sacrifice, Hal's words make it possible for the King to bestow a "father's love" on him (179) without dread. Symbolically, that is, Hal corroborates the old man's immortality in the living crown and in his obedient son, freeing him to die in peace.

Reconciled with his son, the King fulfills Hal's pledge from Part One to "redeem the time" even as he discovers the mysterious fulfillment of his own prediction that he will die "in Jerusalem" (235). The emotional logic of the scene argues that, in part, it is the reconciliation with Hal—to be exact, the recognition of his true nature—that enables the King to discover "Jerusalem." Ironically, like the intuitions that presumably give rise to prophetic conviction in the first place, this Jerusalem turns out to have been at hand all along: a room, as it were, in his own mind. As in a riddle, the revelation comes to the King in a flash of insight, orderly and yet beyond any ordinary problem-solving strategies.

While ironies radically complicate the significance of this Jerusalem, for contemporary audiences the pattern of atonement, death, and triumphal revelation must have had a powerful appeal to the deepest hopes and fears: an appeal which ironies may have qualified or displaced in the minds of spectators, yet probably never merely dispelled. For one thing, the return to Jerusalem is one of the original themes of Judaeo-Christian eschatalogy and, in the tradition that comes down from St. Augustine, an inward process in which mankind, attaining the heavenly city, restores its relation with God and therein achieves wholeness. As Augustine says in the *Confessions*: in the pilgrimage through life "I shall not turn away but shall come to the peace of that Jerusalem, my dear mother, . . . and there Thou shalt collect from my present scatteredness and deformity all that I am."[26] In this vision Jerusalem offers a release from the nightmarish struggle for apotheosis. Instead of wolfish rebellion—and the King himself first conceived his "voyage to the Holy Land, To wash [King Richard's] blood off from my guilty hand" (*R2*,

V.vi.49–50)—Jerusalem offers incorporation into God the almighty father. Instead of "scattered" self ("God knows," Henry laments, "By what by-paths and indirect crook'd ways / I met this crown" [183–85]), the vision promises wholeness. Augustine's vision answers as well to the "deformity" of the insatiably rebellious Richard III, whose violent alienation and birth with teeth cry out for the Jerusalem which is "my dear mother." Not by chance, I suspect, the play invokes Jerusalem just as Shakespeare needs to dramatize the Prince's final integration (in Parts One and Two at least) of his own scattered being. No longer torn between Eastcheap and Windsor, Hal prepares himself to maintain the crown "'Gainst all the world" (224). In effect, the play fetishizes the eschatological city in a room just offstage, as immediate yet separate as the sanctuary in a church. "It hath been prophesied to my mane years, / I should not die but in Jerusalem," the King concludes. Then, with an autonomy corroborated by the uncanny prediction, and a control which for all concerned strongly counters the dread his death must incite, he has himself borne to the adjacent chamber and prophesies: "In that Jerusalem shall Harry die" (236–37, 240). In this way Shakespeare prepares the stage and the cosmos for the ascension of Henry V.

Subsequently Hal "adopts" the Chief Justice—the English law—as his father, defining himself anew and making good his original forecast in Part One. "With my father's spirits," the new king declares, "I survive / To mock the expectation of the world, / To frustrate prophecies, and to raze out Rotten opinion" (V.ii.125–28). Having "falsified men's hopes," he can now exceed or even transcend them by revealing his true nature.[27] Thus astonished, others' imaginations may sense the authority of apotheosis in the King, and "Presume not that I am the thing I was" (V.v.56).

Prophetic behavior, then, can be understood as a means by which Shakespeare tries to validate Hal's heroic stature for us. It is a sign of majesty to be at times intuitively clairvoyant. At Shrewsbury in Part One, for instance, Hotspur's fatalism suggests a gambler's desperation as he urges his comrades on to ill-considered combat: "heaven to earth, some of us never shall / A second time do such a courtesy" (V.ii.99–100). By contrast, Shakespeare endows Hal with a composed prescience. After the battle the Prince addresses the deceptively slain Falstaff "precisely as if he knew he were faking death."[28] In his eulogy he ambiguously foretells Falstaff's resurrection, undercutting any show of grief that would allow Falstaff to leap up later and boast of Hal's love for him. In its eerie way his speech is as equivocal as Hastings' pronouncement of his own death in *Richard III*, although it confirms rather than confutes Hal: "I should have a heavy miss of thee / If I were much in love with vanity! Death hath not strook so fat a deer today" (V.iv.105–07). Were Falstaff truly fallen, the Prince's mockery would be heartless. Implicitly his speech sees through death even as Hal would see through the present time in order to redeem it. His farewell—"Embowell'd will I see thee by and by" (109)—predicts Falstaff's actual embalmed demise even as it foresees him in the near future comically stuffed full of food.[29]

If it were necessary, we could locate the same prophetic pattern that corroborates the Prince in the career of Henry V. As one critic has noticed, "Using the rising sun image of the 'I know you all' speech Henry declares: 'I will rise there with so full a glory / That I will dazzle all the eyes of France'" (*H5*, I.ii.278–79). The King literally predicts a blinding apotheosis. Moreover,

> From this perspective Agincourt is the climax of the plan announced so long before, whereby the sun-king will shine more brightly for the contrast of the "base contagious clouds" which hid it, and "My reformation ... / Shall show more goodly and attract more eyes / Than that which hath no foil to set it off" (*1HIV*, 1.2.206–08). Henry knows all along what he is doing. The glory he looks for in France he wants partly in order to fulfill his own prophecy of a glorious career, partly to cure the insecurity of his title and his psyche.[30]

III

If Hal "knows all along what he is doing," as in the above assessment, then his prophetic behavior stands demystified as so much strategy. The alternative is to credit him with some sort of extra-rational inspiration—perhaps sentimentally abetted by his creator. One assumption tends to produce a more or less Machiavellian prince operating in ironical and conditional history. The other leads to a providential prince.[31]

In the histories, says Professor Rossiter bluntly, Shakespeare "always leaves us with relatives, ambiguities, irony, a process thoroughly dialectical" (p. 22). In *Richard III*, for example, the "'Christian' system of retribution is undermined, counter-balanced, by historic irony" (p. 22). Margaret's prophetic curses appear to be efficacious, enacting a providential judgment. Yet Professor Rossiter rightly calls attention to "the repulsiveness, humanely speaking, of the 'justice.' God's will it may be, but it sickens us: it is as pitiless as the Devil's" (p. 20), more cruelly pagan than Christian.

For the plays to be "thoroughly dialectical" they have to be capable of generating internal critiques of their own substance. And so they do.[32] In *2 Henry IV*, say, Warwick deflates the prophecy of Northumberland's treachery which threatens to demoralize the King. By observing an individual's history, he maintains, one may "prophesy, / With a near aim, of the main chance of things As yet not come to life" (III.i.80–84). In fact, Warwick describes a faculty the dramatist himself might use to develop a given dramatic situation into a play.

Warwick's homely naturalism invites us to understand prophecy as a function of character, while making any providential significance seem incalculable if not purely fantastic. Prescience then becomes a gambler's calculation based on study and chance. A more sophisticated view might add to chance the equally extra-rational contribution of intuition or inspiration—in a word, the unconscious. C. L. Barber would see Warwick's and the King's views in terms of an opposition between magical and empirical views of man. The distinction is a reasonable one but not, I think, without some crucial limitations.

At the close of *2 Henry IV* Professor Barber perceives Shakespeare awkwardly trying to protect the dying King and ascendant Hal from our doubts and dissatisfaction. He scoffs at Henry's opportunistic use of a room named "Jerusalem" to aggrandize his death.

> One can imagine making a mockery of Henry's pious ejaculation about Jerusalem by catcalling a version of his final lines at the close of *Richard II*:
>
> Is this the voyage to the Holy Land
> To wash the blood from off your guilty hand?
>
> An inhibition of irony goes here with Henry's making the symbol do for the thing, just as it does with Hal's expulsion of Falstaff. A return to an official view of the sanctity of state is achieved by sentimental use of magical relations.

Barber has caught the King using the verbal coincidence "Jerusalem" to fetishize the props for his dying scene. Shakespeare, he points out, sentimentally fails to marshal] a critique of the occult resonance attributed to "Jerusalem." Barber then offers his well-known distinction between drama and ritual:

> the drama must control magic by reunderstanding it as imagination: dramatic: irony must constantly dog the wish that the mock king be real, that the self be all the world or set all the world at naught. When, through a failure of irony, the dramatist presents ritual as magically valid, the result is sentimental, since drama lacks the kind of control which in ritual comes from the auditors' being participants.

Then, wisely, comes the acknowledgement that although "the Renaissance moment made the tension between a magical and empirical view of man particularly acute, this pull is of course always present; it is the tension between the heart and the world."[33]

Sensible as it is, this formulation of a "tension between the heart and the world" has something diplomatic or even sentimental about it. To make the heart stand for the irrationality at the center of human life is to do as Henry does, "making the symbol do for the thing." Moreover, this particular symbol complacently gives the irrational a rosy glow. At the same time the idea of a "tension" too conveniently divides experience into objective and subjective spheres, either of which might be pure, whereas in truth, as the critic's own use of "heart" itself inadvertently demonstrates, our experience virtually never escapes some measure of subjectivity or "heart."

These reservations become important insofar as categories such as the heart and world keep us from recognizing the insoluble contradictions at the center of human life which the histories manage to dramatize. For the plays are not simply about government or English society as such. Rather they reenact over and over again the creation and destruction of kings and the life-giving power of the crown. As epitomized in Crookback's career, dread of death and nullity incites a wolfish rage to consume the lives of others in a fantastic struggle for symbolic immortality. To preserve itself, society mounts a compensatory drive to create a hero in whose apotheosis everyone can vicariously share. Divine sanction and dynastic control over the future become signs of the group's power of survival. Whenever that conviction of immortality fails, as it does to some extent in each of the histories, the result is rebellion. And since the ensuing contest unconsciously plays out nothing less than a struggle for being itself, the outcome virtually always means death to the loser, for that death revitalizes the life-giving glory of the crown the victor holds. As Prince John tellingly sums up his defeat of the rebels in *2 Henry IV*, "God, and not we, hath safely fought to-day. / Some guard [these traitors] to the block of death" (IV.ii.121–22). The victors covertly aggrandize themselves by attributing their (treacherous) actions to God and thereby justifying the pitiless slaughter of their opponents, including the innocently disbanded common soldiers. It would not be inaccurate to say that in imagination, apart from any conscious trickery, the winners at once identify with, and dissociate themselves from, a violent God.

Like the histories as a group, the scene at Gaultree forest combines two incompatible perspectives. We may behold a fairly straightforward political action, a drama of state, yet we can also see through the imagery of the scene to an unconscious struggle for apotheosis. To make that symbolic immortality efficacious, culture disguises or denies the reality of death as the play itself manifestly does. In turn, to some extent inevitably, culture can scarcely help but be—as Professor Barber might say—sentimental. Nor should this surprise us. After all, since identity is a symbolic process and potentially limitless, not to say perfectible, we commonly understand ourselves to be godlike as well as the quintessence of dust. We realize that we must die and nonetheless go about our daily business as if we expect to live forever. In subtly compulsive ways we invest ourselves in ideologies, leaders, and objects from art to houses which promise to infuse us with power and permanence. In our own political culture, as in Shakespeare's, we observe painstaking decorum and yet scarcely blink to hear competition for power couched in images of annihilation and apotheosis.[34]

Prophecy calls attention to this insoluble doubleness in human experience, for it may signify a godlike control over time by making the future obedient to the secure past, or it may be a merely natural process of guesswork, even a form of escapism. In a prophetic context the hero's role is usually messianic, and figures such as Richmond and Henry V reflect the same doubleness in their tendency to appear to audiences either as providential agents or as Machiavellian connivers. Similarly, Crookback may strike us as a virtuosic study of Machiavellian psychology, or we may fix on him as a type of the Vice or devil, an anti-messiah.

Rather than argue that one of these extremes—or some nice combination of extremes—is the absolute truth about the plays, I would emphasize that Shakespeare exploited the ambiguities of his medium to create a radically comprehensive play-world. Although his vision of history is aggressively empirical and ironical, it also honors irrational depths of experience. Given our own historical situation, we are disposed to appreciate the way prophecy and prophetic dreams may dramatize the unconscious forces shaping experience. As critics we readily applaud the plays' demystification of historical process. It is less easy for us to evaluate the plays' ambiguous embrace of magical styles of imagination, and to appreciate that demystification can never be complete. In our criticism we are tempted to schematize irrational behavior in systems of belief such as "The King's Two Bodies" which can be sound as critical concepts and yet not adequate to the mentality implied in a complex art such as Shakespeare's.[35]

In part our difficulty in understanding a problem such as prophetic behavior in the plays is that we ourselves are insolubly equivocal about time. We may experience the past as if, as memory, it is still alive somewhere in the back of our minds. As intuition, the future too may feel alive to us already, as it does to a prophet.[36] Extra-rationally, ambiguously, and in the midst of our common sense, that is, we may maintain a mode of imagination which enhances our illusion of control over time and minimizes—even denies—time's irreversible fatality. Although in the world around us ideologies threaten to fight to the death over competing eschatological claims, we tend to protect our own eschatological assumptions and consolations from rational challenge.[37] Ultimately we cannot imagine an end to existence or existence without an end.

It seems likely that, however different, Shakespeare and his culture were no less complex and paradoxical in imagination than we are. Contemporary Christianity, for example, cultivated imaginative forms which embraced mankind's doubleness by meditating on a central figure who is at once person and God, child and father, lamb and shepherd, victim and conqueror, supplicant and king, an alien and yet a presence in all believers. And Christianity is perhaps only the most forthright of examples. In the histories Shakespeare appears to be expanding the imagination of his time, encouraging his audiences to face more openly the immensity and contingency of history. I like to think that the plays serve to demystify history, and therefore represent a healthy assertion of consciousness over intractable and dangerous materials. But I am aware that in Shakespeare as in our own lives there are also strong elements of escapism and self-deception that we need to respect. We should not be surprised that "in tone and sentiments" the benediction and "Amen" at the close of *Henry V* recall "Richmond's final speech in *Richard III*, which also concludes 'God say Amen' and casts a prophetic glow over the coming of the Tudor dynasty." Neither should we be astonished when Professor Prior goes on to insist that, as history, "the happy optimism of the ending [of *Henry V*] is totally unfounded."[38]

Historically, then, Shakespeare's use of prophetic behavior seems to represent a new effort to honor the complexities of experience by dramatizing the dreamlike depths of imagination. Just as Richard III, the angel with horns, plays out a fantasy about omnipotence and revenge against life that resembles in some ways the furious apotheosis imagined by a self-anointed Messiah in the streets of Elizabethan London, so Hal's prophetic destiny evoke—discreetly, even subliminally—the messianic provenance of the English crown.

NOTES

1. G. R. Elton, *Policy and Police* (Cambridge: Cambridge Univ. Press, 1972), p. 33.

2. See Gerard H. Cox, "Apocalyptic Projection and the Plot of *The Alchemist*," *English Literary Renaissance*, 13 (1983), 70–87.

3. Elton, p. 50. In his *Diary* Philip Henslowe lists among his theater's props a cloak of invisibility which, in conjunction with Neville's, witnesses the complexly equivocal attitudes toward the supernatural in Shakespeare's England.

4. Quotations are from *The Riverside Shakespeare*, ed. G. Blakemore Evans et al. (Boston: Houghton Mifflin, 1974).

5. A. P. Rossiter, *Angel with Horns* (New York: Theatre Arts Books, 1961), p. 20.

6. George A. Kelly, *A Theory of Personality* (New York: Norton, 1963). Because his theory "emphasizes the creative capacity of the living thing to represent the environment" and therefore "do something about it if it doesn't suit him" (p. 8), it is especially suggestive when applied to the theater, where characters must create their worlds.

7. Cf. William Neville's ambivalent fantasies at the beginning of this article, in which he wished Henry VIII dead one moment, and the next identified with him by imagining himself slaughtering Henry's enemies "of low blood."

8. In *Dream in Shakespeare* (New Haven: Yale Univ. Press, 1974) Marjorie B. Garber explores Shakespeare's development of dream from a "predictive device" to a "way of presenting the mind at work" (p. 15). Her analyses of dreams in *Richard III* explore imaginative modes akin to the prophetic (pp. 15–25).

9. K. V. Thomas, *Religion and the Decline of Magic* (New York. Scribner's, 1971), p. 398.

10. Glendower illustrates the point by attempting to intimidate the skeptical Hotspur with prophecies which supposedly prove him "not in the roll of common men" (*1H4*, III.i.42). For a discussion of the "Mouldwarp" prophecy which engages Glendower (III.i.147), see Thomas, pp. 399–403.

11. In "'More Than What You Were': Augmentation and Increase in *Macbeth*," *English Literary Renaissance*, 14 (1984), 70–82, James L. Calderwood analyzes Shakespeare's distinction between (perverse) augmentation and (natural) increase, which reflects the taboo. Seeking to be more than what he was, "Macbeth ultimately renders himself—and, in his despairing judgment, all of life—nothing." I have investigated the taboo directly in "Self-Effacement and Autonomy in Shakespeare," in *Shakespeare Studies*, 16 (1983), 75–100.

12. Shadow: "An unreal appearance; a delusive semblance or image; a vain and unsubstantial object of pursuit" (OED, 6a); also "an obscure indication . . . a prefiguration, foreshadowing" (OED, 6c). "Shadow" is also Elizabethan slang for an actor.

13. The Folio prints "spy my shadow," whereas the first quarto gives "see my shadow."

14. Cf. the "cloak of invisibility" which would dissolve the mortal body and confer expansive powers. As a projection of the self out of the body, Richard's repudiation is related to Macbeth's summons of his own will to murder in the form of "seeling night" which can "scarf up the tender eve of pitiful day, / And with . . . bloody and invisible hand / Cancel and tear to pieces that great bond / Which keeps me pale" (III.ii.46–48).

15. My argument here draws upon Ernest Becker, *The Denial of Death* (New York: Free Press, 1973).

16. Muriel Bradbrook, *The Living Monument* (Cambridge: Cambridge Univ. Press, 1976), p. 19.

17. Moody E. Prior, *The Drama of Power* (Evanston, Ill.: Northwestern Univ. Press, 1973), p. 43.

18. Dolores M. Burton, "Discourse and Decorum in the First Act of *Richard III*," *Shakespeare Studies*, 14 (1981), 59.

19. In *Europe's Inner Demons* (New York: Basic Books, 1975) Norman Cohn traces the history of the fantasies which produced the persecution of witches in

Europe, construing the anxious fascination with the devil as "unconscious resentment against Christianity as too strict a religion, against Christ as too stern a taskmaster. Psychologically, it is altogether plausible that such an unconscious hatred would find an outlet in an obsession with the overwhelming power of Christ's great antagonist, Satan" (p. 262).

20. In *The Denial of Death* Becker sees symbolic transcendence as the fundamental project of human personality and culture. He reminds us, "Life cannot go on without mutual devouring of organisms. If at the end of each person's life he were to be presented with the living spectacle of all that he had organismically incorporated in order to stay alive, he might well feel horrified by the living energy he had ingested. . . . To paraphrase Elias Canetti, each organism raises its head over a field of corpses, smiles into the sun, and declares life good" (p. 2). This is precisely the haunting, inadmissible truth about human life dramatized by the biting, "unfinished" Crookback and Henry IV's vision of mankind as insatiable wolves.

21. Henry Howard, Earl of Northampton, *A Defensative against the Poyson of Supposed Prophecies* (1583), sig. D4.

22. Norman Cohn, *The Pursuit of the Millennium* (New York: Harper, 1961), p. 69. My analysis of Hal's behavior here draws upon the dynamics of the apocalyptic fantasy Cohn details. The fantasy has echoes in Shakespeare, but without the revolutionary and chiliastic elements which surfaced again soon after in the behavior of the Ranters.

23. Holinshed attributes Satanic qualities to Worcester, whose aim "was ever (as some write) to procure malice and set things in a broil." In *Shakespeare's English Kings* (New York: Oxford Univ. Press, 1977) Peter Saccio calls Worcester "a born agent of chaos, something like a witch out of *Macbeth*" (p. 50).

24. Ernst Kris, "Prince Hal's Conflict," *The Psychoanalytic Quarterly*, 17 (1948), 487–506.

25. See Carl Bridenbaugh, *Vexed and Troubled Englishmen* (New York: Oxford Univ. Press, 1967), p. 16.

26. See Gilles Quispel's analysis of Augustine's Jerusalem in "Time and History in Patristic Christianity," in *Man and Time*, ed. Joseph Campbell (Princeton, N.J.: Princeton Univ. Press, 1957), p. 106.

27. In *Shakespeare's Creation* (Amherst: Univ. of Massachusetts Press, 1976), I have tried to show in detail how Shakespeare himself will often grossly conventionalize his art in order to violate those conventions and induce in the audience a sense of wonder or tragic awe.

28. James L. Calderwood, *Metadrama in Shakespeare's Henriad* (Berkeley: Univ. of California Press, 1979), p. 83.

29. Embowelled: "That has the bowels full" (OED, 3).

30. Andrew Gurr, "*Henry V* and the Bees' Commonwealth," *Shakespeare Survey*, 30 (1977), 67.

31. See Norman Rabkin's account of these interpretive possibilities in *Shakespeare and the Problem of Meaning* (Chicago: Univ. of Chicago Press, 1981), pp. 33–62, esp. p. 58.

32. In *A Kingdom for a Stage* (Cambridge, Mass: Harvard Univ. Press, 1972), for example, Robert Ornstein contends that *RII* "describes an ideal cosmological scheme in its poetry and mocks it in its dramatic action" (p. 105).

33. C. L. Barber, *Shakespeare's Festive Comedy* (Princeton, N.J.: Princeton Univ. Press, 1959), pp. 219–21.

34. Newspapers described the 1984 presidential campaign, as is customary, in terms of military assault. One candidate spoke of being criticized as "taking incoming" (= artillery). A governor's press secretary was quoted as saying that another candidate for president "hit this state so fast and exploded like an atom bomb." The metaphor naively expressed the dynamics of the fantasy I have been tracing in the histories, in which a leader may be felt capable of annihilating opponents and dominating the collective consciousness with a superhuman power.

35. See Ernst H. Kantorowicz, *The King's Two Bodies* (Princeton, N.J.: Princeton Univ. Press, 1957), esp. his chapter on *RII*, pp. 24–41. Kantorowicz appreciates that Renaissance minds could recognize the fictional nature of the royal ideology without altogether demystifying it.

36. Cf. Hamlet's sense of his own intuition as foreknowledge: "O my prophetic soul'" (I.v.40).

37. In *The Pursuit of the Millennium* Norman Cohn demonstrates that especially in their early stages the Nazi and Communist movements endowed "social conflicts and aspirations with a transcendental significance—in fact with all the mystery and majesty of the final, eschatological drama" (p. 308). Both movements "have been inspired by phantasies which are downright archaic" and "heavily endebted to that very ancient body of beliefs which constituted the popular apocalyptic lore of Europe" (p. 309). But striving for transcendence is by no means limited to these totalitarian movements. Witness the 1912 campaign in which Theodore Roosevelt declared that"we fight in honorable fashion for the good of mankind . . . we stand at Armageddon, and we battle for the Lord." In the early 1980s the American president likewise invokes Armageddon, representing the Soviet Union as an "evil empire" bent upon world conquest and the extirpation of all freedom while characterizing his own ideology, as he did on the evening of his reelection in 1984, as "a prairie fire" which has swept across America from sea to sea. The apocalyptic violence dissociated in the presidential rhetoric is righteously projected onto the demonized rival, the Soviet Union. At the same time 37% of Americans reportedly believe the Russians are their enemies "because they are atheists" (*Harper's*, March 1985).

38. Prior, p. 338.

SHERMAN HAWKINS

Structural Pattern in Shakespeare's Histories

The purpose of this essay is adventurous, even audacious: I wish to propose a structural pattern that comprehends and connects all eight of Shakespeare's major histories. Any such proposal inevitably calls up the unquiet shade of E. M. W. Tillyard. His view of these eight plays as a connected series dramatizing the Tudor Myth is generally discredited today, yet so much energy has been spent in demolishing it that little seems left over to explore alternative patterns. So far has the reaction to Tillyard gone that one current orthodoxy insists on the autonomy of the individual play. Even a critic who explores themes common to the histories, like John Wilders, feels obliged to emphasize that "each one is unique in style, construction, and dramatic effect."[1] Of course, this is true. But for the sake of this truism we are in danger of discarding what seems most imaginative and challenging in Tillyard: his vision of the histories as a unity, a patterned structure that in its final form reflects a single bold conception.

There is, I think, no contradiction between seeing the histories as individual and different, yet also as parts of a larger whole. A distinctive, even unique feature of these plays is their lack of closure. Comedy and tragedy are popularly defined by their happy or unhappy endings, but history goes on happening until the ending End. Of course it is possible to dramatize a given stretch of time in a single play like *King John* or *Henry VIII*, but history's

From *Studies in Philology* 88 (Winter 1991): 16–45. © 1991 by University of North Carolina Press.

essential open-endedness allows—even invites—the ambitious playwright to override these narrow limits. What should strike us first of all in Shakespeare's histories is less the difference or even the discrepancies between his individual plays than the daring and skill of his experiments in multiple form.

The fatal weakness of Tillyard's structural scheme is not that he treats the histories as serial, but that he arranges them in order of their historical events rather than the order of their composition. It is noteworthy that when Tillyard turns from the background to the plays themselves, he reverts from the historical to the literary sequence. In this perspective a different pattern emerges: instead of a single series of eight plays stretching chronologically from Richard II to Richard III, we have two blocks of four plays, each dealing with a continuous but disjunct historic period and culminating in the contrasted portraits of Richard III and Henry V. The ending of each drama in these series looks forward to the beginning of the next; only the last play in each tetralogy concludes with a finality marked by the union of former foes, a prayer for peace, and an echoing "Amen." Shakespeare borrows the death from tragedy and the marriage from comedy to stress this sense of an ending. Each tetralogy, then, constitutes a unit, a continuous whole. Even considered separately, their size and scope represent a formidable structural achievement. But are they really separate?

Tillyard himself recognized the tetralogical pattern—though for him it remained secondary to the overarching Tudor Myth—and the second tetralogy in particular has attracted much critical attention since his time. Yet even critics who show the inner unity and cohesion of its symbols, themes, and actions seem hesitant to analyze its structural pattern, and even more reluctant to extend that pattern to include the four earlier plays. And indeed there are at least two obstacles to such speculation. One obstacle—serious though not insuperable—is our uncertainty whether the first part of *Henry VI* was written before or after the second and third. Most scholars today, I believe, agree that it was written first, as its style and technique suggest. The other obstacle—far more formidable—is the suspicion that Part 2 of *Henry IV* is an unpremeditated sequel, either a carbon copy prompted by the theatrical success of Part 1 or an addition required when Shakespeare's material proved too much for the single play that he originally planned.[2] Harold Jenkins contends that Shakespeare recognized the need for a second play only when he was more than halfway through Part 1. As a result, he was forced to alter the play's shape, improvise an ending at Shrewsbury, and then duplicate Prince Hal's reformation to fill up Part 2. This daring and deftly argued thesis has won wide acceptance. Yet it seems odd that by the time he came to write *Henry IV* Shakespeare was so poor a judge of how much history could fit into a five-act play, and even more surprising that Part 1, with its change of form and improvised ending, emerges as the most shapely and symmetrical of all Shakespeare's histories. The larger structural implications of Jenkins's argument are devastating: even if Shakespeare intended to follow his play about Henry IV with another about Henry V the result would not be the precise balance of four plays against four but an asymmetric sequence of four and three. Indeed, a playwright who proceeds by such haphazard methods in composing a single play seems unlikely to have designed a whole tetralogy, much less two.

There is no room here even to summarize the evidence against Jenkins's theory, which I have examined elsewhere in detail.[3] For the sake of the present argument, I must ask my readers to assume that *1 Henry VI* is the earliest of Shakespeare's histories and that from the first he planned two plays about *Henry IV.* The notion that the second of these is a copy of its brilliant predecessor may make more sense applied to the series of which both are parts. Is it not probable, given the success of the first tetralogy, that Shakespeare should launch another that would resemble it in form and rival it in popularity? If so, may not the diptych form of *Henry IV* offer a key to the pattern of the two tetralogies?

I

The shift to compositional order and tetralogical form changes the whole meaning of these plays. In particular, it gives an entirely different meaning to the reign of Henry V. This provides only a happy but irrelevant parenthesis in the cycle of crime and punishment that makes up the Tudor Myth, whereas in the compositional sequence its position is final and climactic. The significance of this position is suggested by the structural parallel between the last plays in each tetralogy. If Henry V and Richard III are, as Tillyard says, the Good King and the Bad King, we can infer what every schoolboy assumes from the conventional titles of the history plays. We are not watching *The Contention Betwixt the Two Famous Houses of York and Lancaster*—much less *God's Judgment Upon England*—but Henry VI. These are in the first instance plays about kings and kingship, their primary theme, in the words of Polonius, "what majesty should be."[4] Hence their quasi-biographical form. Shakespeare traces the careers of both Richard and Henry through three plays, and these careers move in opposite directions. Gloucester's moral evolution is downward through repeated crimes, while Prince Hal—to the bafflement of many critics—seems to evolve upward towards kingship through repeated reformations. Shakespeare's argument turns on this contrast and opposition: we learn what majesty should be by observing its deformed antithesis. Appropriately, then, *Richard III* is a tragedy, the kind of play which Sidney says shows the fall of tyrants, while *Henry V* is epic, the genre which Sidney says shows heroic virtue, manifested in heroic deeds.

To see that the author of *Henry V* intended this contrast, we need only compare Richard's behavior the night before Bosworth with Henry's the night before Agincourt. The Good King moves incognito among his troops to hearten them, while the Bad King plays the eavesdropper under his followers' tents "To see if any mean to shrink from me." Henry impresses on his soldiers the importance of dying well, but the ghosts of all those he has slain urge Richard to die in despair. The soliloquy in which Henry begs God to overlook his father's crime is often cited as betraying his secret guilt and the illegitimacy of his claim to rule. But when we set this speech against that other nocturnal soliloquy in which Richard despairs of the mercy Henry seeks, we see its meaning in a truer light. Richard condemns himself for crimes he cannot repent, while Henry seeks pardon for a crime that is not even his own. The king is doing exactly what he counsels his followers to do, washing every mote from his conscience, and this repentance itself—as Shakespeare's Protestant audience would be aware—effects what all his works of penance could not achieve. The battles that follow show the judgment of God on these contrasted penitents.

As Moody Prior observes, Richard and Henry embody twin political myths, the tyrant and the true king.[5] This dual myth was not invented by the Tudors and their historians: it stretches back from the Renaissance all the way to Plato's *Republic*. The polar opposition between these images of kingship extends to the tetralogies as a whole, informing their developing action, their political argument, and their didactic strategies. To put it simply, the first tetralogy is essentially negative in emphasis, the second essentially positive. Thus in their very different ways, both Henry VI and Richard III are usurpers: true rule and true obedience prove difficult in their troubled reigns. But in their equally different ways, both Richard II and Henry V are true and valid kings, though Richard's right is his lineage and divine election, while Henry's is finally his own talents and moral qualities, those virtues for which in humanistic theory men were first made kings. The conflict here is between competing truths rather than opposing falsehoods as in the first tetralogy.

The difference between this negative and positive emphasis emerges clearly if we compare the rulers of each series in pairs. Henry VI and Richard II are both kings crowned as children who remain in some sense childish throughout their reigns; who renounce the wise and virtuous uncles who should be their natural counselors and protectors; who, challenged by more able rivals, must surrender their royal title in whole or part; who are finally deposed, imprisoned and murdered. But whereas in the first tetralogy this tragic decline occupies three plays, in the second it is dispatched in only one. The strong and able kings who replace these weaklings govern more effectively and die repenting of their sins. But whereas the reign of Henry IV fills two whole plays, that of Edward—the only prosperous interval in the first tetralogy—lasts barely two acts. Shakespeare keeps us aware of Edward's adulteries and of the factions that divide his court. His final sickness comes upon him as a judgment for his crimes: he dies in fear, and we foresee doom for his son. But Henry IV defeats the rebels who would divide his realm, and though his sudden illness is likewise a sign of judgment, he comes to realize that his fears for the future are mistaken, and we foresee a glorious career for his successor. There is no need to review the reigns of Richard III and Henry V, so plainly are they antithetical: one culminates in an invasion of England from France, the other in an invasion of France from England. In Richard's final defeat and Henry's amazing victory, we see God's verdict not only on them but also on the political claims of York and Lancaster they represent, and on the two eras that end so fittingly with Richard's tragic death and Henry's joyous marriage.

As these diametrically opposed termini suggest, the two tetralogies, like Richard and Henry, move in contrary directions. In the first tetralogy Edward Berry traces a thematic pattern so systematic and coherent that it must be deliberate: play by play, the tetralogy shows the progressive disintegration of political community.[6] Just as deliberately and systematically, the second tetralogy shows its restoration. The earlier series moves downward from loss of empire abroad through civil war at home to absolute tyranny. Reversing this downward trend, the second series moves from despotism through civil war to conquest of empire abroad.

These downward and upward movements are moral as well as political. Consider the decline in *Henry VI* from Talbot's heroic wars against the French in Part 1, to chivalric combat between Englishmen like York and Clifford in Part 2, to the brutal and ruthless vendetta of their offspring in Part 3. The next stages in this violent downward spiral are the summary executions and secret murders of Richard's tyranny. Throughout the first tetralogy we witness tragic falls of the virtuous and innocent, like Talbot, Duke Humphrey, or the hapless princes in the Tower. But we also watch the progressive deterioration of characters at first neutral or sympathetic, like York, Margaret, Warwick, Buckingham. The moral evolution of Henry VI to something like sanctity shines brighter for its isolation in this darkening world. It is countered by Gloucester's descent into demonic evil, as the loyal son and brother turns into the twisted embodiment of the fratricidal spirit that sets brother against brother, father against son, Englishman against Englishman.

The moral logic of the second tetralogy is very different. In these plays one who falls deserves his fate, whether it be a king like Richard II or a rebel like Hotspur. Yet we admire Percy's courage, while Richard's decline in fortune helps to refine and humanize him, preparing for the more drastic transformation of Prince Hal in the plays that follow. The prodigal prince is trained in all the cardinal virtues[7] and proves himself—to his father's surprise—a loyal and loving son. His chivalric combat with Hotspur at Shrewsbury demonstrates his personal and princely courage, but what wins the day at Agincourt is the true king's ability to inspire others to copy him: Henry becomes the embodiment and source of the heroic spirit which converts his motley international army into a band of brothers. Thus in the first tetralogy England is corrupted and divided against itself, while in the second, it is reformed like its future ruler until, under his leadership, it becomes once more a united nation, capable of heroic deeds.

To understand the political aspects of these changes, it will be helpful to glance back to Plato and Aristotle, the classical sources of much renaissance political thought. Plato's *Republic* shows how the state evolves from primitive beginnings into the ideal commonwealth ruled by philosopher kings, and then degenerates stage by stage into timocracy, oligarchy, democracy, and tyranny. This schematized sequence of rise and fall mirrors the great arc of Plato's argument, reflected in miniature by the myth of the cave. In the *Politics* Aristotle's account of how one form of government yields to another is more pragmatic and less mythic. Yet he too arranges the various states in a systematic pattern: the three true polities—monarchy, aristocracy, and constitutional government—are contrasted with their perversions—tyranny, oligarchy, and democracy. The true and valid forms of government all serve the common interest, while the false forms benefit the one, the few, or the many instead of the common good of all.

Timocracy and oligarchy, the rule of the military and the rich, largely disappear in the Renaissance, but the comparative strengths and weaknesses of monarchy, aristocracy, and democracy and the causes for the changes among them remain common topics in political treatises, while Plato's contrast between the king and the tyrant assumes even greater importance. Shakespeare's Roman plays demonstrate his familiarity with all three classical forms of government. Set in a hereditary monarchy, the history plays offer no examples of rule by the aristocracy or commons, but these classes play important parts in Shakespeare's taxonomy of kingship. Thus in the first tetralogy an international empire collapses into a kingdom increasingly divided, and a weak king cedes effective power to his nobles. The rule of his virtuous protector gives way to aristocratic factions, and this strife among the upper classes leads to the rising of the commons. At first the commoners seek only to punish the murderers of good Duke Humphrey, but this demand for justice soon yields to mindless self-interest in the anarchic democracy of Cade's rebellion. The next step is a civil war that involves king, lords, and commons in mutual destruction, and thence the downward path leads ineluctably to the despotism of Richard III.

The upward progress of the second tetralogy is not this simple. Indeed, one reason why the form of this tetralogy seems so satisfying is that it recapitulates the movement of the whole. Just as in *Henry VI* men looked back to the heroic reign of Henry V, so in *Richard II* men recall the heroic reign of Edward and the Black Prince. Richard II, like Henry VI, inherits the crown but not the kingly virtue of his predecessors, and his weak rule is overthrown by his rebellious nobles. In the eyes of these great lords, Bolingbroke is no more than *primus inter pares*, and civil war soon breaks out between the new ruler and those who made him king. Even more dangerous than the revolt of these aristocrats is the anarchy of Falstaff and his lawless plebeians: well may Henry fear that with his death all will be overturned! But the future depends on the character of his successor, and Richard's fall in the first play of the tetralogy is countered by Hal's rise in the remaining three. He moves upward through the classes of the kingdom he must rule and represent, from the riotous democracy of the tavern to the aristocratic rivalry of the battlefield and thence to the royal court, where he assumes his father's crown. At each level he masters what is true and good in its polity, while resisting the selfish temptations of plebeian pleasure, aristocratic honor, and royal ambition. He is ready to rule not for himself but for his people and to lead all England to the field of France, where commons, lords and king fight to regain their lost empire and revive the glories of the past.

The lessons these plays teach are likewise both moral and political. That they have a didactic purpose seems safe to assume: comedies delight, tragedies move, but histories instruct. The positive and negative thrust of the tetralogies suggests two of the recognized functions of the genre in Shakespeare's day. On the one hand is the use of the past to inspire the present and shape the future. Thus Thomas Heywood argues that the lively action of a play has bewitching power to "new mold the harts of the spectators and fashion them to the shape of any noble and notable attempt." What coward would not be shamed, he writes, to see his countryman valiant? And what English prince, inflamed by the royal spectacle of Edward III or Henry V "foraging France" would not be made fit and apt for the like achievement?[8] Here the historical clearly borders on the heroical. But on the other hand there are the familiar lessons of Tudor orthodoxy. So Heywood also maintains that history plays teach subjects obedience to their king, showing the untimely ends of those who rebel and the flourishing estate of those who obey, "exhorting them to allegeance, dehorting them from all trayterous and fellonious stratagems."[9] The monitory tone of such teaching contrasts with the inspirational appeal of heroic deeds. One warns against deviation from a norm, the other urges attainment of an ideal; one argues from negative, the other from positive example. Of course each strategy makes use of the other. Heroism rebukes cowardice as well as inspiring valor, and Pistol has his place and function in *Henry V*. Conversely, dissuasions from rebellion are strengthened by showing the "florishing estate" that rewards obedience: Iden's garden is set against the chaos that engulfs the rest of England in *2 Henry VI*. Thus both ways of teaching, "exhorting" and "dehorting," coexist within a single play, but one or the other is clearly dominant. The epic heroism of Talbot in *1 Henry VI* serves as a foil to the degeneracy of the king and his peers: the main thrust of this play and its sequels is negative and cautionary. Conversely, the tragic fate of Hotspur in *1 Henry IV*, though it shows the "untimely end of such as have moved tumults, commotions and insurrections," serves as a foil to the rise of Prince Hal: the main thrust of this play and its sequels is positive and exemplary. Finally, each tetralogy serves as foil and contrast to the other in a way that heightens the effectiveness of both.

Taken together rather than separately, the tetralogies enforce a larger political lesson. One of the standard arguments for the study of history, repeated over and over in renaissance treatises, is the claim that history explains the rise and fall of nations: "the cause of their encrease, of their prosperous mayntenaunce, and good preservation" and the means by which they "decreased, decayed and came to ruyne," or—to follow Shakespeare's sequence—"the meanes whereby they fall into decay, and agayne whereby they are re-established and restored."[10] What Shakespeare took these "causes" and "meanes" to be is a question too large and complex to be considered here, though the moral character of the ruler is plainly one of them. What matters for our present purpose is that in this view of history as an investigation of the rise and fall of nations, we have a model for the pattern of all eight history plays, a model that is not chronological but conceptual, unified not by sequence but by opposition. This pattern, which connects the two tetralogies and is repeated in the second on a smaller scale, is not evolution and decline, as in Plato, but loss and restoration. And if any myth informs this pattern, it is—as more than one critic has perceived—the mythos of Christian history, of paradise lost and regained, paralleled in the fall and reformation of the individual soul.[11] Plato's philosophic rulers need only to be educated, but in order to redeem his time and become the pattern of all Christian kings, Prince Hal has to undergo conversion, a symbolic death and rebirth.

II

The two tetralogies, then, form a great diptych, shaped by parallel and contrast. At this point I anticipate a rush of skeptical questions. Did Shakespeare actually intend the dual pattern I have sketched? If so, just when was this ambitious plan conceived? What precedents or literary models might have inspired such a vast and complex structure? To me it seems evident that Shakespeare deliberately planned his second tetralogy as counterpart and contrast to the first, but just when he did so seems less certain. Given his use of other early chronicle histories like *The True Tragedy of Richard III* and *The Troublesome Reign of King John*, it is suggestive that the only extant vernacular history that certainly preceded Shakespeare's is *The Famous Victories of Henry V*, a play which eventually became the dramatic model for *Henry IV* and *Henry V*. Thus when he wrote the first part of *Henry VI*, which begins with the funeral of Henry V and is haunted by his memory, it is possible that Shakespeare already conceived a contrasting drama like *The Famous Victories* about England's hero king. But it is one thing to dream of such a play or plays, another to design a whole tetralogy. Nothing in my argument requires the second tetralogy to have been planned before the theatrical success of the first invited a sequel.[12]

An immediate stimulus and model for such a project is at hand in *Tamburlaine*, whose influence pervades Shakespeare's earlier histories and whose diptych structure juxtaposes the hero's rise and fall, epic and tragedy.[13] The still larger historical sweep of Shakespeare's two tetralogies finds precedent in the miracle cycles, whose influence on the histories has been explored by Emrys Jones.[14] These stretch from the beginning to the end of time, and their pattern of fall and redemption dramatizes the mythos that underlies Shakespeare's double series. But of course Shakespeare would have found this pattern in the Bible itself with its diptych structure of Old and New Testaments. And he was surely familiar with the typology by which earlier figures in this sacred history prefigure or contrast with later ones.

Here, however, Shakespeare's probable model is not Christian but classical. From his schooldays, as David Riggs points out, Shakespeare was familiar with the exercises in *comparatio* exemplified by Fluellen's comparison of Henry V to Alexander the Pig.[15] This involves both similitude (not only are there rivers in Monmouth and Macedon but "there is salmons in poth") and contrariety (Alexander slays Cleitus "in his ales and his cups," whereas Henry turns away Falstaff "in his right wits and good judgments").

As Riggs observes, the same technique underlies Plutarch's *Lives*, which Shakespeare already uses as a source in Titus Andronicus.[16] Here we move from rhetoric to history and to comparatio on a grand scale. Plutarch's method is to pair biographies of Greek and Roman worthies who resemble each other in character, career, or historic role. "Thus," writes Geoffrey Bullough, "Theseus goes with Romulus (both founders of states and civilization), Alcibiades with Coriolanus (traitors), Alexander and Caesar (conquerors cut off in their prime), Dion and Brutus (liberators), Demetrius and Antony (extreme vice and virtue)."[17] The parallels Plutarch finds between these figures might excite envy even in Fluellen:

> Now surely, methinks that Theseus in many things was much like Romulus. For being both begotten by stealth, and out of lawful

matrimony, both were reputed to be born of the seed of the gods. . . .
Both joined valiancy with government. The one of them built
Rome, and the other by gathering into one dispersed people erected
the city of Athens: two of the most noble cities of the world. The
one and the other were ravishers of women; and neither th' one nor
th' other could avoid the mischief of quarrel and contention with
their friends, nor the reproach of staining themselves with the blood
of their nearest kinsmen. Moreover, they say that both the one and
the other in the end did get the hate and ill will of their citizens.[18]

One notices here several different kinds of likeness: the lineage of the
heroes, their public virtues and private vices, their position in the evolution
of their countries, the shape of their own career and its final outcome. Such
topics also inform the short comparative essays that follow each pair of biographies, but here likeness often gives way to antithesis:

Numa accepted the kingdom, and Lycurgus gave it up. The one
received it, not seeking for it; and the other having it in his hands
did restore it again. The one being a stranger and a private man
was by strangers elected and chosen their lord and king. The other
being in possession a king, made himself again a private person. . . .
Virtue brought the one to be in such a reputation that he was
judged worthy to be chosen a king, and virtue bred so noble a mind
in the other that he esteemed not to be a king.[19]

In such branching and balanced sentences we seem very close to the structural
and thematic patterning of Shakespeare's histories. And there are hints for the
careers of his kings, as in the story of Cimon, who in his first youth had a "very
ill name and report" as a great drinker and rioter, yet proved a brave captain
and a wise and virtuous governor.[20] These biographies, moreover, find their
place in the larger "lives" of Greece and Rome, so that according to Amyot,
Plutarch's French translator, the reader learns not only what to shun or copy
in the careers of individual captains, governors, and kings, but also the ways in
which states have been "established, and afterward maintained and increased;
or contrariwise, changed, diminished, and overthrown."[21]

III

The pattern of Shakespeare's histories, then, is in both form and method less
an act of creation *ex nihilo* than of adaptation, development, and synthesis. But
the pattern itself is more ingenious than I have yet shown. The most immediate model for the second tetralogy is the first, but it is a model that works

in reverse. Does this reversal apply to the structure of the tetralogies as well as their action and meaning? Is it an accident that in one series, three Henry plays lead to a Richard, while in the other, a Richard play is followed by three Henries? These dramas are as different in genre as in title. Both *Richard II* and *Richard III* are tragedies as well as histories. Both seem relatively disjunct and self-contained, whereas the Henry plays are comparatively open-ended and continuous. This continuity permits them to approximate the third of the great classical genres, whose obvious distinguishing mark, like the happy or unhappy ending of comedy and tragedy, is sheer size. That *Henry V* is intended as epic is obvious from its opening lines. But I would extend this epic analogy backward to include both parts of *Henry IV.* Thus the "Henriad"—a title I would reserve for the three plays of which Henry of Monmouth is actually the hero—forms an epic of princely education, whose classical precedent is the *Cyropaedia* of Xenophon. In contrast, the three parts of *Henry VI* form a negative epic of national collapse and civil war, whose classical model is the *Pharsalia* of Lucan.[22] Thus we have one tetralogy in which a negative and cautionary epic trilogy leads on to tragedy balanced by a second where tragedy gives way to an epic trilogy which is positive, heroic, and exemplary.

Let me press the argument one step further. Is it possible that this pattern of reversal works play by play, so that the first in one series corresponds to the last in the other, and the two central plays match in reverse order? (See Table, p. 31.) Certainly we do not find such correspondences between the two tetralogies when we consider the plays in their normal order. Except for the battles that conclude them, *Richard III* does not much resemble *Henry V.* But when we compare *Richard III*, the last play of the earlier tetralogy, to *Richard II*, the first play of the later one, parallels and contrasts leap to the eye. If we consider their political action, both plays dramatize successful usurpations of the crown, though in one the usurper is ultimately himself deposed while in the other he retains the throne. True to the negative and positive emphasis of the two tetralogies, the usurpation in *Richard III* is a sinister conspiracy prompted by personal ambition, while in *Richard II* it is a national uprising prompted by real and legitimate grievances. Gloucester is determined to prove a villain while Bolingbroke aspires to become a just king, and their methods differ accordingly. Bolingbroke's open challenge to Mowbray contrasts with Gloucester's secret plot against Clarence, and if divine justice is thwarted in the ritual trial by combat, it is diabolically perverted by the bloody baptism in the Tower. Gaunt and Edward, the last guardians of order and the past, die in the second act, and Gaunt's prophecy, like Margaret's, foreshadows the disorder to come. Though the rightful rulers, Richard and young Edward, come back to claim their own, their protectors prove ineffectual or malign, and the conspirators seize control of the state. This shift in power is marked by the execution of Rivers, Grey, and Vaughan in one play and of Bushy, Green, and Wiltshire in the other. It culminates near the end of Act III in scenes strikingly alike in their staging. From below, the willing tools of the conspirators, Northumberland and Buckingham, address their hypocritical eloquence to Richard and Gloucester, who appear with bishops on the castle walls above them. One Richard descends to the "base court," all too ready to be deposed; the other exits still "aloft," all too eager to be king. Thus at the beginning of Act IV, one Richard is crowned and the other abdicates. Gloucester straightaway plots with Tyrrel to murder the princes in the Tower while Bolingbroke indirectly prompts Exton to the murder of Richard at Pomfret. Typically, Gloucester rewards his accomplice and pretends repentance only in order to win his victim's sister, while Bolingbroke seeks to repudiate both his accomplice and his crime. Our pity for these falls of princes is increased by the figure of a weeping queen, the lamenting wife of *Richard II* and the mourning mother of *Richard III*. Now counter-forces begin to conspire against the usurper, but Bolingbroke defeats his foes while Gloucester is overthrown by his. In the penultimate scenes, both Richards die fighting bravely, and both plays conclude with their successors firmly established in power.

TABLE: CHIASMIC PATTERNING IN THE TWO TETRALOGIES

A. Political Evolution:

Fall	Rise
1 Henry VI—foreign conquest	*Richard II*—tyranny
2 Henry VI—civic rule	*1 Henry IV*—civil war
3 Henry VI—civil war	*2 Henry IV*—civic rule
Richard III—tyranny	*Henry V*—foreign conquest

B. Genres:

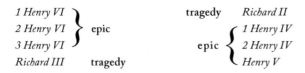

1 Henry VI				tragedy	*Richard II*
2 Henry VI	}	epic			*1 Henry IV*
3 Henry VI			epic	{	*2 Henry IV*
Richard III		tragedy			*Henry V*

C. Individual Plays:

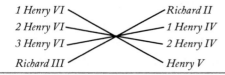

1 Henry VI	*Richard II*
2 Henry VI	*1 Henry IV*
3 Henry VI	*2 Henry IV*
Richard III	*Henry V*

If the political action invites comparison between the usurpers, as tragedies the plays focus on the two protagonists. Both Richards are bad kings, the only genuinely bad rulers in either tetralogy. Each seizes the inheritance that belongs to another, and each is guilty of a kinsman's blood. Both are duly punished by an invasion from France, led by a charismatic rival who unites England against its dubious king. Both Richards might be described as tyrants in the sense that each rules for his own selfish interest. And it is this self-absorption that explains the strange kinship of these namesakes, who are outwardly so unlike. As Coppelia Kahn points out, they are actors, self-dramatizing narcissists: "Both are fascinated with their mirror images, Richard III descanting on his shadow . . . Richard II dramatizing his crisis of identity in a real mirror."[23] The twisted shadow, the shattered glass epitomize the defective sense of self that produces the isolating egotism of each. In renaissance terms, these despots rule their outer kingdoms so badly because they fail to order the kingdom within. And by a different kind of mirror logic, each Richard is destroyed by a Henry who is his exact antithesis.

But these similarities only point to the contrasts so characteristic of the two tetralogies. Nature seems to sanction the lineal king and stigmatize the usurper by their very appearance. Richard is as beautiful as Gloucester is deformed, and the self-love of the "sweet lovely rose" seems natural compared to the self-loathing of the "foul bunch-backed toad." Both are soliloquists, but one is tragic and lyrical, the other ironic or blackly comic, their styles correspondingly "high" and "low." These contrasts in looks and speech reflect the crucial political difference between the two kings: Richard III really is a tyrant both by usurpation and misrule, whom it is almost a duty to overthrow, while Richard II is the kind of bad but legitimate ruler whom it is still a duty to obey. Their offenses against justice are not equal. Though Richard II seems clearly responsible for Woodstock's death, that event happens outside the play, and the precise nature and degree of Richard's guilt is not spelled out. The worst crime we actually see him commit is seizing Bolingbroke's inheritance. He is a thief, his robbery the first of a series that runs through the plays that follow. And that "false thief" Prince Hal gradually redeems the act of robbery itself by giving back what he had stolen—Falstaff's gold, Hotspur's honor, the King's crown—and ultimately by claiming in France the inheritance of another which he proves to be his own. In contrast, Richard III takes not only his nephew's crown but his life: he is a murderer, and the killing of helpless children climaxes not only his own earlier crimes, but all the increasingly brutal deeds of violence in the preceding plays. Blood will have blood, and Richard III pays for his murders with his own life. By the same logic and justice, Richard II pays for usurping Bolingbroke's lands and titles when Bolingbroke in turn usurps his. But

Richard's death falls outside this balanced scheme of crime and punishment. Though the murder at Pomfret tacitly recalls Woodstock's fate at Calais, it has further meaning. More are men's ends marked than their lives before, and in death Richard's courage proves the native royalty he asserts with his last breath, whereas the desperate valor of the other Richard only confirms his doom: he has hazarded all—and lost.

Thus in these two tragedies, the inner logic of the action is directly contrary: the sufferings of the hero are punitive in one play and expiatory in the other, aligning the plays with two basic but contrasted versions of the genre. *Richard III* is a tragedy of damnation, whose hero, like Macbeth, first rises and then falls in outer fortune, while progressively losing our sympathy and his own soul by his repeated crimes, till at the end he seems almost the common Enemy of mankind. Richard II, on the other hand, is a redemptive tragedy, whose hero, like Lear, undergoes a progressive fall in fortune but after his initial crime or error regains both audience sympathy and his own soul, till in the end his sufferings can be compared to those of Christ. Punitive and redemptive tragedy, enacting crime and punishment in one case and purification through suffering in the other, are variants of the genre that go all the way back to Aeschylus, and their contrasted patterns of rise and fall versus fall and rise seem to be archetypal.[24] Thus in the fourth act of these plays, the two Richards reach opposite points on Fortune's wheel: Richard III gains the crown and Richard II surrenders it. From here the outer fortunes of both heroes lead down to death, but the inner action points in opposite directions. In his last soliloquy, Richard III judges himself and despairs: there is no creature loves him—not even Richard. In the corresponding soliloquy, Richard II is still struggling to know himself, but the music that helps prompt his tormenting self-awareness is a sign of love. Richard III is slain in a fair fight, and Henry Richmond rejoices that "the bloody dog is dead." In contrast, the murder of Richard II is the very crime against kin that Henry Bolingbroke set out to punish. But the blood that stains his guilty hand has finally washed Richard clean: "Mount, mount, my soul! thy seat is up on high. . . ."

IV

In contrast to the two Richards, Henry V and VI are both good kings. But their goodness differs in ways that reflect the different emphases— providential and humanistic—of the two tetralogies. Henry VI's virtues are religious, Henry V's moral and political: one becomes a saint and martyr, the other a model of the just governor and the good man. Henry V unites and extends his realm; his are the virtues needed to rule the kingdoms of this world. Henry VI loses first France and then England but gains another kingdom and a higher royalty: "My crown is in my heart, not on my head. . . ." Nevertheless, the unworldly piety of "holy Harry" costs him and England everything his heroic father gained, confirming the prophecy that "Henry born at Monmouth should win all / And Henry born at Windsor should lose all."

Shakespeare's epic trilogies dramatize this losing and winning, the decline of one Henry and the rise of the other. But whereas Prince Hal is obviously the real protagonist even of *Henry IV*, the titular hero of *Henry VI* seems less clearly central to the plays that bear his name. This is precisely Shakespeare's point: the weak king fails to dominate the trilogy as he fails to rule his kingdom. Hence both dramatic interest and political power in *Henry VI* are divided among a number of contending rivals. As a result we shall find that a single character or action in "Henriad" is often mirrored—as it were prismatically—by several in the fragmented world of *Henry VI*.

The two central plays in each tetralogy set Henry VI's deterioration as a king against Hal's education as a prince. The disintegration of England in the earlier plays and its reform in the later ones reflect the increasing misgovernment of one Henry and the other's progressive mastery of the arts of rule. What qualities does a true king need? According to a tradition that goes back to the *Institutes* of Justinian, he must rule with valor in war and justice in peace. And valor and justice are the twin virtues that Hal learns in *1* and *2 Henry IV* and Henry signally fails to exhibit in *2* and *3 Henry VI*.[25]

The opening lines of *1 Henry IV*, with their plangent evocation of civil butchery, might equally well begin *3 Henry VI*. Both are dramas of civil war, but their moods could hardly be more different. Falstaff's festive comedy could find no place in the sanguine tragedy of *Henry VI*, but it fits the buoyant and optimistic ethos of *1 Henry IV*, where even Hotspur's revolt is conceived at first as chivalric adventure. War here is the field of honor, the test of manhood by which Hal proves himself. His courage is an authentic virtue, defined by contrast with its excess and defect in Hotspur and Falstaff. Indeed, it is Hal's angry eagerness to outdo Hotspur in valor that reconciles him to his father, and at Shrewsbury the two fight side by side. In contrast, Henry VI is incapable of striking a blow; on the field of battle he can only meditate. His pusillanimity in surrendering the succession to York alienates him from his wife and son, but this Prince of Wales is too young to defeat his father's foes, while Margaret's unwomanly ferocity is as much a perversion of fortitude as Falstaff's unmanly cowardice. No one here—not even the weakling king—lacks physical courage, but courage seems closer to vice than virtue, hardly distinguishable from savage cruelty and ruthless ambition. Civil war is here a scene of nightmare violence and communal crime, whose emblem is the slaying of a son by a father and a father by a son. These anonymous and accidental crimes against kin dramatize in symbolic form the less direct way in which parents and children destroy each other in these plays: thus it is Margaret's murder of York which begets the murder of her own son. In contrast to this pervasive parricide is Hal's rescue of the king at Shrewsbury: the son saves his father's life—and England.

Both plays show the reigning house of Lancaster struggling to put down rebellions, and typically Lancaster wins in one play and loses in the other. But the issues are broader than that: *1 Henry IV* shows the victory of order, *3 Henry VI* the triumph of discord. In *1 Henry IV*, despite Hotspur's valor and Mortimer's lineal claim, we never doubt which side is right: the rebels would split up England between themselves while Henry seeks to unite it. In *3 Henry VI*, however, York and Lancaster divide our sympathies as they do England. In the first scene, the rival claimants confront each other like mirrors:

> Henry:
>   I am thy sovereign,
> York:
>   I am thine.

In the episodes that follow, the leaders of both sides break oaths, slaughter prisoners, conquer and flee, are captured and escape, are exiled and return. From a Lancastrian viewpoint, York and his kin are like the rebel Percies, with Edward or Gloucester in Hotspur's role. But from a Yorkist perspective, the rebels are Henry and his followers, with Hotspur divided between Clifford and Warwick. The analogies thus created are bafflingly profuse but sometimes quite exact: compare Hotspur to Warwick, who helps make Edward king, quarrels with him because he feels his honor slighted, allies himself with former enemies, but is betrayed by a trusted kinsman (for Clarence is his son-in-law) and finally defeated by overwhelming royal forces. We do not see the combat in which he is fatally wounded, but his dying lines create echoes we shall hear again:

> Lo, now my glory smeared in dust and blood;
> My parks, my walks, my manors that I had,
> Even now forsake me; and of all my lands
> Is nothing left me but my body's length.
> Why what is pomp, rule, reign, but earth and dust?

Events as well as characters are prismatically multiplied, so that Shrewsbury is refracted in Wakefield and Towton and Barton and Tewkesbury. The fortunes of war toss either side now up, now down, and these giddy revolutions, repeated in battle after battle, create a patterned image of chaos. But morally both York and Lancaster seem caught in a spiral of violence that punishes crime with crime. In contrast, the political plot of *1 Henry IV* shows a single decisive turn of fortune's wheel, as Hotspur plunges from victory at Holm-edon to defeat at Shrewsbury and Hal rises to take his place. Our sense of order is here moral no less than structural. The slaying of one Harry by the other is a chivalric exploit that glorifies the victor. In contrast, the murder of one Edward by another at the end of *3 Henry VI* is a deed of shame which dooms all who share in it.

V

The Elizabethans, as Paul Jorgenson informs us, viewed war and peace as phases in an alternating cycle.[26] Thus in *2 Henry IV* and *2 Henry VI* the civil wars that occupy their two companion plays are ending or beginning. The terrifying visions of disorder evoked by Northumberland and Clifford come, significantly, in the very first scene of one play and the next-to-last scene of the other. True to the antithetical patterning of the tetralogies, *2 Henry IV* moves from war to peace, *2 Henry VI* from peace to war. The Archbishop's revolt is really the aftermath of Hotspur's, while Cade's rebellion is but the prologue to York's. And both these uprisings are defeated not by arms but by eloquence and cunning, by the word rather than the sword. For despite such wars and rumors of wars, these are plays centrally concerned with peace. This peace, however, is not to be equated with civic harmony: England is divided by faction in *2 Henry VI* and diseased by corruption in *2 Henry IV*. Such disorders require the exercise of justice quite as much as war demands the proof of valor.

It typifies this difference that in Part 1 of *Henry IV* we see Falstaff leading his troops to battle while in Part 2 we observe the chicanery with which he recruits them. The theme of justice is dramatized by just such vignettes of its administration (or maladministration): the baffled petitioners, the pretended blind man, the farcical trial by combat in *2 Henry VI*; the attempted arrest of Falstaff or Shallow's handling of the suit of Visor against Perkes in *2 Henry IV*. Human justice in these scenes seems to fail more often than it succeeds, but the plays intimate the workings of a higher justice which is divine. We glimpse it in the sudden sickness that strikes down Beaufort and Bolingbroke at the very moment when they seem to have triumphed over their enemies. The king, however, dies repentant, the cardinal in madness, terror, and despair.

In each play political order is threatened both by high and low, by rebellious peers and riotous commoners. But the ambitious York is clearly more dangerous than the idealistic Archbishop or the guilty and enfeebled Northumberland. So at the lower end of the social scale, Falstaff's squalid revels seem genial and benign compared with the bloody anarchy of Cade. No doubt Sir John would applaud his namesake's wish to have London's conduits flow with wine; in practice, however, Cade makes them run with blood. Comedy here turns black indeed. But Falstaff's real threat to justice is not as a rebel but as the "false favorite" whose counsels may mislead and corrupt the young king. This suggests that his actual counterpart in *2 Henry VI* is not Cade but Margaret. She becomes Henry's evil genius as Falstaff is Hal's, and her rivalry with Duke Humphrey foreshadows Falstaff's rivalry with Henry IV and his surrogate, the Chief Justice.

The choice the young kings make between these rivals turns out to be directly opposite. The good duke and the wise judge clearly stand as symbols of order and justice. There is a crucial change of government as Humphrey surrenders his staff of office to one Henry and Henry IV gives up his crown to the other. Henry VI, incited by Margaret and her confederates, renounces Humphrey's paternal protection, while Henry V, renouncing Falstaff and his followers, adopts the Chief Justice as a second father. The balanced scenes of judgment in which Hal banishes his seeming friend and honors his apparent foe show vice punished and virtue rewarded. The harsh words of the young king to Falstaff are intended to reform and cure him, and it is no accident that they echo those of a higher King and Judge: divine and human justice at last come together.[27] In contrast to these final acts of judgment are the central scenes in *2 Henry VI*, where Henry fails first to defend Humphrey from his accusers and then to punish his murderers as they deserve. It remains for God to strike down Beaufort and pirates to execute Suffolk—but that way chaos lies. Indeed chaos has been imminent throughout *2 Henry VI* from its opening scene, where the facade of harmony in a court met to welcome its new queen is stripped away to reveal faction, ambition, and conspiracy. In contrast, near the end of *2 Henry IV* a frightened and demoralized court, mourning its dead king, finds a new and unifying object of allegiance in his successor. Thus at the end of these plays, Henry V prepares to lead a reunited England against France, while Henry VI must face an England bloodily divided between York and Lancaster.

VI

Of all these histories, the first and the last, *1 Henry VI* and *Henry V*, are the most clearly parallel and antithetical. The cycle that begins with the funeral of Henry V ends with his marriage, and these opposed events typify the mood and meaning of the tetralogies and the two plays they introduce and conclude. The announcement in the first scene of *1 Henry VI* that the French have rebelled gives both plays a common action, the recovery of France. And in fact every English defeat in *1 Henry VI* is promptly reversed:

Joan is captured and burned; the Dauphin finally pledges fealty to Henry. Yet by the end of *1 Henry VI* we know that France is lost, while at the end of *Henry V* France is won.

It is a myth as well as an empire that is built up in *Henry V* and dismembered in *1 Henry VI*, the myth of Henry himself. Though he is buried at the beginning of *1 Henry VI*, in a real sense he is not yet dead. As Talbot teaches the Countess of Auveigne, a man's physical being is but his "shadow." And just as Talbot's real "substance, sinews, arms and strength" are his soldiers, so Henry survives in his virtuous brothers, Gloucester and Bedford, and in the brave comrades in arms like Salisbury and Talbot who keep alive his heroic example. The deaths and funerals of these, punctuating the play at ritual intervals, mark the gradual demise of the hero king, reflected in the moral, political, and geographic collapse of his realm. But Henry also dies as the meaning of his life is denied or betrayed, as his right to rule is challenged by York and his miraculous conquests are parodied by the demonic victories of Joan. Thus the funeral that opens the play symbolizes the action of the whole. And we see what the counter-action of *Henry V* must be: not just the conquest of a kingdom but the renewal of a myth, the recreation of "that ever-living man of memory."

The themes of dissension and unification so central to the two tetralogies are reflected in the very form of these plays. The child king who is the titular hero of *1 Henry VI* does not even appear until the third act, and even then he seems overpowered dramatically as well as politically by his turbulent and contentious peers. The hero of *Henry V*, on the other hand, dominates his world and our attention so powerfully that he has no rival or real antagonist; he seems almost to absorb his followers into himself. The same principles of unity and multiplicity apply to action: compare the several empty English victories in *1 Henry VI* to the single, decisive triumph of Agincourt, or the repeated sieges of Orleans, Rouen, and Bordeaux to the taking of Harfleur. Its multiple plots make *1 Henry VI* fragmentary and episodic; the setting shifts back and forth between France and England; even the style is so various as to provoke theories of multiple authorship. But the comic subplot of *Henry V* with its appropriately lower style merges increasingly with the main plot as the action grows more connected and the play moves in a single forward impulse from England to France.

This formal unity and deliberate disunity match the internal politics of the two plays. The death of Falstaff early in *Henry V* marks the end of anarchy. His followers, less comic and less dangerous, are gradually eliminated from the body politic: the fever that has infected England ever since *Richard II* ends here. But Mortimer's death at almost the same point in *1 Henry VI* signals the approach of chaos as his claim, so long suppressed, passes to the far more perilous Richard of York. Henry V easily detects and crushes the conspiracy of York's father, the Earl of Cambridge; Henry VI, failing even to recognize the ambition of Cambridge's son, restores his titles and makes him regent of France. The whole movement of *1 Henry VI* is towards disintegration as the quarrel between the red rose and the white spreads from noble to commoners and from England to France, leading to the final defeat of Talbot. The heroic mutuality which Talbot and his son achieve in death contrasts with the stubborn feuding of York and Somerset, foreshadowing the civil wars that will set Englishman against Englishman in subsequent plays. But the movement of *Henry V* is towards unity, reconciling the civil and national divisions of the preceding plays. The comic plebeians, Pistol and Nym, patch up their quarrels; captains from Scotland, Ireland, and Wales learn to fight side by side under an English king; York and Suffolk, whose very names by now betoken strife, die embraced. Cornered and outnumbered like Talbot at the same point in *1 Henry VI*, the English overcome their quarreling French antagonists through this new unity, and it is sealed in the reconciliations that resolve the comic bickering over gloves and leeks, antitypes of the fatal roses of *Henry VI*. The source and inspiration of this heroic community is, of course, Henry himself: the real victory we see at Agincourt is the renewal of a myth.

Whatever we today may think of Henry's imperialism, it is important for Shakespeare's argument that the play's unity and reconciliation extend to include both peoples, French and English. Ironically, the arguments that Burgundy uses to make peace between two nations in *Henry V* echo those Joan uses in *1 Henry VI* to persuade Burgundy himself to break his alliance and make war with England:

> Look on thy country, look on fertile France,
> And see the cities and the towns defaced
> By wasting ruin of the cruel foe.

Both plays end in peace, but in one this masks English defeat and in the other crowns English victory. In both the English king marries a French princess, but whereas Margaret is a princess only in title who must be bought at the price of Anjou and Maine, Katherine's dowry is a kingdom. Thus one marriage portends the division of England itself, while the other symbolizes the union of England and France. The same contrasting principle applies at the personal level. It is noteworthy that Suffolk woos both Margaret and the youthful Henry VI, while Henry V speaks for himself. One courtship is really a seduction that will lead to adultery; the other, despite its political setting and purpose, achieves genuine romance. Henry VI chooses to ignore the welfare of his country to satisfy his own desires: he divides the man from the king. But it is in pursuing England's good that Henry V finds his own happiness: as he woos Katherine, the king and the man become one.

Throughout this argument, I have assumed a positive, even idealistic view of Henry. In the overall tetralogical pattern, that is the only one that makes sense. But we should remember that this project was carried out over a long period in which Shakespeare himself grew and changed: what he originally planned to do in *Henry V*, what his earlier plays and his general argument required him to do, may not have been quite what he wanted to do when he finally came to write the play—and the resulting tensions are felt throughout *Henry V*. But if we would know Shakespeare's final judgment of his hero, is it not suggested in the way that Hal, who to so many critics seems to banish personal affection and his own humanity along with Falstaff, finds both in the French princess who for him in the end is simply Kate?

VII

The structural pattern I have traced is not complete. There are significant comparisons to be drawn within each tetralogy, between the saintly Henry VI and the demonic Richard III, between Richard II, the bad ruler who cannot become a man until he ceases to be king, and Henry V, the good ruler who cannot become king until he learns to be a man. But our main concern here is the connection between the two tetralogies—and in any case I have traced as many likenesses and oppositions as even the most tolerant reader can be expected to stomach. Did Shakespeare really intend all of them? Or indeed any?

Before even attempting an answer, we should note that the stuff of Shakespearean history consists of a limited range of events: conspiracies and battles, revolts and invasions, murders and executions, coronations and royal marriages. Such restricted material, spread through eight plays, inevitably produces repetition. Consider, for example, the motif of the prince murdered in prison: one thinks at once of Duke Humphrey and Henry VI, Clarence and the princes in the Tower, Woodstock and Richard II. The question is whether these repetitions are casual and meaningless or deliberate and systematic.

Elizabethan views of history encourage us to look for significance in such recurrence. One obvious example is the stress on crime and providential punishment. Thus the second in each pair of murders listed above could be seen as replicating and punishing the first. Tillyard's Tudor Myth is simply a large-scale elaboration of this idea: the deposition of Henry VI balances the deposition of Richard II by Henry's grandfather. We no longer mistake Tillyard's myth for the single, authoritative interpretation of these events: in the *Mirror for Magistrates*, for instance, Henry VI does not mention any ancestral sin; instead, he attributes his fall to his own breach of contract in marrying Margaret. That such errors are indeed punished—often by iteration or reversal—was a belief widely and deeply held. But the chroniclers often tacitly assume such causal relations or offer alternate formulations of them. This leaves a dramatist like Shakespeare free to choose or create connections for himself.

Again, the study of history was regularly justified on the ground that we learn to foresee the future by studying the past. This assumes that history repeats: the political or moral choice one faces today resembles choices made by the heroes or villains of yesteryear. Such study of history was not only academic: in view of our recurrent motif, it is fascinating to read that the warders of Mary Stuart decided it was not "convenient or safe" to do away with the imprisoned queen in part because they recalled the precedents of Edward and Richard II.[28] The motif of the impolitic marriage, important in Shakespeare's histories, was also a vital public issue of the time: Mary lost her throne by wedding Bothwell, who was thought to have murdered her husband, while Elizabeth refrained from marrying Leicester, who was suspected of murdering his wife. It is doubtful that either royal lady had historical precedents in mind as they weighed the choice between prudence and desire. But the precedent was there in Edward IV, whose unwise marriage to Lady Grey repeats the similar mistake of Henry VI, with equally fatal results. Hall makes no explicit connection between these events, but no reader as keen as Shakespeare could fail to see the parallel. Of Henry's marriage Hall declares that

> God with this matrimony was not content. For after this spousage the kynges frendes fell from hym, both in Englande and in Fraunce, the Lordes of his realme, fell in division emongest themselfes, the commons rebelled against their sovereign Lorde, and naturall Prince, feldes wer foughten, many thousandes slain, and finally the kyng deposed, and his sonne slain, and this Quene sent home again, with as muche misery and sorowe, as she was received with pompe and triumphe.[29]

Likewise Hall speculates that "God was not contented, nor yet pleased" with Edward's match, observing

> what miserie, & what troble ensued by reason of this mariage: for it can not be denied, but for this mariage kyng Edward was expulsed the Realm, & durst not abide, And for this mariage was therle of Warwycke & his brother miserable slain. By this mariage were kyng Edwards ii. sonnes declared bastardes, & in conclusion prived of their lifes. And finally by this mariage, the quenes bloud was confounded, and utterly in maner destroyed.[30]

It seems only a step from such implicit parallelism to Shakespeare's patterned correspondences. The marriage of Henry V, which concludes the histories, takes on its full meaning only in contrast to these fatal choices earlier in the cycle.

History offered a vast repertory of such exempla, both positive and negative. We see why its study was believed to confer wisdom, whose parts—in Cicero's familiar definition—are the past, the present, and the future, and whose essence is understanding what we should imitate or shun, the knowledge of good and bad.[31] Just this drastic and simple polarization, as we have seen, underlies Shakespeare's contrasted portraits of Richard III and Henry V and informs the structural pattern of his two tetralogies. Even though it does not match some universally agreed Tudor monomyth, this pattern seems to fit his audience's sense of how history is shaped and what it means.

The very fact that the pattern itself is so elaborate and precise may render it less plausible in an age as disordered as our own. In fact ordered neatness is exactly what we should expect. Only recently have we begun to recognize and appreciate Shakespeare's mastery of structural form. In his pioneering study *Shakespearean Design*, Mark Rose shows how Shakespeare arranged scenic divisions in skillfully balanced diptychs and triptychs. The opposition of such diptych forms, he observes, extends to the pairing of characters, the doubled plots and contrasted settings, the antithetic image patterns and thematic contraries of Shakespeare's drama: bipolar opposition seems one law of his "symmetrical imagination,"[32] This delight in pattern Shakespeare shared with most of his contemporaries. As Rose points out, it was grounded in the metaphysical assumptions of his time, for art imitates nature, and nature is an order contrived by the supreme artist. It was further inculcated by training in rhetoric. Elizabethan schoolboys were taught to admire and employ those schemes and figures whose very names are now familiar only to scholars. Ingrained by practice, such intricate devices of repetition, parallel, and contrast can become not only features of style but instinctive paradigms for ordering the largest as well as smallest elements of form. Thus the pattern of reversal we have traced in the histories is everywhere in Shakespeare, from the "foolish figure" of chiasmus or antimetabole to which Polonius is addicted—"'Tis true 'tis pity, / And pity 'tis 'tis true"—to the structure Rose finds in *The Tempest*, whose scenes balance in chiasmic order, turning on that central moment when Ferdinard and Miranda declare their love. Such ingenuities are not unique to Shakespeare. Perhaps even in the Sonnets there is no antimetabole so brilliant as Donne's "My face in thine eye, thine in mine appears," where the words reflect as do the lovers' eyes and the line becomes an emblem of what it describes.[33] An example of the same device raised to epic proportions is *The Faerie Queene*, which appeared—rather like Shakespeare's tetralogies—in two sections of three books each, which mirror one another so that Book I corresponds to Book VI, Book II to Book V, Book III to Book IV.[34] Yet in his passion for order and the skill that expresses it, Shakespeare surpassed all his rivals—even Spenser, even Donne: in him it became a special and individual gift or power. I suggest that he organized his tetralogies on the same principles and with the same ingenuity that he designed a play, a scene, a line. It would be the absence of pattern that should astonish us.

As with *The Faerie Queene*, the pattern of the histories is essentially thematic, though in Shakespeare, as we have seen, correspondences in characters and events are sometimes surprisingly precise. Many readers will dismiss some or all of these detailed parallels and contrasts as coincidental, unimportant, or illusory, while other readers will detect some that I have missed—for this is a field that invites further investigation. It is the larger overall patterns on which I would insist: the cycle of national decline and restoration, the movement from foreign conquest through civil strife to tyranny and back again, the basic distinction between epic and tragedy and the contrast between positive and negative versions of these kinds, the systematic balance of good and bad kings, royal misgovernment and princely education, empire lost and empire won. This pattern seems objectively present in the two tetralogies, and it cannot be accidental. It compels us to look at both the author and his works with a fresh eye: to see in Shakespeare a dramatist capable of working on the largest and most ambitious scale, and in his historical diptych a major feat of architectonic imagination.

Notes

1. *The Lost Garden: A View of Shakespeare's English and Roman History* Plays (Totowa, N.J.: Rownan and Littlefield, 1978), ix.

2. See for the first view Matthias Shaaber, "The Unity of *Henry IV*" in J. G. McManaway, et al., eds., *Joseph Quincy Adams Memorial Studies* (Washington: Folger Library, 1948), 217–27, and H. E. Cain, "Further Light on the Relation of *1* and *2 Henry IV*," *SQ* 3 (1952): 21–38. For the second view, see Harold Jenkins, *The Structural Problem in Shakespeare's "Henry the Fourth"* (London: Methuen, 1956).

3. "*Henry IV*: The Structural Problem Revisited," *SQ* 33 (1982): 278–301. The essay discusses the theories of Shaaber and Cain as well as Jenkins.

4. Quotations from the plays—with some changes in punctuation—are taken from the Pelican edition of *The Complete Works*, ed. Alfred Harbage (Baltimore: Penguin Books, 1969).

5. *The Drama of Power* (Evanston, Ill.: Northwestern UP, 1973), 183 ff.

6. *Patterns of Decay: Shakespeare's Early Histories* (Charlottesville: U of Virginia P, 1975).

7. See "Virtue and Kingship in Shakespeare's *Henry IV*," *ELR* 5 (1975): 313–43.

8. *An Apology for Actors* (1612), ed. Richard Perkinson (New York: Scholars' Facsimiles and Reprints, 1941), sig. [1341.

9. *An Apology*, sig. [F3ᵛ].

10. Lily B. Campbell lists five such generally recognized uses of history: see *Shakespeare's "Histories": Mirrors of Elizabethan Policy* (San Marino: Huntington Library, 1968), 19–20. The phrases quoted in my text are by Philippe de Comines, quoted in the introductory material to Thomas Nicoll's translation of Thucydides (1550) and by John Brende, dedication to his translation of Quintus Curtius (1553), in Campbell, 46.

11. See Berry's final chapter in *Patterns of Decay*, and Alvin Keman, "The Henriad: Shakespeare's Major History Plays," in Alvin Keman, ed., *Modern Shakespearean Criticism: Essays on Style, Dramaturgy, and the Major Plays* (New York: Harcourt, Brace, & World, 1970), 245–75.

12. It is worth emphasizing the spectrum of possible meanings of "plan," ranging all the way from a general intention or a rough outline to the most exact scenario. If (as I believe) Shakespeare intended from the first to write a play or plays about Henry V but only designed these after completing *Richard III*, then the first tetralogy provided a detailed model for the second—see the next section of this essay. The parallels could be as loose or exact as Shakespeare chose to make them in writing the second series, and my argument certainly does not preclude the possible effect of hasty composition, extensions and alterations in design, or changes of mood and attitude. The pattern that emerges is in part retroactive. A thematic example of this backward process is the way that Carlisle's great prophecy in *Richard II*—"O, if you raise this house against this house"—reinterprets the events of *Henry VI* in retrospect, misleading Tillyard and his followers. But not even Shakespeare could change beyond a point the meaning of plays he had already written. A structural example of the same retroactive process is the renaming of Oldcastle, which produces the parallel episodes in which a cowardly Sir John Falstaff, or Fastolfe, makes haste but comes too late to a coronation and is rebuked and banished by a young king. But the placing of these episodes does not fit the antithetical scheme outlined in this essay, and if Shakespeare had originally planned the parallelism—or even identity—of the two knights, one wonders whether he would have named the second one Oldcastle to begin with. The epilogue to *2 Henry IV*, with its promise to continue the story "with Sir John in it" suggests that much of the design remained open even while the later plays were being composed.

13. On the diptych structure of *Tamburlaine*, see G. K. Hunter, "*Henry IV* and the Elizabethan Two-Part Play," in *Dramatic Identities and Cultural Tradition* (New York: Barnes and Noble, 1978), 303–18. For its influence on Shakespeare's earlier histories, see David Riggs, *Shakespeare's Heroical Histories: Henry VI and Its Literary Tradition* (Cambridge, Mass.: Harvard UP, 1971), especially Chapter 4. I discuss its importance for Shakespeare in "Aggression and the Project of the Histories," in Sidney Homan et al., eds., *Shakespeare's Personality* (Berkeley: U of California P, 1989).

14. *The Origins of Shakespeare* (Oxford: Oxford UP, 1977), Chapter 2.

15. *Shakespeare's Heroical Histories*, 41–42.

16. On the indebtedness of *Titus* to the lives of Scipio and Coriolanus, see Geoffrey Bullough, *Narrative and Dramatic Sources of Shakespeare* (London: Routledge and Kegan Paul, 1966–78), 6: 23–26. Dates suggested for Titus range from the mid-eighties to 1594, points at which Shakespeare may have been planning the first or the second tetralogy (though 1594 seems impossibly late on stylistic grounds). Shakespeare's constant recourse to Plutarch from his very earliest to his very latest

tragedies seems a strong argument for the influence of the *Lives* on the conception and structural pattern of the histories.

17. *Narrative and Dramatic Sources* 5: 13.

18. *The Lives of the Noble Grecians and Romans*, trans. Sir Thomas North (New York: Heritage Press, 1941), 1:6.

19. *Lives* 1: 218.

20. Lives 2: 817.

21. "To the Reader," in *Lives* 1: xxxiv.

22. Almost forgotten today, the *Cyropaedia* was widely admired in the Renaissance. It was translated into English in 1576 and repeatedly cited by Sidney in his *Defense* and by Spenser in the Letter to Raleigh. The *Pharsalia* was even better known: Shakespeare drew upon it for the omens in *Julius Caesar*, and it became the model for Daniel's *Civil Wars*.

23. *Man's Estate: Masculine Identity in Shakespeare* (Berkeley, U of California P, 1981), 66.

24. I trace the varying forms of punitive and redemptive tragedy in *Hamlet*, *Macbeth*, *Othello* and *King Lear* in "Religious Patterning in Shakespeare's Major Tragedies," forthcoming in *Transactions of the Connecticut Academy of Arts and Sciences*.

25. See Ernst Kantorowicz, "On Transformations of Apolline Ethics," in *Selected Studies* (Locust Valley, N.Y: Augustin, 1966), esp. 404–406. This formulation has been standard ever since Dover Wilson's *Fortunes of Falstaff*, and it is supported by the tradition just noted. It underlies the parallel and contrast between *1* and *2 Henry IV* and *2* and *3 Henry VI*. But in "Virtue and Kingship" (see n. 7 above), I cite evidence that the cardinal virtues were also traditionally regarded as attributes of the good ruler and argue that Hal's princely education includes temperance in Part 1 and wisdom in Part 2. If so, Shakespeare in the second tetralogy elaborates the simpler thematic pattern of the first.

26. *Shakespeare's Military World* (Berkeley: U of California P, 1956), 192 ff.

27. "I know thee not" recalls three separate New Testament passages: Matt. 7.21–23, 25.11–13, Luke 13.24–28. The staging as well as the allusion is apocalyptic: the king whom Falstaff last saw in the form of a servant now comes in glory, heralded by trumpets, his crown upon his head. Indeed the Folio, which has Henry and his train pass over the stage and then return, makes this literally his second coming!

28. Sir John Neale, *Elizabeth I and Her Parliaments, 1554–1601* (London: J. Cape, 1953–57), 2: 140.

29. *Narrative and Dramatic Sources* 3: 103.

30. *Narrative and Dramatic Sources* 3: 187. Hall mentions an alternative interpretation: men divined that God was displeased with Edward's marriage or punished his deceitfulness to Warwick.

31. *De Inventione* 2.52.

32. *Shakespearean Design* (Cambridge, Mass.: Harvard UP, 1972), 65 ff.

33. "The Good Morrow," I. 15, in *The Complete English Poems*, ed. A. J. Smith (Baltimore: Penguin, 1973), 60.

34. See Thomas P. Roche, Jr., *The Kindly Flame: A Study of the Third and Fourth Books of Spenser's "Faerie Queene"* (Princeton: Princeton UP, 1964), 200–201.

MAURICE CHARNEY

King John

King John reigned from 1199 to 1216, and Shakespeare's play covers more or less those years (without, of course, mentioning the Magna Carta in 1215). Unlike the events of the Major and the Minor Tetralogies, which lead up to the accession of the Tudors in 1485, King John's reign is isolated and remote from contemporary concerns. There are 161 years between the death of King John and the coming of Richard II to the throne in 1377. What happens in *King John* is not close to history as we know it. For example, Shakespeare represents the struggle between John and his nephew Arthur for legitimacy as a real conflict that opens the play, whereas historically John was the undisputed successor of his brother, Richard the Lion-Hearted (Richard I). Arthur is deliberately infantilized, and great weight is given to his grieving and querulous mother, Constance of Brittany, who is modeled on Queen Margaret, especially as she is represented in *3 Henry VI*.

There is a certain confusion and inchoate quality in the historical narrative of *King John*. At one moment John, like Henry VIII, is defying the Pope in a way that could only please Shakespeare's Protestant audience. He refuses the orders of Pope Innocent III to appoint Stephen Langton as Archbishop of Canterbury, and speaks in a high patriotic style:

What earthy name to interrogatories [= legal questions]
Can task the free breath of a sacred king?
    (3.1.73–74)

From *All of Shakespeare*, pp. 150–59. © 1993 by Columbia University Press.

John speaks of the Pope as having "usurped authority" (86) and vows that "no Italian priest / Shall tithe or toll in our dominions" (79–80). Unlike Richard II, King John doesn't speak further about the divine right of kings, and this passage seems to be John's only moment of asserting that he is a "sacred king" (74) and that "we, under God, are supreme head" (81).

Later in the play, John is basely yielding up his crown to Pandulph, the Papal legate, in order to be crowned again by him:

> Take again
> From this my hand, as holding of the Pope,
> Your sovereign greatness and authority.
> (5.1.2–4)

Pandulph asserts his power to end the war with Lewis, the French Dauphin, which he himself has stirred up because of John's "stubborn usage of the Pope" (18): "But since you are a gentle convertite, / My tongue shall hush again this storm of war" (19–20).

John is baffled in this scene and turns over the rule of England to the Bastard: "Have thou the ordering of this present time" (5.1.77). His virtual abdication at this point increases the shapelessness of the play, and he is soon dead, having been poisoned by a monk. Suddenly, John's son, whom we have never heard of before in the play, emerges to become Henry III. In the dramatic logic of the action, we expected the heroic Philip Faulconbridge, the bastard son of Richard I who dominates the play, to assume the kingship. He makes the final vaunting speech of the play:

> This England never did, nor never shall,
> Lie at the proud foot of a conqueror
> But when it first did help to wound itself.
> (5.7.112–14)

The tone of this speech is echoed in the dying Gaunt's exclamations in *Richard II*.

The affinities of *King John* with *Richard II* suggest that both plays were written close to each other, around 1595. My intuition is that *John* precedes *Richard*, because once Shakespeare started on the Major Tetralogy he probably wasn't distracted to write another unrelated history play. There are apparently no allusions in *King John* that might be helpful in dating. I doubt very strongly whether *King John* can be dated to 1590, as the Arden editor, E. A. J. Honigmann, and others propose. It is quite different in style from the plays of this period, such as the three parts of *Henry VI*. Its relation to *The*

Troublesome Raigne of Iohn King of England, published in two parts in 1591, which used to be thought the source of Shakespeare's play, is problematical, since *The Troublesome Raigne* may echo *King John.*

The Bastard is unlike any of the early protagonists of Shakespeare, although he has some of the witty bravado of Richard III. Despite his addiction to "policy" (2.1.396), he is not by any stretch of the imagination a villain. He is, in fact, the savior of England, whose patriotic, bluff, but heroic style looks forward to Henry V. But he is much more stylistically self-conscious than Henry V. After Hubert's extremely rhetorical speech about the merits of a match between Lady Blanch and Lewis the Dauphin, the Bastard launches a satirical attack on the terms of art he has just been bombarded with: "Zounds! I was never so bethumped with words / Since I first called my brother's father dad" (466–67). It is expected of a bastard to be blunt and forthright in speech, as Edmund is in *King Lear*, but the Bastard goes beyond this to a mockery of rodomontade like Hamlet's of Laertes' rant in the graveyard scene.

Hubert launches a swollen period to exaggerate the merits of the proposed match:

> But without this match,
> The sea enraged is not half so deaf,
> Lions more confident, mountains and rocks
> More free from motion, no, not death himself
> In mortal fury half so peremptory,
> As we to keep this city [= Angiers].
>   (2.1.450–55)

The Bastard makes fun of Hubert's hyperboles:

> Here's a large mouth, indeed,
> That spits forth death and mountains, rocks and seas,
> Talks as familiarly of roaring lions
> As maids of thirteen do of puppy-dogs.
>   (457–60)

Hubert "gives the bastinado with his tongue: / Our ears are cudgeled" (463–64). The Bastard is wittily aware of rhetorical amplification, and the much-trumpeted match hardly outlasts act 3, scene 1.

The Bastard is an almost wholly unhistorical figure, drawn from Shakespeare's general acquaintance with bastards in the medieval period. This is another problem with *King John* as a history play, because it takes as its leading figure the Bastard, who has as tenuous a connection with historical accuracy as Falstaff. Both the Bastard and Henry V embody mythic characteristics of the great leader. On his first appearance in the play, the Bastard is accepted by King John as "A good blunt fellow" (1.1.71) and a "madcap" (84), and John's mother Elinor confirms that the Bastard "hath a trick of Cordelion's [= Richard I's] face" (85). She seems eager to acknowledge that she is his grandmother.

Philip Faulconbridge rejects his inheritance from his supposed father to pursue honor and glory as King John's nephew. He asserts his noble ambition in the style of Chapman's Bussy D'Ambois and other powerful figures from early Jacobean tragedy: "And I am I, how'er I was begot" (1.1.175). In the first of his many long soliloquies, he claims that he is a "mounting spirit" (206), a close observer of the times, who, like a successful, flattering courtier, will know how to deliver "Sweet, sweet, sweet poison for the age's tooth" (213). The Bastard's determination for his own "rising" (216) depends upon a cynical understanding of the corruption of the times. In this sense the Bastard is a much more sophisticated and complex character than Henry V.

The Bastard's first political triumph is his suggestion to the Kings of England and France to attack the city of Angiers and end its politic equivocation. It is a brilliant stratagem, which breaks the standstill in negotiations. Interestingly, the Bastard thinks in terms of histrionic imagery:

> By heaven, these scroyles [= scoundrels] of Angiers flout you, kings,
> And stand securely on their battlements
> As in a theater, whence they gape and point
> At your industrious scenes and acts of death.
>   (2.1.373–76)

It is the theatrical mockery that the Bastard objects to, and he calls Angiers "this contemptuous city" (384) and "this peevish town" (402). Angiers manages to slide out of certain destruction by proposing a marriage between Blanch and Lewis, but the Bastard is skeptical of their good intentions: "Mad world! Mad kings! Mad composition [= compromise]!" (561).

In his most famous soliloquy in the play, the Bastard inveighs against Commodity in all of its many derogatory senses:

> That smooth-faced gentleman, tickling commodity,
> Commodity, the bias of the world . . .
>   (2.1.573–74)

This is the business ethic Antonio speaks of in *The Merchant of Venice* that supports Shylock's bond and that the Duke cannot possibly refuse:

For the commodity that strangers have
With us in Venice, if it be denied,
Will much impeach the justice of the state,
Since that the trade and profit of the city
Consisteth of all nations.
  (*The Merchant of Venice* 3.3.27–31)

Commodity, or essentially convenience and expediency for businessmen, rules Venice rather than equity or natural law; without commodity Venice as a center of trade between East and West will disappear.

This commercial sense is not exactly what the Bastard means by *commodity*, but his political meaning follows directly from the connection of the word's root with wares, goods, and merchandise. It is "tickling commodity," like Thersites' invocation of "the devil Luxury," who, "with his fat rump and potato finger, tickles" Diomedes and Cressida together (*Troilus and Cressida* 5.2.54–55). The Bastard calls the personified Commodity "This bawd, this broker" (2.1.582) and "That daily break-vow" (569). Cynically, he vows allegiance to the political expediency of Commodity, who hasn't wooed him yet. He ends his soliloquy with a ringing, ironic declaration:

Since kings break faith upon commodity,
Gain, be my lord, for I will worship thee!
  (597–98)

This is the way of the world, to which disinherited bastards are especially sensitive.

Similarly, the Bastard opposes the "mad composition" that Pandulph, the papal legate, tries to impose on the wars between England and France. When John has basely yielded his crown to the Pope, the Bastard tries to stir him up to fight off the Dauphin's invasion of England: "glister like the god of war" (5.1.54). As he takes over "the ordering of this present time" (77) from John, the Bastard is at his most patriotic and his most glorious in defying the Pope and making war against Lewis the Dauphin:

  Shall a beardless boy,
A cockered silken wanton, brave our fields
And flesh his spirit in a warlike soil,
Mocking the air with colors idly spread,
And find no check?
  (69–73)

This is the heroic defiance of France that we shall hear later from Henry V. In the next scene the Bastard speaks, in the voice of the King, his utter contempt for the French invaders: "This harnessed masque and unadvised revel, / This unhaired sauciness and boyish troops" (5.2.132–33). At this point in the play, the Bastard is effectively the King of England.

Only at the end of the play, when he is poisoned, does King John seem memorable. He speaks distractedly from the effect of the poison and he has a passion now that he never had before, especially in the early scenes when he was directed by his mother Elinor (as Arthur was ruled by his mother Constance). John is burning up: "There is so hot a summer in my bosom / That all my bowels crumble up to dust!" (5.7.30–31), but no one will help him: "And none of you will bid the winter come / To thrust his icy fingers in my maw" (36–37). Shakespeare excels at metaphors of madness, but we have no previous development of John to support his present passion. John's suffering and guilt are powerful:

> Within me is a hell, and there the poison
> Is as a fiend confined to tyrannize
> On unreprievable condemned blood.
>   (46–48)

These are strong speeches but the play doesn't make any effort to dramatize why there is a hell within King John.

Shakespeare is much more successful in evoking passion at the attempted blinding and killing of little Arthur by the King's loyal servant Hubert (the same Hubert who so skillfully defends the city of Angiers). Arthur, the son of John's older brother, Geoffrey, is an active claimant of the English throne who makes John seem a usurper. Although Arthur was in fact twelve when John came to the throne, Shakespeare keeps him a child in order to increase the sense of outrage and pathos at his death, which occurs when Arthur is already sixteen in 1203. His mother, Constance, shames him by speaking in baby talk about his grandmother Elinor, who supports her son John: "Give grandam kingdom, and it grandam will / Give it a plum, a cherry, and a fig" (2.1.161–62). The bitterness of Constance overwhelms her maternal feelings for her son.

The scene between Arthur and Hubert, who comes to murder him, is the most effective in the play, and it strongly anticipates the blinding of Gloucester in *King Lear* (3, 7). Hubert is responding to John's express comment that Arthur "is a very serpent in my way" (3.2.71), and, like all Shakespeare's murderers, he wants to be serviceable to his king: "I'll keep him so / That he shall not offend your Majesty" (74–75). In act 4, scene 1

Hubert provides executioners who hide in the room where he plans to murder Arthur. They are to heat irons for Hubert and to bind Arthur fast to his chair at Hubert's command—this is the way Gloucester is dealt with in *King Lear*. Unknowingly, the innocent Arthur treats Hubert as his friend, but his loving comments have a bitter irony: "I would to heaven / I were your son, so you would love me, Hubert" (4.1.23–24). Hubert's wavering is specifically indicated in his asides: "If I talk to him, with his innocent prate / He will awake my mercy, which lies dead" (25–26). Unable to speak directly, he gives Arthur a paper that informs him of his fate: Hubert must burn out both his eyes with hot irons.

Arthur indulges in elaborate conceits like those in *Richard II* to counter Hubert's determination:

> Ah, none but in this iron age would do it!
> The iron of itself, though heat red-hot,
> Approaching near these eyes, would drink my tears
> And quench this fiery indignation
> Even in the matter of mine innocence!
>   (4.1.60–64)

The point of the conceits is that they cannot stop, and Arthur continues with an excess of rhetorical ingenuity:

> Nay, after that, consume away in rust,
> But for containing fire to harm mine eye!
> Are you more stubborn-hard than hammered iron?
>   (65–67)

Arthur persuades Hubert to send away the executioners: "O save me, Hubert, save me! My eyes are out / Even with the fierce looks of these bloody men" (72–73).

Hubert finally relents after an extraordinary long scene of pleading, in which Arthur as a young Metaphysical poet works endless changes on the emblematic theme of eyes. He even offers his tongue for his eyes in a grotesque piece of pleading:

> Or, Hubert, if you will, cut out my tongue,
> So I may keep mine eyes. O, spare mine eyes,
> Though to no use but still to look on you!
>   (4.1.100–102)

Hubert cannot resist this eloquence "For all the treasure that thine uncle owes" (122). Ironically, Arthur afterward kills himself by jumping off the walls of the castle in his ship-boy's disguise:

> O me! my uncle's spirit is in these stones!
> Heaven take my soul, and England keep my bones!
>   (4.3.9–10)

It is an affecting, childlike, animistic end, which seems to presage John's own evil fate.

The Bastard defends Hubert against Salisbury's accusation of murder in words that are echoed by Othello: "Your sword is bright, sir; put it up again" (4.3.79); Othello tells Brabantio and his followers: "Keep up your bright swords, for the dew will rust them" (*Othello* 1.2.58). The Bastard's sense of mastery and command is similar to Othello's and in this scene he underscores the pathos of Arthur's death. He tells Hubert that he is damned "Beyond the infinite and boundless reach / Of mercy" (4.3.117–18) if he did this murder. In his deep passion, the Bastard invokes extravagant hyperboles of despair for Hubert:

> A rush will be a beam
> To hang thee on. Or wouldst thou drown thyself,
> Put but a little water in a spoon
> And it shall be as all the ocean,
> Enough to stifle such a villain up.
>   (4.3.129–33)

Although the Bastard finally comes to believe Hubert, he sees the fate of England compromised by Arthur's death:

> England now is left
> To tug and scamble and to part by th' teeth
> The unowed interest of proud swelling state.
>   (4.3.145–47)

Henry V opens with the Archbishop of Canterbury talking about a bill against the Church "that the scambling and unquiet time / Did push . . . out of farther question" (1.1.4–5), and Henry will win Kate "with scambling" (5.2.207), or scrambling and scrimmaging like a soldier. "To tug and scamble" is to fight for something that one would assume to be inviolable and not to be disputed. These are the evil fruits of Commodity, by which even good political intentions come to grief. In his soaring imagery, the Bastard uncovers the truth of what is happening to the realm of England, which prepares us for his heroic final speech: "Naught shall make us rue / If England to itself do rest but true!" (5.7.117–18).

King John does seem an odd history play in relation to the tumultuous events of the Minor and Major Tetralogies. It has some connection with the anti-Catholic, antipapal issues of *Henry VIII*, and the defiance of the French is familiar from Shakespeare's other histories, especially *Henry V*, but *King John* still seems anomalous. Why would Shakespeare want to go back to the early thirteenth century and completely overlook the Magna Carta, which seems so important to us? The Bastard provides an outspoken, witty, and heroic model for such later figures as Henry V, and his bluffness and honesty stand as a bulwark against the political chicanery of the rest of the play. But the Bastard is suddenly at the end deprived of the kingship he so richly deserves. The conclusion is strikingly indeterminate, as if there must be some other play or plays to wind up the historical action. We expect a miniseries that never comes.

HARRY LEVIN

Sitting upon the Ground (Richard II, *IV, i*)

Kingship (or queenship) has established a highly traditional framework—
or, at all events, a frame of reference—for the perspectives of English life.
Shakespeare confronted that institution directly and dealt with it upon a
duly majestic scale. A succession of eight kings parades through his double
set of historical tetralogies (the later kings appearing in the earlier set): two
Richards and four Henries, plus two Edwards (the younger one assassinated
before he could be formally crowned), with still another Henry to preside
over an updating afterpiece. Those last two Henries belonged to the more
recent house of Tudor, having staked their claim through a marital alliance
with the Lancasters and reinforced it by a subsequent intermarriage with
the Yorks, so that their own accession could be looked upon as a happy ending to the wars so bitterly fought in the name of the Roses. That preceding
Richard could be looked back upon as a terminal figure in England's for-
mative dynasties, a childless son whose father, the legendary Black Prince,
had died before succeeding to the throne, and who himself would bequeath
it to the contentions of his York and Lancaster cousins through the greater
part of the fifteenth century. Thus Shakespeare had ample occasion to ring
the changes on the monarchic theme; and the unhappy reigns of those two
dissimilar Richards—the Second all too passive, as contrasted with the

From *Shakespeare's Universe: Renaissance Ideas and Conventions: Essays in Honour of W. R.
Elton*, edited by John M. Mucciolo with the assistance of Steven J. Doloff and Edward A.
Rauchut, pp. 3–20. © 1996 by the contributors.

hyperactive Third—gave him a deepening opportunity to tilt his histories in the direction of tragedy.

Neither Richard could justly be regarded as a hero in the honorific purport of the term, which may be more readily accommodated to the epic than to the drama. Richard III looms large, both physically and morally, as the very archetype of the arch-villain, his inner nature scarcely masked by his avowed hypocrisy; a man of action whose external acts constitute a series of unalleviated misdeeds, more melodramatic than tragic in their utter disregard for the ethical implications. Richard II, in contrast, is rather a weak than a wicked human being, prone to irresponsibility rather than malevolence. Over-indulged and self-indulgent, coddled into that seat of grandeur which Richard III would struggle toward so ferociously, he neglects its duties and obligations while enjoying its privileges and exploiting its prerogatives. Yet, quite unlike his misshapen namesake, he cuts a self-consciously personable figure, and responds with increasing sensitivity to the circumstances that turn against him. Experience is enlarged, not by his vainglorious round of public appearances, but by the cramping retreat that overtakes and confines him, while his evolving private voice engages our belated sympathies. Words come to him easily, while deeds do not; he is at ease when surrounded by the court, but less so when afield—least of all on the battlefield. Unlike that other Richard, who strives so brashly for it, worldly greatness has been thrust upon him, and he hesitates in facing its emergent demands.

A man of passion rather than action—passion in its primary sense of suffering—Richard feels those sufferings all the more keenly because he has been spoiled by his privileged status. Hence he bears and bespeaks his feelings with greater eloquence than any Shakespearean characters have previously done. None of them will more fully express or personify what Walter Pater would call 'that irony of kingship': the histrionic routines, the long-winded protocols, the childish punctilio, the authorized egocentricity, the merely human limitations under the awe-inspiring mantle of majesty—viewed from the inside, an all but impossible job. The earliest history-plays must come to terms with the wickedness of Richard III, with the weakness of Henry VI, with both of those faults in King John. Shakespeare would sound the depths with Richard II, before addressing himself to the upward mobility of the fourth and fifth Henries. 'Up, cousin, up', is Richard's descending counsel to his successor, Bullingbrook (III, iii, 194). But except for the latter, who will wear his crown with some uneasiness, and more distinctively his son, Prince Hal/Henry V (despite a notably wayward apprenticeship), none of Shakespeare's English rulers could serve as models for their exalted roles. Shortcomings too obvious to be overlooked would have to be rationalized by the medieval doctrine of the king's two bodies, the ideal of divinely hedged supremacy cohabiting with the realization of mortal frailty.

Yet royalty, so often at war with itself, held self-evident dangers as a corpus of subject-matter, even more through the exposure of its weaknesses than through the abuse of its powers. *Richard II*, by dwelling on both of those recurrent issues, would bring Shakespeare as precariously near as he ever came to the political complications and troubles of his own day. Viewed from a more classical, an Aristotelian standpoint, his elevated protagonist could hardly have seemed more nonchalant in his *hubris*, more self-centred in his *hamartia*, or more abject in his *peripéteia*. Crowned heads are ideally supposed to betoken a glorified incarnation of humanity at large, which cannot altogether look up to them when they themselves do not really live up to their own exceptional standards. Their inherent pride will sometimes risk, and always exacerbate, an ominous fall. We are invited to sympathize, and to a certain extent we do, with such failures in the highest places. But, while we are witnessing the downfall of those who have lorded it over such ordinary mortals as ourselves, our reactions may be shaded with a slight tinge of *Schadenfreude*. In sharing that shock of reversal on the kingly plane, we may also feel some democratic release in rehearing the humiliations of *lèse-majesté*. That makes for an ambivalent catharsis, though it subserves the ends of poetic justice, allowing us to commiserate with the fallen even while we are welcoming the forces that have been destined to supplant them.

Tragedies, as composed in the Middle Ages, were not plays but narratives illustrating the scriptural dictum, 'How are the mighty fallen!' Boccaccio had transcribed and collected a good many salient examples, from the primal Adam to the Renaissance despots, with his *De Casibus Virorum et Feminarum Illustrium*, which would be emulated in Middle English verse by John Lydgate's *Fall of Princes*. Chaucer's Monk defined the genre in outline as the story of a falling-off from the height of prosperity to the most wretched misery, each successive case exemplifying the mutability of worldly fortunes. Claiming to have gathered together a hundred such case-histories, and prompted to recite a number of the earliest ones, he had been cut off by his bored fellow pilgrims after the seventeenth. The influential compilation, *A Mirror for Magistrates*, would be published, several times reprinted, and augmented by various poetic hands throughout the Elizabethan period. Its title evoked a conventional symbol for the didactic function of literature, as a cautionary reflection of life which edified its viewers by showing up the exemplary mistakes of their official predecessors. Its *Induction* by Thomas Sackville, Earl of Dorset, framed the whole sequence within the nightmare-vision of a journey to the underworld, while the ghosts of worthies mainly from the British past would deliver their respective plaints. More than thirty histories would be dramatized from these versified lives of illustrious but ill-starred men and women.

Richard II was brusquely and adversely reflected in the *Mirror for Mag-istrates*. Shakespeare's treatment had more in common with the balanced metrical narration of Samuel Daniel's *Civil Wars*. He would also draw upon conflicting accounts in the prose chronicles of Raphael Holinshed, Edward Hall and Jean Froissart; and certain French witnesses may have inclined him toward a rather more sympathetic view of his subject. His Richard is supremely conscious of his personal visibility in the magistral looking-glass. Hastening back from his inauspicious war in Ireland to face the crisis of Bullingbrook's return from banishment, the execution of his own sycophantic henchmen, and the defection of supporting forces from Wales and the North, he eloquently oscillates from one extreme to the other, from reassertions of regal authority to admissions of helpless defeat. But the trend runs down-ward: from the divine right of his anointed sovereignty to his 'talk of graves, of worms, and epitaphs' (III, ii, 145). Weeping for joy when he lands at its Welsh shore, he immediately salutes what he takes to be the compliant soil of his loyal kingdom. Within a few minutes his body sinks down upon what has suddenly become that 'barren earth', like another job bemoaning his fate. Whereupon this prodigal prince aligns himself with the figures in Sackville's ghostly procession:

> For God's sake let us sit upon the ground
> And tell sad stories of the death of kings:
> How some have been deposed, some slain in war,
> Some haunted by the ghosts they have deposed,
> Some poisoned by their wives, some sleeping kill'd,
> All murthered . . .
> (155–60)

Later on, while playing his own part in that hapless spectacle, taking leave of his queen, and gravitating toward his own obituary, he will enjoin her: 'Tell thou the lamentable tale of me' (V, i, 44). Only then, when her listeners' tears will have put out its fire (V, i, 40–49), will the blackness of its ashes attest 'the deposing of a rightful king' (50). Now, to depose means literally to put down, a customary paradigm in tragedy. That thematic stricture, ring-ing through the play, has by then reached its denouement and been acted out in what has come to be known as the Deposition Scene. The basic verb falls from Richard's lips repeatedly; and it will prove ironic that he himself first used it (in another sense) with reference to the armed rival claimant, Bullingbrook, when asked for a deposition (a sworn statement of his inten-tions): 'Depose him in the justice of his cause' (I, iii, 30). A mock-heroic echo—'Depose me?'—will be voiced in the playacting scene of *1 Henry IV*, when Falstaff is called upon by the Prince to step down from his impersonation of the King.

But there remains a generic difference between Richard and his storied precursors. We listen to their sad stories; we witness his, from step to step, as it is being enacted; and, while their storytelling points a collective moral for us to reconsider from our own vantage-point, his dramatic characterization offers a psychological bond that enables us to participate in his actions and to suffer through his emotions vicariously. For this we find a closer prototype in Marlowe's *Edward II*, which is equally if not more intensely concerned—in Charles Lamb's phrase—with 'the reluctant pangs of abdicating royalty', and which would be set above *Richard II* by Swinburne and Rupert Brooke. Shakespeare's pioneering contemporary had made the most spectacular impression through his overreaching protagonists, and through such 'sky-aspiring and ambitious thoughts' as Richard would vainly attempt to suppress in others (I, iii, 130). By centring upon a royal weakling, influenced at that stage perhaps by the *Henry VI* plays, Marlowe for once could work out a more Shakespearean pattern of interaction with the other characters. The weakness that makes Edward seem most vulnerable, as rendered in Marlowe's tenderest lyrical strains, is the King's homoerotic infatuation with his French courtier, Piers Gaveston. Their vengeful challenger, the Earl of Mortimer, is due to break down in his Machiavellian turn, whereas Richard's triumphant antagonist, Henry Bullingbrook, now Duke of Lancaster, will dethrone him and assume his crown as Henry IV.

If *Richard II* formed a sorrowful prologue to the cycle of a more auspicious regime, it had been preceded—possibly suggested—by the sorrows of another drama, the anonymous *Thomas of Woodstock*. Here the titular character, officially Duke of Gloucester, is victimized for his principled opposition to the caprices that have been leading his nephew, the youthful monarch, astray. By farming out gainful franchises to his self-serving favourites, and thus empowering them to collect the revenues from taxes and from leases on public lands, Richard has been negligently squandering the resources of his country, and will be forced to pay the price himself in Shakespeare's sequel. There the death of Woodstock will be recalled by his mourning Duchess, and his patriotic admonitions will be carried on by the two surviving brother-uncles, the Dukes of Lancaster (John of Gaunt) and of York. Since so much of Richard's 22-year reign had been crowded into *Thomas of Woodstock*, *Richard II* would be free to concentrate upon its two last years—the last two years of what Barbara Tuchman would designate as 'the calamitous Fourteenth Century'. Its most fearful calamity almost seemed to have been ordained from on high; countless lives were lost by the intermittent visitations of the bubonic plague, the Black Death. Military strife throughout this epoch, the Hundred

Years' War on the Continent, was aggravated at home by movements of social protest that culminated in the Peasants' Revolt.

We can revert more happily to those years while we are reading Chaucer; but, if we open Wycliffe's contemporaneous Bible, we are reminded of the heretical Lollards, of the dissidence and persecution that ushered in the Reformation. What was broadly and gradually happening would become an embattled transition from feudal oligarchy to centralized monarchy. But that would not take place until the baronial claimants had eliminated one another's claims, and a more popular rule had taken command through the dynamic personality of Henry V. It will be he who confides, on the eve of Agincourt, speaking incognito to three common soldiers, 'I think the King is but a man, as I am.... His ceremonies laid by, in his nakedness he appears but a man'. And Shakespeare's Henry, going on to invoke 'thou idol Ceremony', will soliloquize over those undemocratic distinctions which it has so arbitrarily raised between man and man. Richard II, seen in that retrospective light, has ruled by taking advantage of such distinctions, and has maintained his princely rank by proceeding from one ceremony to the next. His First Act is prearranged accordingly, with formal pomp, theatrical display and heraldic flourishes. He inaugurates it by mounting a scaffold and standing high before Windsor Castle, while two contending peers appeal to his less than decisive judgment. Ominously Herford (Bullingbrook) and Mowbray (Duke of Norfolk) accuse each other of treason, recapitulating past conflicts and portending eventual disasters.

That ceremonious opening soon deteriorates into an unheroic anticlimax. Richard keeps trying to reaffirm, with all his wavering dignity, that he was 'not born to sue, but to command' (I, i, 196). Yet his mediation is powerless to resolve the quarrel or to appease the irreconcilable rivals, who press their mutual accusations by flinging down their gauntlets (as 'gages' of their determination), and thereby exchanging knightly challenges to a trial by single combat. This opens the way for an even grander—and consequently more anticlimactic—ceremonial, set in the chivalric lists at Coventry. Trumpets sound, banners wave and armour flashes, as the heralds marshal in the hostile champions. Their militant steeds are conventionally declared to be awaiting them backstage, and will not be needed as it turns out (conveniently for the staging), though the prospective riders will figure on horseback when Mowbray's son recalls and narrates the episode in 2 Henry IV. Here, at the most expectant moment, Richard throws down his own gage, the ruling baton, and with that commanding gesture calls the tournament off. Both of the would-be combatants will instead be banished. 'The note of banishment', as the self-exiled James Joyce would comment, 'sounds uninterruptedly' throughout Shakespeare's works; and it is sounded here with a special poignance through

Mowbray's lament, because it will exclude him forever after from hearing or speaking the English language:

> What is thy sentence then but speechless death,
> Which robs my tongue from breathing native breath?
>   (I, iii, 172f.)

On the other side, the rare word 'regreet', dropped negatively by Richard and picked up twice by Bullingbrook, will become a positive augury (I, iii, 67, 142, 186). Bullingbrook's expatriation will be temporary, somewhat commuted in deference to his grieving father, John of Gaunt, and actually to be cut short by Gaunt's imminent death. Richard's sudden and arbitrary decision has marked an end of the usages of chivalry, as well as the beginning of his own reverses, the first in a sequence of guidelines pointing downward. 'Oh, when the King did throw his warder down . . .', the younger Mowbray will pronounce in his later reminiscence, 'Then threw he down himself' (*2 Henry IV*, IV, i, 123, 125). Gaunt's deathbed speech—enunciated at the play's moral centre, like the dream of Clarence in *Richard III*—is both a warning and a prophecy for the condition of England. 'This blessed plot, this earth, this realm' is patriotically eulogized up to a point—a critical point where the apprehension and insights of the dying man downgrade that fertile terrestrial metaphor into a paltry piece of real estate, a heavily mortgaged farm (II, i, 50). When Richard pays his frivolous visit, he is admonished that, in his extravagance and exploitation as 'landlord of England', he has been acting to depose himself (113). Callously he meets the announcement of his uncle's death by appropriating the ducal estates, in order to finance his ill-advised Irish expedition; and this is what motivates Bullingbrook to return and reclaim his Lancastrian inheritance.

Meanwhile the reported voices of both nobles and commons have been rising to a virtual chorus of resentment and disaffection. It is York, the very last survivor among the seven sons of Edward III, appointed as governor during the sovereign's absence from England, who likewise inherits from his older brother the conscience of a *raisonneur*. Under that twofold commitment, his articulate but ineffectual position must be 'neuter'; he must disregard the family connection ('uncle me no uncles'); he can neither abet nor oppose the *coup d'état* dethroning Richard and enthroning Henry (II, iii, 87, 159). More and more widely recognized and accepted, as both of the rivals turn homeward from opposite directions, and as the followers of the straying leader desert him for the ranks of his more purposeful adversary, the overturn becomes inevitable. Each encounter is a comedown for Richard, after the bad news greets him in Wales and pursues him to Flint Castle. His initial response is to stiffen his haughty posture as God's deputy. But, as the pressures mount, he lapses into self-pitying monologues: 'Cry woe, destruction, ruin, and decay ... ' (III, ii, 102). I have already quoted part of the passage in which he relates himself to the bygone spirits of deposed and murdered kings. Sitting there on the ground (this blessed plot? this barren earth?), and waiting now to be royally unseated, he continues by tragically dramatizing his less than stately role:

> ... for within the hollow crown
> Keeps Death his court, and there the antic sits,
> Scoffing his state and grinning at his pomp,
> Allowing him a breath, a little scene,
> To monarchize, be fear'd, ... and humor'd thus
> Comes at the last and with a little pin
> Bores through his castle wall, and farewell king!
>   (160–70)

The funereal jester will have the ultimate word, even as a mirror for magistrates foreshadows a dance of death. Ready now to surrender without resisting, Richard discharges his dwindling retinue: ' ... hence away, / From Richard's night to Bullingbrook's fair day' (217f.). That daylight is the habitual ambience of royalty, radiating from the sun itself, from the King himself. The earlier farewell of Bullingbrook—'This must my comfort be, / That sun that warms you here shall shine on me'—will in the long run be less polite than portentous (I, iii, 144f.). Under the immediate stress upon Richard, his imagery is shifting to sunsets and clouded skies. In the next play, reviewing the train of events, Henry IV will candidly recount to his wayward prince how he braved comparison with 'the skipping king' and managed to appropriate Richard's aureole of 'sunlike majesty'.

Their confrontation eventually comes to pass at Flint Castle, which 'royally is mann'd', now that Richard has taken refuge there (III, iii, 21). So Bullingbrook is informed by young Harry Percy, who will be better known afterwards as Hotspur, and much less friendly to the Lancastrian party. Richard again makes his formal appearance aloft ('*on the walls*'), looking down from the battlements. The elevation is still kinglike, but the illumination is darkling—a modulation likened by Bullingbrook to that of 'the blushing discontented sun' when 'the envious clouds are bent / To dim his glory' (63, 65–6). A preliminary interview pits Richard's stern reproof against the more conciliatory approach of Northumberland (Percy's father, Bullingbrook's spokesman). But Richard has come a long way from his angry rhetorical question, 'am I not king?', when he beseeches his captors, 'What must the

King do now?', and counterbalances the changing alternatives: 'My gorgeous palace for a hermitage, . . . And my large kingdom for a little grave' (III, ii, 83; iii, 143, 148, 153). He cannot refuse the bidding to come down into the lower courtyard, where Bullingbrook, whose 'heart is up', awaits him; yet he is acutely sensitive to the symbolism implicit in this descent, and Shakespeare's stage was well suited to the blocking of these bodily ups and downs (194). Richard goes through the motions ceremonially and histrionically, reproving his foes and critics in rhymed couplets that formalize his predicament on a literary plane:

> Down, down I come, like glist'ring Phaeton,
> Wanting the manage of unruly jades.
> In the base court? Base court, where kings grow base,
> To come at traitors' calls and do them grace.
> In the base court, come down? Down court! down king!
> For night-owls shriek where mounting larks should sing.
>   (178–83)

The classical allusion is an admission; for the scion of the mythical sun-god, Icarus, was disastrously unable to drive Apollo's blazing chariot across the sky; and Richard, while blaming the horsemanship (*manège*) for the mismanagement, ignores what Shakespeare elsewhere mentions: that the earth was badly scorched by Phaeton's disaster. A double pun is unfolded in the following couplet: if that lowest courtyard (not the *cour d'honneur* but the workaday *basse cour*) befits the abasement of the degraded king, then the adjective *base* can also be accorded to his treacherous courtiers. In the concluding trope the visual antitheses of *night/day* and *sunlight/clouds* are vocalized into bird-calls.

Whenever a climax looms ahead, we may hopefully speak of rising to it; and this can be said of Richard's behaviour, which becomes more outstandingly eloquent as the difficulties arise before him; yet each consecutive encounter sustains and accentuates a falling movement, which abases him more deeply than the last one. The scene that intervenes between his surrender and his condemnation functions as a choric interlude in much the same vein as Gaunt's dying prediction, which was placed between the two scenes presenting court assemblies. Here we get our clearest glimpse of Richard's touching queen, whose mutually affectionate relations with her husband diverge very strikingly from the estrangement of Marlowe's indifferent Edward and his faithless Queen Isabel. Shakespeare has embroidered upon the historical facts, since Richard's first wife (Anne of Bohemia) was dead, and the spouse of his diplomatic second marriage (Isabelle of France) was barely adolescent at this time. The Queen, as Shakespeare conceives her, is seeking but not finding a few moments of relief from her conjugal worries. The setting that attracts and fails to distract her is a garden (the Duke of York's), which colours the ensuing diction with the cluster of images that Caroline Spurgeon has traced—as a characteristic point of departure and return—through all of Shakespeare's writing. The Wars of the Roses were launched in the Temple Garden; the Battle of Agincourt is resolved by a peace that should recultivate France into 'this best garden of the world'.

Iago will humanize the metaphor: 'Our bodies are our gardens'. Ophelia's madness will seek expression by handing out flowers, King Lear's in distributing weeds. 'Richard, that sweet lovely rose' is invidiously compared with 'this thorn, this canker Bullingbrook' amid the Percies' afterthoughts in *1 Henry IV*. With *Richard II* it is the play itself that elicited Pater's comment, 'What a garden of words!', and Shakespeare has gone beyond his sources to introduce this scene. It is a gardener in person who recites the *topos* and elucidates the allegory, likening the cultivation of the land to the proper tending of a commonwealth. That suggests a query from his assistant which will bring out his overheard disclosure: why should this little patch of ground be tended so conscientiously, when 'our sea-walled garden, the whole land,' has been so neglected, and indeed is now so overgrown and 'swarming with caterpillars?' (III, iv, 43, 47). Those pernicious worms denote Bushy, Bagot, and Greene, 'The caterpillars of the commonwealth', the self-serving courtiers who have so grievously misled their king and so shamefully profited from their flattery (II, iii, 166). The Gardener's answer is to report their deaths, along with Bullingbrook's capture of Richard himself, who is 'depress'd' (put down) if not yet 'depos'd' (III, iv, 68). The idiom of gardening extends to the round of seasons, with autumn—in its vividly Anglo-Saxon synonym—as the visible embodiment of tragic decline:

> He that hath suffered this disordered spring
> Hath now himself met with the fall of leaf.
> (III, iv, 48–9)

The oracular significance of this dialogue is rounded out when the Queen envisages the Gardener as old Adam, re-enacting 'a second fall of cursed man'; and, after her departing curse upon this other Eden, he plants 'a bank of rue' for ruth—for pity—in commemoration of her plight (76, 105). Their anxious colloquy brings down to earth the restless visions expounded so much more schematically by Ulysses in *Troilus and Cressida*, the cosmic oscillation from order to disorder.

Everything in the first three acts builds up to the single continuous scene that comprises the fourth. This might well be termed a *scène à faire*, in the language of Francisque Sarcey—or, as phrased by William Archer, an 'obligatory scene'. For both of those very practical critics, the most clear-cut test of a playwright's talent was his ability to pick out and treat that segment of his narrative material which would best lend itself to effective dramatization. In the present instance the material happened to be associated with problems that extended far beyond the stage. During the final period of the Virgin Queen's long sovereignty, the unsettling issue of what would come next—of who would become her successor—was much in the air. Analogies would be discerned, most sharply by Elizabeth herself, between the Earl of Essex's conspiracy and that of the future Henry IV against Richard. A suspiciously opportune revival of *Richard II* in 1601, a private performance half a dozen years after its premiere, was officially countered by the arraignment and interrogation of Shakespeare's company. Perforce the Deposition Scene was omitted from the text of the first three quartos, and not published until the fourth, after King James had more or less comfortably settled down on the throne. Shakespeare in the mean time was advancing from the histories toward his tragical period, and the play is entitled a tragedy in all the quartos. In the Folio its title reads: *The Life and Death of King Richard the Second*.

There does not seem to be much valid historical basis for this grand scene, which interlinks Richard's abdication with Henry's coronation. Two disparate and mutually antagonistic episodes seem to have been fused together, through a propagandistic twist of the chronicles in smoothing the way for the Lancastrian dynasty. Contemporaneous testimony, most expressly from a French fellow prisoner in the Tower of London, Jean Créton, handed on the report that Richard raged and wept when he received the parliamentary judgment against himself, and that he accused Henry of committing treason. Shakespeare has transferred the background to Westminster Hall—just in time, since that edifice had been erected at the King's command only a few years before. There, even while divesting himself of the office he has abused, Richard comes to dominate the proceedings of parliament. The act has started out with the wrangling nobles ready to throw down their gages once more, and will end with the clerics expressing their expectations of further turmoil. It pivots around a speech of prophetic protestation from the loyal Bishop of Carlisle, who defends the legitimate line of kingship, and foresees the consequent disasters 'if you raise this house against this house' (IV, i, 145). He is arrested at once, and what should ensue is the requisite climax: lines 154–318, which came under the Elizabethan censor's ban, and would be printed as 'new additions' in the Fourth Quarto (and from a more authoritative Jacobean text in the Folio).

Enter Richard then, heralded by York as 'plume-pluck'd', stripped of his majestic feathers, and followed by attendants bearing the contested regalia, the crown and the sceptre (161). Summoned as a prisoner to acknowledge his capitulation and act out his humiliation 'in common view' before the national assembly, he is just beginning to shake off his own 'regal thoughts' (155, 163). His successful competitor, having taken full charge, is ready to publicize their new relationship, which Richard proclaims his discomfiture in accepting, or bending a courtier's knee to this usurper. Recalling how very recently he himself has been the object of such flattering salutes, he cannot but reproach the surrounding courtiers for their disloyalty. If their hypocritical 'All hail!' is to be paralleled with that of Judas, it follows that he is casting himself in the role of Jesus—an identification that he confirms at a later stage by recasting them as 'Pilates', unable to wash away their sin of delivering him to a kind of martyrdom (169, 240). Richard's own career could hardly qualify as an *imitatio Christi*; yet some of his chroniclers, notably Créton, were willing to draw that sacrosanct analogy; and Richard has now involved himself in the enactment of a passion-play. The ambiguity of the situation is heightened when the abdicating monarch cries 'God save the king!', and no one cries 'amen' because no one definitely knows for which potential incumbent that blessing has been invoked (172).

Submissively Richard inquires: 'To do what service am I sent for hither?' (176). York answers by reminding him that his 'tired majesty' has freely offered to resign in Henry Bullingbrook's favour, and that his resignation must here and now be made public (178–80). If this is an enforced renunciation of authority, for Richard it is also an open invitation to stage a culminating ceremonial. 'Give me the crown' is his very last command—not that he would wrest it back from his conqueror, but that a meaningful act of abdication should be fully realized and nobly enacted (181). Grasping one side of that golden diadem and enjoining Henry to hold up the other side, he visualizes their opposing fortunes as a pair of buckets within it, moving downwards and upwards respectively through a figurative well: Henry's bucket 'ever dancing in the air', continually ascending even while Richard's, heavily laden with all his griefs, completes its lachrymose descent—and the doleful noun 'grief' is more frequently heard in this play than anywhere else in Shakespeare:

> You may my glories and my state depose,
> But not my griefs; still am I king of those.
>   (192f.)

The tongues of both men, like Scroop's in a previous scene, have become 'care-tun'd' (III, ii, 92). When Henry matter-of-factly speaks of 'cares' that are being passed on, this inspires four lines of Richard's wordplay in which the keyword reverberates nine times (IV, i, 195–8). For the former it signifies the assumption of responsibilities; for the latter it can only mean the continuation and intensification of anxieties. Responding to the former's straight question, 'Are you contented to resign the crown?', again Richard plays upon words, upon the most elementary monosyllables: 'Ay, no, no ay'. *Yes* and *no* are meaningless, 'for I must nothing be' (200–1). There can be no identity under such conditions: no 'I', and 'Therefore no, no', neither assent nor denial (202).

Yet he is never more personally himself than when he proceeds, slowly and proudly, to renounce the ancestral rights of royalty and give up its vested trappings, to

> ... give the heavy weight from off my head,
> And this unwilling sceptre from my hand,
> The pride of kingly sway from out my heart.
>   (204–6)

A ritual is being uniquely improvised, a coronation in reverse, wherein every intimate gesture reinforces an attitude of widening detachment from his consecrated grandeur:

> With mine own tears I wash away the balm,
> With mine own hands I give away my crown,
> With mine own tongue deny my sacred state.
>   (207–9)

And, as it moves through the legal and political to the religious consequences of his decision, Richard's blank verse is formalized into rhyme, grimly seining off his own retirement, graciously congratulating his opponent, and envisaging the next regime in its brightest aura:

> God save King Henry, unking'd Richard says,
> And send him many years of sunshine days!
>   (220–1)

This is where the speaker might well have preferred to conclude his demonstration. But he has still to reckon with Northumberland, who steps forward to demand a confession, so that the detailed articles of indictment will show the commons that their erstwhile king has been 'worthily depos'd' (227). Weeping, Richard demurs and condemns himself for having complied with these encircling enemies by lending himself to their treacherous accusations. It has left him, after living through the chill of so many winters, in a seasonal change with 'no name, no title'—since name and title depended upon the rank that has just been 'usurp'd' from under him (255, 257). He envisions his repudiated self in the serio-comic image of a snowman, deliquescing under the solar radiance of his ascendant rival for the kingship:

> O that I were a mockery king of snow,
> Standing before the sun of Bullingbrook,
> To melt myself away in water-drops!
>   (260–2)

When Northumberland produces a legalistic script and urges him to sign it, Richard's hesitation finds its voice in a self-conscious expression of undiminished vanity. Not that he is reluctant to confess; after all, that is the best opportunity he has left to talk about himself. But a piece of paper is not the source of inspiration he needs; he can best peruse his sins in the book of his own face. It is a looking-glass, therefore, that he requests, and with Bullingbrook's permission receives; to crystallize the occasion: 'Give me that glass, and therein will I read' (276). To hold it up to himself should induce a mood of introspection, and yet his first reaction is to be gratified that his features have not been wrinkled more deeply by his griefs. But that cannot be the truest reflection of the saddening part that he has been walking through. The mirror-image may unduly flatter him, as—he now understands—his opportunistic followers have so guilefully done. Scrutinized more thoughtfully, his glass becomes another mirror for magistrates, and he becomes another passer-by in that weary procession of failed authorities. Nearing a rhetorical climax, Shakespeare conjures up the most romantic precedent, 'the face that launch'd a thousand ships' in the unforgettable salutation of Marlowe's Doctor Faustus to Helen of Troy:

> Was this the face
> That, like the sun, did make beholders wink?
> Is this the face which fac'd so many follies,
> That was at last out-fac'd by Bullingbrook?
>   (283–6)

Richard will no longer shine in the light of, nor abide comparison with, the tutelary orb of kings, whose very brilliance caused men's eyes to blink. This valediction is coupled with two further wordplays on 'face': the realization that he has countenanced too many follies, and the concession that he has now been put out of countenance by Bullingbrook.

It is Richard's climactic stroke, at this juncture, to signalize the 'brittle glory' of his face and of his office by dashing down the glass against the ground into 'an hundred shivers' (287, 289). To Bullingbrook, the 'silent king', he divulges a moral: 'How soon my sorrow hath destroy'd my face' (290–1). To this his more businesslike and literal-minded listener interposes a word of correction: 'The shadow of your sorrow hath destroy'd / The shadow of your face' (292–3). The darkness of his troubles has momentarily cast its shade upon his perception of himself. Richard, in his melancholy, is willing to embrace that umbrageous revision: 'Say that again, / The shadow of my sorrow!' (293–4). Shadow, as the antithesis to sunlight, befits his current unkingly stance; and, even more profoundly, as the insubstantial counterpart of substance, it redirects him from the world of outer appearances to a sphere of innate realities. For this shared insight he thanks King Henry, and asks for but one more courtesy. And it is Henry's condescension that elicits Richard's final irony: since a king is politely flattering him, he must now be 'greater than a king' (305). The granted boon is simply 'leave to go'; and, since no destination has been named, Henry issues the order to his attendants: 'Go some of you, convey him to the Tower' (313, 316). His choice of verbs prompts Richard to a parting shot of linguistic one-upmanship, inasmuch as—to the Elizabethans—'conveyer' was a euphemism for 'thief':

O, good! convey! Conveyors are you all,
That rise thus nimbly by a true king's fall.
    (317f.)

This concludes what the Abbot of Westminster describes as 'a woeful pageant' (321). Like the other spectators and incidental speakers, he has consciously fallen in with the overt theatricality of Richard's stage-managed departure. Predictably, if not anticlimactically, the Fifth Act will do all it can to tie up the looser ends of unfinished business. The Queen has but two appearances of any importance, the one before and another just after the Deposition Scene, and the latter is the only scene that brings her onstage with her husband. Together only to separate forever, she is retiring to her native France, while he—in a shifted sentence—will be imprisoned not at the nearby Tower of London but far north at Pomfret Castle. Their leavetaking could not be more formally observed, dwelling upon his posthumous reputation, evoking such allusions as ancient Troy, and trading verses in stichomythy. Richard's prophetic rebuke to Northumberland, when the Earl interrupts this elegiac duet to send them on their penitential ways, will be recollected ironically by the King in *2 Henry IV*, after the former allies have turned against one another

as predicted. 'As in a theatre', but at a second remove, we overhear the Duke
of York telling his Duchess about the triumphal procession in which King
Henry is hailed and ex-King Richard is humbled (V, ii, 23). Horses prance
verbally, if not literally, through Elizabethan drama. To ride in triumph, for
Marlowe's Tamburlaine, was to achieve his imperial ambitions.

If horseback could be seen as a mode of enthronement, then to be
unhorsed could stand for dethronement, as was so conclusively demonstrated
by Richard III. The equestrian deposal of Richard II will be tearfully brought
home to him when his last visitor, a groom from the royal stable, tells of
Henry riding to his coronation on Richard's favourite steed, Roan Barbary.
This will round out the reversals of Act V. Conspiracy will have raised its head
again; and the Yorkist plot of Aumerle will be thwarted, exposed by York himself and pardoned by Henry: yet its impact will continue to be felt as a threat
undermining Lancastrian prospects. So long as Richard is alive, however, he
dominates his prison cell as he did his courtly surroundings, now revelling in
the moods and changes of his adversity. Having cried woe and destruction,
having arrived at ruin and decay, he is well aware that 'The worst is death' and
prepared to accept the fact that 'death must have its day' (III, ii, 102–3). His
receding thoughts move up and down through 66 lines of soliloquy, recapitulating his course from the worldly pride of kingship to the suicidal dejection
of beggardom, grasping ineffectually at the consolations of proverbial wisdom,
and belatedly evincing an empathy for other roles than his own:

> Thus play I in one person many people,
> And none contented
>   (V, v, 31)

Then the unexpected sound of music in the distance—broken music—shifts
his meditation to the rhythms of time, with the recognition that his time
is up. 'I wasted time, and now doth time waste me' (49). His murder is
unavoidable but ambiguous, since Henry is not to be held responsible for the
regicide, but must repudiate the assassin who is doing him such a service,
Pierce Exton, and then must rather guiltily promise to do penance with a
crusade—a promise that will soon be intercepted by battles to retain his
English conquest. Richard is aroused at long last to redeem his stature with
a valiant fight against his murderers, and to reverse the emphasis on his
descension with an expiring gasp:

> Mount, mount, my soul! thy seat is up on high,
> Whilst my gross flesh sinks downward, here to die.
>   (111f.)

It is a pious sentiment; but from the lowest depths, the absolute bottom of his imaginary well, the sole remaining outlook for him cannot be other than upwards; and Richard has shown less resistance as he has been sinking from one station of his pilgrimage to the next. At his last agony he is still clinging to hope and pretension, though he might more definitely be declaiming the tag-lines of Jonson's *Sejanus*:

> For whom the morning saw so great and high,
> Thus low and little fore the 'even doth lie.

Jonson would be translating loosely from the *Thyestes* of Seneca; but this *sententia* was also quoted from the original Latin by Marlowe in *Edward II*; and, as a concise formulation of tragedy, it was often quoted during the English Renaissance. The composition of *Richard II* has been singled out, by some of Shakespeare's interpreters, as a dress rehearsal for *Hamlet*. Composed in the mid-1590s, it might be considered to mark his literary coming-of-age, using what he had learned from the widespread experimentation of his apprentice years and prefiguring mature developments. Richard may indeed anticipate Hamlet in the full disclosure of his mind, but his is a shallower mind. Hamlet not only lamented the cursed spite that kept opposing him; he deliberately sought it out and, however unsuccessfully, tried hard to strike back. An undramatic lack of bilateral conflict led Yeats to criticize *Richard II* as 'a play without a hero'. Coleridge had said that it was 'for the closet', and George Pierce Baker would argue that it provided 'no good acting part'. Those cavils could be somewhat neutralized by E.K. Chambers' description of Richard as 'a born actor', even though he fails so crucially in living up to his inherited role. Moreover, his role-consciousness can be partly attributed to Shakespeare's medium-consciousness at the verge of his fullest technical mastery. If Richard seems continually aware that he is acting a part, Shakespeare leaves us similarly aware that he has been writing a play.

Happily, the matter suits the manner—and even the mannerisms, which might not have fitted so neatly into a less elaborate or symmetrical context. The earlier plays are more open and more uneven; the later ones range more freely through their individualized effects; this one seems to have been moulded into its ornate artistic form. The formalities of its construction are matched by the regularities of its style. It never stoops from verse to prose, as do nearly all of the others. The absence of comic characters has helped to eliminate that relaxing convention; even the earthy Gardener has his moralistic vein of iambic pentameter. To walk with Richard from scene to scene is like turning the illuminated pages in a medieval Book of Hours. Shakespeare, writing at the apogee of what we regard as his Lyrical Period, was moving from history and light comedy toward tragedy with *Romeo and Juliet*. But he would still be celebrating the brightest span of history itself by moving on with the Henries, and incidentally cutting through the Ricardian grandiloquence to a more colloquial vein. Prince Hal is conspicuous by his absence from *Richard II*, notoriously 'at London, 'mongst the taverns' (V, iii, 5). As the diction moves from hollow court to mellow tavern, so does the ethos. Bullingbrook will be denounced as a 'vile politician' by the chivalric Hotspur, 'policy' being commonly understood as Machiavellian realism. To the cynical Bastard in *King John*, the watchword for the interplay of motives had been 'commodity' (self-interest).

The backward glance does not seem altogether fair, when we reconsider the sixteenth-century Shakespeare in the forward-looking light of his Jacobean achievements. Doubtless with maturity and practice he came to understand more comprehensively and to render more convincingly the psychology of his dramatic personages. But latterday critiques may not have made due allowance for the formalism and the conventions of his still-developing medium, when G.I. Duthie could denominate Richard 'an artist miscast as a king', or when Mark Van Doren could recast him as 'a minor poet, not a king'. Reversing that formula, a modern poet, Louis Aragon in 1940, could ease the strains of German occupation and French resistance with a recollection of Richard accepting the loss of his state and glories, but not of his griefs: 'Still am I king of those'. That became the consolatory refrain of '*Richard Deux Quarante*': '*je reste roi de mes douleurs*'. (Aragon would go on to commemorate a more heartening exemplar, the crusader buried in France, with '*Richard Coeur-de-Lion*'.) But, although England's second King Richard might have seemed outdated in his own or in Shakespeare's lifetime, his reappearance may strike us today as quite timely. It is *Richard III* that no longer holds the favourite place it occupied in the repertory of the eighteenth and nineteenth centuries. That became the first—and for many years the most popular—Shakespearean production in the United States, possibly because it transmitted so adverse a picture of royalty.

Such a chronological reversion from Richard III to Richard II may symbolize a significant permutation in the cultural climate, while the strong-minded century of Balzac was being displaced by Kafka's age of anxiety. It would be hard to imagine the same actor as both kings, as Richard the ranting tragedian and Richard the lyrical self-questioner; but styles of acting change too, along with the times. It is easy to think of John Gielgud as Richard II: slight in stature, sensitive in mien, mellifluous in enunciation. The part is his by nature, and he has played it well. As for the play itself, it somehow became the most familiar vehicle for Maurice Evans, who patterned his interpretation on Gielgud's and who managed to set records with it on both sides of the Atlantic. Gielgud, in his turn, appeared successfully in the title role of a new play on the same subject, *Richard of Bordeaux*, written for him under the pseudonym of Gordon Daviot. At any rate, our century has refuted those prior criticisms regarding the actability of this Shakespearean history. And, though its stage history is fairly sparse in the early record, there were some unusual occasions, such as the problematic revival that got itself implicated with the Earl of Essex against Queen Elizabeth. And just a few years after that unique episode—to be exact, the recorded date is 30 September 1607—*Richard II* was performed by the crew of the good ship *Dragon*, off the coast of Sierra Leone on its voyage to East India.

Those sailors were allowed to engage in dramatics, as we learn from the journal of their captain, William Keeling, in hopes that such recreation might divert them from indulging in games more unlawful, or from the sleep or silence into which they might otherwise have bogged down. But why they should have chosen this particular offering, in addition to two shipboard performances of *Hamlet*, rather than two easier choices for so amateur a group of players, fosters speculation if not explanation. Both offerings were deeply rooted in the Europe from which they were being carried away, but neither could have imbued its nautical cast with much nostalgia. Though the *Dragon* was heading for an older world, it was animated by the adventurous spirit that had currently begun to settle a new one. In the developing culture of that new world even the unkinged Richard would find some recognition, as we have noticed (and Hamlet, the disinherited prince, would find a good deal more). Walt Whitman, the self-proclaimed bard of democracy, would take his hand-bound copy of *Richard II* along when he rode on a Broadway bus, and would counteract the street noises by loudly spouting from it to his fellow New Yorkers. Even more surprisingly, Abraham Lincoln, who was fond of reading Shakespeare aloud or reciting from memory to his friends, seems to have weathered some of his discouragements by quoting from an unlikely speech and speakers: 'For God's sake let us sit upon the ground / And tell sad stories. . . .'

To have drawn together such polar opposites is to touch upon the canon of universality, in spite of some readers who may have been put off along the way by the palpable artifice and the residual preciosity of a talent so consciously realizing itself. In its resulting fusion of poetry into drama, in what E.M.W. Tillyard has reckoned as the 'most formal and ceremonial' of Shakespeare's plays, music has been more than a recurrent metaphor; it has become an operatic *lietmotif*. That note is sounded first on Mowbray's expulsion, and linked with language—but negatively, since he must put English behind him. Henceforth his tongue can mean no more to him

Than an unstringed viol or a harp,
Or like a cunning instrument cas'd up,
Or being open, put into his hands
That knows no touch to tune the harmony.
    (I, iii, 162–5)

If departure means silence for Mowbray, the last words of Gaunt are accorded a special attention, 'like deep harmony' (II, i, 6). And he introduces his predications by linking the image of a dynastic sunset with the dying fall of a musical composition, together with a couplet that echoes Shakespeare's thirtieth sonnet ('remembrance of things past'), which will be re-echoed in the latterday context of Proustian memories:

The setting sun, and music at the close,
As the last taste of sweets, is sweetest last,
Writ in remembrance more than things long past.
    (12–14)

But for the moribund Richard, as the timing broke down, the sweetness turned sour. Alas, that, after all those elegant intonations, it should come to this! 'So is it in the music of men's lives' (V, v, 45). And, since history can be perceived as the music of time, it is fitting that the close of Richard's life should have its musical accompaniment, but also that its tones should orchestrate the discordant pitch as well as the faltering rhythms of his career in office: the neglected 'concord of my state and time' (47). Projecting that same metaphor, the chronicler Hall had given it a more affirmative twist by looking ahead toward the victorious Lancasters: 'Things decay through discord, . . . through concord they are revived'. But this is not quite yet their hour; it is the end of Richard's; and his erstwhile glories are overwhelmed by his present griefs. That, of course, is the fundamental outline of all tragedies, and his is an archetypal example because its comedown is so steep and spectacular. The sweet fruition for Richard III, as for Marlowe's most heroic protagonist, was an earthly crown. For Richard II it is a crown of sorrows.

ALEXANDER LEGGATT

The Death of John Talbot

Our habitual division of Shakespeare's plays into comedies, histories, and tragedies, each play fitting one category, is largely based on the Folio of 1623. But title-page evidence suggests that in Shakespeare's time the lines could be drawn differently and the divisions were not so absolute. The Quarto texts of *Richard III* and *Richard II* identify them as tragedies. The play we know as *3 Henry VI* was first published as "*The true Tragedie of Richard Duke of Yorke, and the death of good King Henrie the Sixt. . . .*" *King Lear* in its Quarto version is a "*True Chronicle Historie.*" The Folio division that has shaped our thinking probably does not reflect the way Shakespeare himself thought of his plays. Certainly the layout of the Folio obscures the fact that the history play as a genre, while it sometimes goes its own way, frequently intersects with the established, traditional genres of tragedy and comedy—for Shakespeare, more often with tragedy. The plays the Folio presents as the *Henry VI* trilogy function also as a collection of individual tragedies in the manner of *The Monk's Tale* and *The Mirror for Magistrates*. The title page of *The true Tragedie of Richard Duke of York* also advertises the play's second major death, that of Henry VI, and the two deaths get equal billing in the running titles. The title page of "*The First part of the Contention betwixt the two famous Houses of Yorke and Lancaster*" goes on to list the deaths of Gloucester, Suffolk and Winchester. A title page functions as a

From *Shakespeare's English Histories: A Quest for Form and Genre*, edited by John W. Velz, pp. 11–30. © 1997 by the Arizona Board of Regents for Arizona State University.

blurb, and Shakespeare's public liked a good death scene. But in addition to being a come-on, the title page is a fair reflection of the contents. In this early experiment in historical drama Shakespeare evidently found himself thinking of history, in part, as a series of tragedies. Only in part, of course. The fact that it is a series, not the story of one hero, marks a break with the usual dramatic form of tragedy (though it may also anticipate such Jacobean group tragedies as *Women Beware Women* and *The White Devil*). The way the story sweeps on past the deaths of even the most important characters forms a distinction between history and tragedy that Shakespeare goes on using in later plays. What we have in the *Henry VI* trilogy is an intersection of two forms, tragedy and history, each one shaping and affecting the other. The heroes of individual tragedies are brought down by historical forces. Humphrey of Gloucester is a key example: it is not so much his own *hamartia* that undoes him as the fact that his political enemies are too strong for him, and the kind of civil order he represents is crumbling as England slips into anarchy. At the same time an interest in tragedy makes the play pause over the fates of individuals in a way that the simple chronicling of events would not require. In *2 Henry VI*, the deaths of Gloucester and Suffolk slow the action down, as each death is held in a freeze-frame to let us contemplate it before the pace picks up again and history moves on. It is as though history and tragedy took place at different speeds, tragedy being the slower; or as though each individual death made time stop for a while to let us contemplate human fate *sub specie aeternitatis*.

The first striking episode of this sort is the death of Talbot in *1 Henry VI*, which seems designed as the climax of that play. We have no Quarto version in this case, but if we did it would not be surprising to find it called something like *The Famous Life and Lamentable Death of Lord Talbot Earl of Shrewsbury*. In a much-quoted passage, Thomas Nashe testifies to the power Talbot's death had over the play's first audience:

> How would it have joyed brave *Talbot* (the terror of the French) to think that after he had lain two hundred years in his tomb, he should triumph again on the stage, and have his bones new embalmed with the tears of ten thousand spectators at least, (at several times) who, in the tragedian that represents his person, imagine they behold him fresh bleeding![1]

The focus on Talbot as a national hero ("the terror of the French") whose death was "the last stand of English chivalry,"[2] whose final defeat was a defeat for his nation, makes the scene a communal welling up of grief, even a "ritual experience."[3] At the same time the actor who plays him is a "tragedian." We are watching a turning point in English history, and the death of a hero. We are also watching, I would like to argue, one of the critical moments in Shakespeare's artistic development, a scene that reverberates not only through the other *Henry VI* plays but through Shakespeare's later work, particularly his later tragedies. It tells us how much Shakespeare as a writer of tragedy owed to his first experiments in historical drama. Its importance has, I think, been underestimated: partly because its artificial manner is frigid and offputting to modern readers; partly because we have not fully grasped the significance of the fact that it involves the death of not one hero but two.

The central importance of the Talbot sequence is established early in the play. The first scene reports two critical events: the death of Henry V, and the defeat and capture of Talbot at Orleans. In the development of the scene the second event displaces the first in importance, and foreshadows Talbot's end. At Orleans he is betrayed by the desertion of Falstaff; at Bordeaux he will be betrayed by York and Somerset who, locked in their own squabble, refuse to send him aid. The last Talbot episode circles back to the first, giving a sense of tragic inevitability. Early in the play Joan la Pucelle breaks off a combat with him and walks away, declaring, "Talbot, farewell; thy hour is not yet come" (I.v.13).[4] It is as though she knows, through her communion with spirits, of Talbot's ultimate end. When we come to that end the play slows down and its concentration tightens. According to Robert Y. Turner, "The plotting indicates that Shakespeare intends these scenes to be the emotional high point of the play. As nowhere else he devotes three scenes to preparation." He also introduces a new character, "who has never before appeared or even been mentioned in the play,"[5] Talbot's son John. In dramatic terms, he is born only to die. In that way he resembles Young Cato in *Julius Caesar* or Young Siward in *Macbeth*. They too are the sons of famous fathers, and that is about all we get to know of them. But while they flash through their plays very briefly, John Talbot is held up, like his father, for contemplation, and though Nashe does not mention him, his tragedy and his father's are bound together in a sequence that made Elizabethan audiences weep.

John has the same fated quality as his father does. The first reference to him comes from Lucy, whose frustrated attempts to rouse York and Somerset to action show the net tightening around Talbot:

Then God take mercy on brave Talbot's soul,
And on his son young John, who two hours since
I met in travel toward his warlike father!
This seven years did not Talbot see his son,
And now they meet when both their lives are done.
   (IV.iii.34–38)

In later Shakespeare, family reunions will create the ultimate images of fulfillment in comedy and romance; the Talbot reunion is marked by death, as
though John, in finding his father, has found his own doom. Moreover, this
is how John finds and asserts his identity. He is his father's son, and that is
all he is; as his father's son, all he can do is die:

> Is my name Talbot? And am I your son?
> And shall I fly? O, if you love my mother,
> Dishonor not her honorable name
> To make a bastard and a slave of me!
> The world will say he is not Talbot's blood,
> That basely fled when noble Talbot stood.
>   (IV.v.12–17)

The name he finds for himself is not "John" but "Talbot." His mother has
no name, no identity other than that of a medium through which the family
blood and honor are transferred from father to son. The identity of name
leads John to imagine an identity of nature so total it is as though their bodies are fused together, and must act together:

> No more can I be severed from your side
> Than can yourself yourself in twain divide.
> Stay, go, do what you will—the like do I;
> For live I will not, if my father die.
> TALBOT.
> Then here I take my leave of thee, fair son,
> Born to eclipse thy life this afternoon.
>   (IV.v.48–53)

Talbot's reply sees John's death as foreordained; but John sees it not as a
function of a particular time, but as a function of a relationship. In an identification Talbot himself makes twice, they are Daedalus and Icarus (IV.
vi.54–55, IV.vii.16). (Was the image suggested to Shakespeare by Hall's
reference to Talbot's danger as "the imminent jeopardy and subtile labyrinth
in which he and hys people were enclosed"?)[6] John dies as his life is about to
begin, doomed like Icarus for being his father's son.

This terrible paradox runs through the whole sequence: the man who
gave John life now, for all his attempts to prevent the tragedy, gives him death.
John summarizes the paradox with the social ritual, an everyday routine in
Elizabethan England, of the child kneeling down to ask the parent's blessing:
"Here on my knee I beg mortality" (IV.v.32). Talbot, in giving John life in

the first place, has already given him mortality. (The gravedigger of Elsinore began his work the day Hamlet was born.) In the following exchange—

TALBOT.
Shall all thy mother's hopes lie in one tomb?
JOHN.
Ay, rather than I'll shame my mother's womb.
(IV.v.34–35)

—the rhyme of "womb" and "tomb" makes the same imaginative connection between birth and death, this time through the unnamed mother. In both cases the play on language universalizes John's fate; we all owe mortality to our parents. The irony is compounded when Talbot rescues John on the field of battle:

TALBOT. . . .
Where is John Talbot? Pause, and take thy breath.
I gave thee life and rescu'd thee from death.
JOHN.
O, twice my father, twice am I thy son!
The life thou gav'st me first was lost and done,
Till with thy warlike sword, despite of fate,
To my determin'd time thou gav'st new date.
(IV.vi.4–9)

This gives new force and immediacy to the idea of Talbot giving his son life, thereby sharpening the final paradox. Later, knowing that he is dying, Talbot sees John's potential for giving *him* life: "Where is my other life? Mine own is gone. / O, where's young Talbot? Where is valiant John?" (IV. vii.1–2). The way Talbot goes from "my other life" to "valiant John" suggests an attempt to bestow on his son the separate, individual identity that John has persistently denied himself, the separate identity that (paradoxically again) allows parents to live on through their children. But by the end of the speech it is clear that Talbot already knows his son is dead. His opening question shows his imagination's refusal to accept his death. The identification of birth and death is sealed with a final play on words as the Servant signals the entrance of John's corpse: "O my dear lord, lo, where your son is borne!" (IV.vii.17).

A related paradox is that John's death is also a rite of passage, an initiation into full adulthood.[7] Talbot makes the point clear in his first words to his son: "O young John Talbot, I did send for thee / To tutor thee in stratagems of war" (IV.v.1–2). He urges him to leave after his first taste of battle, his rite of passage completed: "Wilt thou yet leave the battle, boy, and fly, / Now thou art seal'd the son of chivalry?" (IV.vi.28–29). But John's true initiation is into death. The speech in which Talbot describes his son's full emergence into manhood, rescuing his father as his father had rescued him, shows the young man in his first battle transformed into a powerful warrior:

> When he perceiv'd me shrink and on my knee,
> His bloody sword he brandish'd over me,
> And like a hungry lion, did commence
> Rough deeds of rage and stern impatience.
>   (IV.vii.5–8)

But this is also the speech that describes his death.

The military rite of passage is described in language that suggests a sexual rite of passage. Earlier in the play, Joan's disturbing power is identified as partly sexual: fighting her is an erotic thrill for the Dauphin, who suddenly declares, "Impatiently I burn with thy desire" (I.ii.108). She has a witch's power to unman Talbot senior, who finds himself incapable of defeating her. Shakespeare imagines her as a witch, and many of the fantasies surrounding witchcraft in his time were sexual. John, however, rejects her with a virginal pride that Shakespeare would later see in Adonis and the young man of the Sonnets. After his death, Joan describes her failure with him:

> Once I encount'red him, and thus I said:
> 'Thou maiden youth, be vanquish'd by a maid.'
> But, with a proud majestical high scorn,
> He answer'd thus: 'Young Talbot was not born
> To be the pillage of a giglot wench.'
> So, rushing in the bowels of the French,
> He left me proudly, as unworthy fight.
>   (IV.vii.37–43)

It is Orleans who takes John's virginity, and Talbot avenges the act as though avenging a daughter who has been violated:

> The ireful bastard Orleans, that drew blood
> From thee, my boy, and had the maidenhood
> Of thy first fight, I soon encountered,
> And interchanging blows I quickly shed
> Some of his bastard blood; and in disgrace

Bespoke him thus: 'Contaminated, base,
And misbegotten blood I spill of thine,
Mean and right poor, for that pure blood of mine
Which thou didst force from Talbot, my brave boy.'
   (IV.vi.16–24)

The Talbots dwell so much on John's legitimacy, and on the bond of father and son, that it seems appropriate his first encounter should be with a bastard, as though John, like a Spenserian knight, is testing himself against an allegorical opponent who represents the vice most opposed to his virtue. Appropriately, it is Orleans who, on finding the Talbots dead, wants to desecrate the bodies and has to be restrained by the Dauphin (IV.vii.47–50).

Birth, loss of virginity, initiation into manhood—all these experiences, which ought to mark entries into a new life, mark John Talbot's entry into death. The risk Shakespeare takes in writing the whole sequence in heroic couplets, "a form which Shakespeare never uses elsewhere in a tragic passage"[8] and one "not customary in the formal lament by his contemporaries"[9] has the effect not just of heightening the scene by stylizing it, but of making the Talbots seem boxed in, stymied. The relentless click-click of the rhymes reinforces the point that for John Talbot all arguments are arguments for death; as every other line ending is countered by a rhyme, so every argument Talbot gives for John to flee becomes an argument for staying. As Talbot is trapped at the military level by the French, and by the treachery of York and Somerset, so John is trapped at the level of argument by his determination to die:

TALBOT.
  Thy father's charge shall clear thee from that stain.
JOHN.
  You cannot witness for me, being slain.
  If death be so apparent, then both fly.
TALBOT.
  And leave my followers here to fight and die?
  My age was never tainted with such shame.
JOHN.
  And shall my youth be guilty of such blame?
   (IV.v.42–47)

Stylistically, the Talbot sequence looks forward to plays like *The Conquest of Granada* in which, no matter how often the characters change their minds, the rhyming couplets make every decision they take seem final.

Early in the play, when an English hero dies the torch can pass to his comrades. So it is with the dying Salisbury's last, unspoken message to Talbot:

> He beckons with his hand and smiles on me,
> As who should say 'When I am dead and gone,
> Remember to avenge me on the French.'
> Plantagenet, I will. . . .
>   (I.iv.92–95)

John's determination to die explicitly blocks that possibility. As Talbot warns him, "In thee thy mother dies, our household's name, / My death's revenge, thy youth, and England's fame" (IV.vi.38–39). When the captured York, about to be killed by his enemies, threatens that a phoenix will rise from his ashes to avenge him (*3 Henry VI*, I.iv.35–36) we know that the prophecy will be fulfilled in his son Richard. But when Lucy predicts of the Talbots, "from their ashes shall be rear'd / A phoenix that shall make all France afeard" (IV. vii.92–93) the prophecy—unusually for the *Henry VI* plays—comes to nothing. Deaths in history are as likely to start an action as to finish it: think of Richard II. The Talbots' deaths, like the deaths of heroes in later tragedies, truly constitute an ending. After this, not only is the English cause in France doomed, but Talbot and his son are forgotten. *1 Henry VI* opens with an act of remembrance, the funeral of Henry V. It closes with a passage of forgetting: no sooner are the Talbots dead than we see Henry and Gloucester planning a peace treaty, and when in the first scene of *2 Henry VI* Gloucester summarizes England's wars with France he makes no mention of Talbot. John D. Cox has argued that the *Henry VI* plays were written not in a flush of patriotic fervor at the defeat of the Armada but as a reflection of the bitter disillusionment that set in afterwards "as the reality of a costly, bloody and enervating war of attrition sank in."[10] This disillusionment may be reflected in the aftermath of the Talbot scenes: the fate of English heroes is to die, and the habit of the English community is to forget them.

Shakespeare's aim, as in later tragedies, is not to explore the future that lies beyond the hero's death but to explore the death itself. The Talbots die apart (dying is the most private, solitary thing we do) and together (it is something we all share). John dies in battle, separated from his father; Talbot dies with his son's body cradled in his arms. The trap has closed and—paradoxically again—this means the dying Talbot can speak with a new freedom. No longer in a back-and-forth debate with John, a debate that always ends one way, Talbot can explore what death, now they have attained it, means for both of them. His mind plays around the experience, shifting and experimenting:

Thou antic Death, which laugh'st us here to scorn,
Anon, from thy insulting tyranny,
Coupled in bonds of perpetuity,
Two Talbots, winged through the lither sky,
In thy despite shall scape mortality.
O thou, whose wounds become, hard-favored Death,
Speak to thy father ere thou yield thy breath!
Brave Death by speaking, whether he will or no;
Imagine him a Frenchman and thy foe.
Poor boy! He smiles, methinks, as who should say,
Had Death been French, then Death had died today.
Come, come, and lay him in his father's arms. . . .
My spirit can no longer bear these harms.
Soldiers, adieu! I have what I would have.
Now my old arms are young John Talbot's grave.
   (IV.vii.18–32)

The grinning skull of Death, like the antic that keeps his court in the hollow crown of Richard II, has the last laugh on the Talbots; then they escape him, free in spirit as they were trapped in body. But the triumph is brief. Suddenly Talbot, like Lear with Cordelia, cannot accept his son's death and asks him to speak. He cannot speak, but he can smile. His smile counters the grin of death, but it may also mirror it: just as Macbeth becomes withered murder, a human character transformed to an allegorical figure, so John Talbot becomes the grinning Death of a few lines earlier. Then he becomes (again, like Cordelia) a child cradled in his father's arms. Birth and death fuse; the father's body becomes a grave. As the survivors debate the appropriate response to the bodies—Lucy, with unconscious irony, asks for Talbot by listing all his titles and Joan retorts, "Him that thou magnifi'st with all these titles / Stinking and fly-blown lies here at our feet" (IV. vii.75–76)—the sheer length of the debate protracts the time we have to look at the stage picture of the dead father cradling his dead son. This picture embodies deeper ironies in its fusion of love and death than the obvious ironies of Lucy's debate with Joan. The image of embracing corpses will return in the wedding night in the tomb that ends *Romeo and Juliet* (the only time we see the lovers lying together), the tragic loading of the bed in *Othello*, the terrible *pietà* that ends *King Lear*.

The image of the Talbots linked in death has a more immediate power within the *Henry VI* trilogy itself. They may be forgotten by the other characters—that, in fact, is part of their tragedy—but they are remembered by the play. The image they present goes on reverberating. The first strong echo takes the form of parody. Shakespeare understood, as Marx did, that all great historical events are played twice: once as tragedy, once as farce. All through *1 Henry VI* Talbot has been contrasted, explicitly and implicitly, with Joan la Pucelle, the English hero and the French witch. The contrast is sharpest at the end when Joan, under sentence of death, is met by her father. Like John Talbot, the Shepherd is a new character, who has sought out his daughter only to find her on the point of death. The reversal of generations is only the beginning:

SHEPHERD.
   Ah, Joan, this kills thy father's heart outright!
   Have I sought every country far and near,
   And, now it is my chance to find thee out,
   Must I behold thy timeless cruel death?
   Ah, Joan, sweet daughter Joan, I'll die with thee!
JOAN.
   Decrepit miser, base ignoble wretch!
   I am descended of a gentler blood.
   Thou art no father nor no friend of mine.
    (V.iv.2–9)

Joan's response to her father's offer to die with her is to deny the link of paternity that means so much to the Talbots. As John kneels to his father, so the Shepherd asks Joan to kneel to him. Her refusal is too much for him:

   Kneel down and take my blessing, good my girl.
   Wilt thou not stoop? Now cursed be the time
   Of thy nativity! I would the milk
   Thy mother gave thee when thou suck'dst her breast
   Had been a little ratsbane for thy sake!
   Or else, when thou didst keep thy lambs a-field,
   I wish some ravenous wolf had eaten thee!
   Dost thou deny thy father, cursed drab?
   O, burn her, burn her! Hanging is too good. *Exit.*
    (V.iv.25–33)

The Shepherd's startling change of tone turns what looked like pathos into savage farce. That tone continues as Joan—eager to live as John Talbot was to die—claims to be pregnant but keeps changing the name of the father. York cuts her off with, "Strumpet, thy words condemn thy brat and thee" (V.iv.84). As in the Talbot sequence, but with very different effect, parent and child will die together.

Once as tragedy, once as farce. One result of Shakespeare's experiment of seeing history as a collection of tragedies is that episodes, sometimes widely separated episodes, echo each other, producing a structure based on connected images rather than a connected action, drawing out the meaning of history on the level of ideas rather than on the level of story. The human bond reflected by the Talbots works one way for them, a very different way for Joan and the Shepherd. And as Joan is replaced by Margaret, Reignier's cool indifference to losing his daughter—

> Suffolk, what remedy?
> I am a soldier, and unapt to weep
> Or to exclaim on fortune's fickleness.
>   (V.iii.132–34)

—shows that the breakdown of piety and natural feeling is spreading, and it matches the farce of Joan's last scene with a wry comedy of its own. In *2 Henry VI*, the issue of paternity returns in Jack Cade's first scene:

CADE.
  We John Cade, so term'd of our suppos'd father—
DICK. (*Aside*)
  Or rather, of stealing a cade of herrings.
....
CADE.
  My father was a Mortimer—
DICK. (*Aside*)
  He was an honest man, and a good bricklayer.
CADE.
  My mother a Plantagenet—
DICK. (*Aside*)
  I knew her well; she was a midwife.
CADE.
  My wife descended of the Lacies—
DICK. (*Aside*)
  She was, indeed, a pedler's daughter, and sold many laces.
    (IV.ii.31–45)

Later, Cade produces a grim parody of the joining in death of the Talbots when he orders the severed heads of Lord Say and his son-in-law Sir John Cromer, impaled on poles, to "kiss one another, for they lov'd well when they were alive" (IV.vii.125–26).

The parent–child configuration returns in more serious forms throughout the trilogy. In a notoriously sentimental image, Henry, lamenting the fall of Gloucester, compares himself to a cow unable to save her calf from the butcher (III.i.210–20). But its principal use is to drive the machinery of private revenge, which increasingly dominates the public action towards the end of *2 Henry VI*. Old Clifford, slain in battle by York, dies with a motto that makes his death seem a dignified and significant finish to his life: "La fin couronne les oeuvres" (V.ii.28). But Young Clifford, who has appeared for the first time just before this battle, thereby strengthening the parallel with John Talbot,[11] draws a very different meaning out of his father's death as he looks down on the body:

> Even at this sight
> My heart is turn'd to stone; and while 'tis mine,
> It shall be stony. York not our old men spares;
> No more will I their babes. . . .
> Henceforth I will not have to do with pity.
> Meet I an infant of the house of York,
> Into as many gobbets will I cut it
> As wild Medea young Absyrtus did.
> In cruelty will I seek out my fame.
> (V.ii.49–60)

As he carries out the body he compares himself to Aeneas bearing Anchises; but this Anchises is dead, and in Clifford piety has turned to savagery. We see the results early in *3 Henry VI*, when Clifford sets about killing the innocent schoolboy Rutland simply because he is York's son:

> CLIFFORD.
>   In vain thou speak'st, poor boy. My father's blood
>   Hath stopp'd the passage where thy words should enter.
> RUTLAND.
>   Then let my father's blood open it again.
>   He is a man, and, Clifford, cope with him.
>   (I.iii.21–24)

While John Talbot was eager to die, Rutland, like Joan, pleads desperately for life; and the pathos of the scene darkens into brutality as we realize what Rutland is saying: don't kill me, I'm too young; kill my father.

One of the most striking of the individual tragedies in the trilogy is the one that gives the Quarto version of *3 Henry VI* its title, the death of York. Alone, defeated, he recalls how his sons tried to save him:

My sons—God knows what hath bechanced them;
But this I know, they have demean'd themselves
Like men born to renown by life or death.
Three times did Richard make a lane to me,
And thrice cried 'Courage, father, fight it out!'
And full as oft came Edward to my side
With purple falchion, painted to the hilt
In blood of those who had encount'red him.
   (I.iv.6–13)

But while the Talbots manage to save each other before they die, and come together in death, York finally confronts his enemies alone. He is given, not the body of his son to cradle, but a napkin dipped in the blood of Rutland to dry his tears. The Talbots never wept; the audience wept for them. Whatever the audience does in this later scene, York weeps openly—and so does Northumberland, drawing Margaret's rebuke (I.iv.169–74). The Talbots largely had the stage to themselves, freely displaying their courage and piety, talking of how they encountered their enemies. York is beset by enemies, like a baited bear; he and Margaret engage in a ferocious exchange of insults that replaces the dignity of the earlier scene with a more savage idiom. It is also far more painful. The scene immediately following begins with Edward's question, "I wonder how our princely father scap'd" (II.i.1), emphasizing how father and sons have been separated so that York must face his death alone. Piety, as in the case of Clifford, can act itself out only through revenge, with a touch of grotesque futility as York's sons are reduced to taunting Clifford's corpse, having missed their chance to kill him,[12] and a savagery that matches the deaths of Rutland and York as they take turns stabbing the captured Prince Edward at Tewkesbury.

Prince Edward's relations with his father King Henry are another variation on the Talbot–John relationship, again fragmented into parody. When Henry disinherits Edward as part of his settlement with the Yorkists, the unnatural Clifford rebukes him for unnaturalness, declaring that even "unreasonable creatures" (3 Henry VI, II.ii.26) fight to defend their young. When Henry knights him it is a rite of passage, but one that shows the separation of the two men, as Edward takes Clifford's side in the debate against his father:

KING HENRY.
  Edward Plantagenet, arise a knight,
  And learn this lesson: Draw thy sword in right.
PRINCE. (*Rising*)
  My gracious father, by your kingly leave,

> I'll draw it as apparent to the crown,
> And in that quarrel use it to the death.
> CLIFFORD.
> Why, that is spoken like a toward prince.
> (II.ii.61–66)

Yet there is a curious bond between father and son. When Edward is stabbed at Tewkesbury Margaret laments and curses at length, but Henry's reaction is more striking. Richard, immediately after the killing of Edward, rides "all in post" (V.v.84) to London to kill the King. Yet even before Richard arrives, Henry, imprisoned in the Tower, knows what has happened. Dramatic economy, perhaps; but perhaps it is also Henry's prophetic insight, of which there is other evidence in *3 Henry VI*. As in the case of York, father and son die separately, but there is a bond between them. Henry's characteristically sentimental image of himself as a bereaved bird leads Richard to develop, and Henry to extend, a classical image that recalls the Talbots:

> KING HENRY.
> ... I, the hapless male to one sweet bird,
> Have now the fatal object in my eye
> Where my poor young was lim'd, was caught, and kill'd.
> GLOUCESTER.
> Why, what a peevish fool was that of Crete,
> Who taught his son the office of a fowl!
> And yet, for all his wings, the fool was drown'd.
> KING HENRY.
> I, Daedalus; my poor boy, Icarus;
> Thy father, Minos, that denied our course;
> The sun that sear'd the wings of my sweet boy,
> Thy brother Edward; and thyself the sea
> Whose envious gulf did swallow up his life.
> (V.vi.15–25)

It is significant that this echo of the scene that has given the strongest image of the human bond in *Henry VI* is followed not only by Richard's murder of Henry (we have gone from the final defeat of the English army in France to the murder of the English king in London) but by Richard's ultimate denial of all human ties: "I am myself alone" (V.vi.83). (The Quarto version of his soliloquy includes a specific denial of the link that bound the Talbots: "I had no father, I am like no father.") He goes on, in grim asides in the final scene, to threaten his brother's newborn son.

The most terrible echo of the Talbot scenes is the Towton allegory. The identification of its principal characters as a son who has killed his father and a father who has killed his son makes the main point with piercing simplicity, but Shakespeare does not stop there. While the Talbots were driven by an old-fashioned code of honor, the Son and Father have killed, not just in feudal obedience, but more particularly for money. The Son, before he realizes whom he has killed, declares,

> Ill blows the wind that profits nobody.
> This man, whom hand to hand I slew in fight,
> May be possessed with some store of crowns....
> (*3 Henry VI*, II.v.55–57)

The Father begins in a similar vein: "Thou that so stoutly hast resisted me, / Give me thy gold, if thou hast any gold" (II.v.79–80). They are in this war, like ordinary sensible people, for what they can get out of it. Their motives are those of Pistol and his cronies in *Henry V*. This only sharpens the horror, since it turns them from the cardboard cutouts they might have been to people we can recognize. It also sharpens the parody of the Talbot sequence, a parody that is strengthened by a number of echoes. One is the paradox of the father who gives his son both life and death. The Son declares, "And I, who at his hands receiv'd my life, / Have by my hands of life bereaved him" (67–68); and the Father, "O boy, thy father gave thee life too soon, / And hath bereft thee of thy life too late!" (92–93). The unseen wives and mothers are also involved, but not this time as conduits of honor:

> SON.
> How will my mother for a father's death
> Take on with me and ne'er be satisfied!
> FATHER.
> How will my wife for slaughter of my son
> Shed seas of tears and ne'er be satisfied!
> (103–6)

Finally, the *pietà* of father and son is recalled:

> SON.
> I'll bear thee hence, where I may weep my fill....
> FATHER.
> These arms of mine shall be thy winding sheet....
> (113–14)

Whatever dignity there may be in the image is lost in pain and horror; and, as in the death of York, the weeping spectator is now on stage in the person of the King: "Weep, wretched man, I'll aid thee tear for tear" (76). They give no sign of hearing him, or of hearing each other. As the Talbots die separately and together, this is a scene of group tragedy in which all three figures suffer together, and alone.

While the Towton scene seems to most modern readers more powerfully written than the death of Talbot,[13] it draws some of its power from its memories of that earlier scene. By the same token the individual tragedies of the *Henry VI* trilogy, though they are fixed, held, and isolated, are also involved with each other, and are all episodes in the tragedy of England. Though a father–son confrontation is central to *Henry IV*, and the death of Hotspur (abandoned by his father Northumberland) is an individual tragedy after which history sweeps on, Shakespeare never quite returned to this method again. Even in *Henry VIII*, the play that comes closest, the individual falls of Buckingham, Katharine and Wolsey seem to be contributing more to a tragicomedy than to a tragedy. But it gave Shakespeare a way of thinking about history as a series of individual stories that are also the stories of a group, in which no one finally suffers alone (the blows that kill Richard II also destroy any chance that Henry IV will have a peaceful reign) and public events take domestic configurations, as in Henry V's wooing of the French princess, which stands for his conquest of France.

As *Henry VI* is both history and tragedy, so the death of John Talbot in particular feeds more directly into the later tragedies, though it is beyond the scope of this essay to offer more than a few suggestions as to how this happens. The rite of passage that ends in disaster returns in the near-contemporary *Venus and Adonis* where Adonis, challenged to prove his manhood with Venus, would rather prove it in the hunt, and the result is the grotesque love-death inflicted by the boar. Like John Talbot he is a virgin, just at the start of his manhood, and he gets no further. Romeo takes Tybalt's life and Juliet's virginity on the same day; both are rites of passage for him, and identify their love as death-marked. Macbeth has proved his manhood in battle, but still has to prove it to Lady Macbeth by killing Duncan. But the killing leads only to a sterile kingship, "No son of mine succeeding" (III.i.63), and to his own death. The rite of passage fails. The close bonding of the Talbots is recalled in *Titus Andronicus*. The mutilation of Lavinia is designed to destroy her as a social being by denying her language; the family group responds by tightening around her as never before, and Titus, whose relationship with her has previously been so formal, develops an intimate bond with her. He claims that he can read her thoughts, and when he kills her it is—in most productions—a matter agreed between them. Yet though the text allows that possibility it does not dictate it; and we can never be sure that Titus, when he claims to speak for Lavinia, is speaking true. Father and daughter, like the Talbots, are together and apart. The final image of the father cradling his dead son, with its grim message that in this world the young die first, will return at the ending of *King Lear*, a play that begins with rites of passage, Lear's retirement and Cordelia's betrothal, that go terribly wrong. Shakespeare's tragic figures are not isolated, titanic heroes with only the cosmos for background; their tragedies come from the most intimate relations, the most normal passages of life: the need for love, the demands of loyalty and piety, the turmoil of sexual awakening, the need to prove oneself at whatever cost. The Talbot scene is Shakespeare's first exploration of that kind of tragedy. Nashe reports the audience's tears at the death of a single hero; but it mattered to Shakespeare that he did not die alone.

Notes

1. *Pierce Pennilesse*, quoted from Gamini Salgado, ed., *Eyewitnesses of Shakespeare* (New York: Barnes and Noble, 1975), 16.

2. David Riggs, *Shakespeare's Heroical Histories* (Cambridge, Mass.: Harvard Univ. Press, 1971), 109.

3. J. P. Brockbank, "The Frame of Disorder—'Henry VI,'" in John Russell Brown and Bernard Harris, eds., *Early Shakespeare* (London: Arnold, 1961), 74.

4. All references to Shakespeare are to *The Complete Works of Shakespeare*, ed. David Bevington (Glenview, Ill.: Scott, Foresman, and Company, 1980).

5. *Shakespeare's Apprenticeship* (Chicago: Univ. of Chicago Press, 1974), 25, 26.

6. Geoffrey Bullough, ed., *Narrative and Dramatic Sources of Shakespeare* (London: Routledge, 1960), 3:73.

7. Marjorie Garber discusses Shakespeare's interest in this theme in *Coming of Age in Shakespeare* (London: Methuen, 1981). She does not mention the Talbot sequence.

8. Emrys Jones, *The Origins of Shakespeare* (Oxford: Clarendon Press, 1977), 158.

9. Turner, 97.

10. *Shakespeare and the Dramaturgy of Power* (Princeton: Princeton Univ. Press, 1989), 83.

11. See Turner, 94.

12. See Jones, 189.

13. See, for example, Robert B. Pierce, *Shakespeare's History Plays: The Family and the State* (n.p.: Ohio State Univ. Press, 1971), 72–3.

HARRY BERGER JR.

Food for Words:
Hotspur and the Discourse of Honor

In *Richard II*, Thomas Mowbray, the Duke of Norfolk, having been accused of grievous crimes and challenged to judicial combat by Henry Bolingbroke, addresses the following piece of ceremonial bluster to the throne:

> However God or Fortune cast my lot,
> There lives or dies true to King Richard's throne,
> A loyal, just, and upright gentleman.
> Never did captive with a freer heart
> Cast off his chains of bondage and embrace
> His golden uncontroll'd enfranchisement,
> More than my dancing soul doth celebrate
> This feast of battle with mine adversary.
> Most mighty liege, and my companion peers,
> Take from my mouth the wish of happy years;
> As gentle and as jocund as to jest
> Go I to fight: truth hath a quiet breast.
>   (1.3.85–96)

Such ritual self-representation has the obvious purpose of turning the speaker as completely as possible into a conventional icon, of emptying out

From *Making Trifles of Terrors: Redistributing Complicities in Shakespeare*, edited by Peter Erickson, pp. 251–86, 453–55. © 1997 by the Board of Trustees of the Leland Stanford Junior University.

his particularity so that he may fully embody and signify the discourse of honor. It is insurance against potential detraction should he be defeated. Its value is commemorative: in what may be his last performance the speaker designs his own death mask, speaks his own epitaph, tries to preempt the honor-giving function by stamping his ritualized *idea* on the future. The speech concludes not with one but with two rhymed couplets—double insurance. The message Mowbray intends is that he has already been enfranchised, that he is inwardly untouched by the "chains" of falsehood and corruption that bind him, and therefore that his truth, his probity, can't be affected by the outcome. Everything in this speech, however, strains against this message, qualifies it, contradicts it.

The initial strain is felt in the parallelism of the first two lines: his lot will be cast by God if he lives but by Fortune if he dies. This distinction may serve the rhetorical purposes of his message, but it is, to say the least, theologically difficult, and it is an evasive modification of the juridical logic that governs trial by combat, in which to lose is to be judged guilty by God. Another strain is suggested by Mowbray's insistence that he is true to "King Richard's *throne*"; his effort in 1.1 discreetly to distance himself from complicity with Richard insinuates a distinction into this phrase: truth to the throne may not be identical with truth to Richard. Mowbray is implicated in the Gloucester murder as well as in other unpalatable Ricardian projects. After he deflects blame for the murder from himself to Richard he goes on gratuitously to mention his participation in another failed ambush directed at John of Gaunt (1.1.133–41). Since nothing more is said about this episode we are left to wonder whether that was another Ricardian project, and the speculation only increases our sense of the snarled factional networks, the deep divisions, papered over by the ritual formulas that shape the language and actions of these public scenes.

Given the conventional demands of ceremonial speech, Mowbray's assertion of complacent conscience need not be belied by the catachrestic violence of his wild figural dance. Such a dance is expected to fulfill the pastoral function of ritual without succumbing to the deadly iterability of the clichés of self-praise. The function is pastoral because it is a simplified and artificial procedure that conspicuously excludes and therefore alludes to the complicated network of motives, purposes, and interests to which it responds. Yet because of his unhappy relation to this network Mowbray's defense of his probity and freedom from guilt is compromised from the start. He is not only placed in a false position; he is also in a no-win situation. He would be disgraced if Bolingbroke were to defeat him, but were he to win he would uphold the disgraced regime that taints him by association, and he would validate the king he had all but accused of murder (1.1.132–34). Furthermore, it seems clear to everyone involved that both Richard and Bolingbroke are using him as a factor, an expendable decoy, to further their own designs. For all these reasons the very assertion of truth, autonomy, and quiet conscience must be assumed to jeopardize the self-esteem of any speaker whom we imagine to cherish those values, and the phrase "truth hath a quiet breast" takes on ominous vibrations: given the situation Mowbray finds himself in, there can be no truth in words. He thus welcomes the feast of battle as a liberation from the silenced truth of the network in which he is hopelessly entangled. He throws himself into it as an escape from the effeminizing—because (in his case) castrating—battle of words, "the trial of a woman's war" (1.1.48), in which he has been forced to defend his honor in terms that can only further compromise it. There is no escape from this bondage except in the enfranchisement his language orgiastically solicits and anticipates: death. "Take from my mouth the wish of happy years": not only "I wish you many happy years" but also "let me not wish for happy years"; "let me die now." Mowbray's dilemma is a harbinger, a proleptic epitome, of the dilemma that faces Hotspur in *1 Henry IV.*[1]

* * *

The discourse of honor lurches like a sick horse toward the field it pastures and sickens on—the field beneath which problems of gender, speech, and gift exchange twist along in rhizomes whose bad fodder crops up everywhere. Harry Percy alias Hotspur rides into the field on that same horse, but misperceives the poor critter as his roan, his throne, and foolishly—or dashingly—disregards one of the symptoms of what ails it: it is, he says, "a crop-ear" (2.3.70). My topic in this essay is Hotspur's crop-eared dash toward death. More specifically, I am interested in Hotspur's talk and in things mucking about among the rhizomes of his language that the speaker seems not to hear, or not to want to hear. But before following Hotspur into the field, I want to set the stage for his entry by describing the field itself.

One of the many fine moves Pierre Bourdieu makes in *Outline of a Theory of Practice* is to map the discourse of honor onto Mauss's famous account of the discourse of the gift. In that account, Mauss writes that to give "is to show one's superiority, to show that one is something more and higher, that one is *magister*.... To accept without returning or repaying more is to face subordination, to become subservient, a client, a debtor," for "charity wounds him who receives, and our whole moral effort is directed toward suppressing the unconsciously harmful patronage of the rich alms-giver"—the patronage, for example, of such figures as the Christian Father and the Jewish Mother, both of whom, taking a page from King Lear's book, continually remind their children that "I gave you all."[2] In the course of sketching out what may be called a "gift-act theory," Bourdieu chooses for his first example the game of honor and goes on to offer a conspectus of its strategies and misfires, which, he claims, conform to "a logic of challenge and riposte."[3]

This move is interesting because the dialectic of honor is more than a casual example of the dialectic of the gift. To superimpose challenge-and-riposte on gift-and-return is to bring out the ambivalence in each (the aggressiveness of giving, the generosity of the challenge) and in fact to suggest that the two form a reversible fabric, each side the inner lining of the other. Bourdieu insists that the logic of honor is inherent in the more general practices of gift exchange: just as a gift "is a challenge which honors the man to whom it is addressed, at the same time putting his point of honor ... to the test," so a challenge is a gift because it credits its recipient "with the dignity of a man of honor."[4] This general view of the relationship, however, fails to engage the particular difference that distinguishes the special discourse of honor from the contribution its logic makes to the ambivalence of gift exchange. For gift-giving as Mauss discusses it may be aggressive and challenging, but it needn't be *discussed* by anyone but the anthropologist. The semiotics of gift exchange can operate with only nonlinguistic signs; the periodic deposit and removal of material objects (mineral, vegetable, animal, human) could conceivably take place in total silence. Not so the discourse of honor, which entails a linguistic component because it is not a closed or circular interaction but always subtends the arbitration and authority of a third party.

If two men meet in the forest, draw their swords over a point of honor, and one falls, but nobody hears him, has the other won honor? Not unless he returns to tell the tale, and the tale is accredited, and it reaches the right ears. *Percipi est esse*—and therein hangs a problem. Aristotle noted that while many think honor to be the *telos* of the political life, it is too superficial to be the final good because "it appears to depend on those who confer it more than on him who receives it."[5] According to Bourdieu's account, when the claimant to honor challenges others to recognize his claim, he may be said to confer honor on them because the challenge credits them with the capability of "playing the game of honor" and obligates them to respond. But since the challenge is a request, it also confers *power* on them. Even if the honor-seeker feels he deserves the gift, it remains a gift for which he incurs an obligation. Thus the struggle between honor-seekers and honor-givers generates the need on both sides for strategies that control the flow of power and indebtedness.

The coupling of honor and gift exchange goes back at least as far as Aristotle, who says that "a gift is at once a giving of a possession and a token of honor." This remark may be coupled with another in which he indicates that honor itself is a gift, and with still another in which he notes of the "great-souled man"—who above all others prizes and deserves honor—that he "is fond of conferring benefits, but ashamed to receive them, because the former is a mark of superiority and the latter of inferiority." This suggests a problem, because if honor is a benefit conferred, shouldn't the great-souled lover of honor be ashamed to receive it, especially since he knows himself to be superior and "is justified in despising other people"?[6] Aristotle secures the great-souled man from this dilemma by arguing that he will be justified in feeling he receives "only what belongs to him, or even less, for no honor can be adequate to the merits of perfect virtue, yet all the same he will deign to accept their honors, because they have no greater tribute to offer him."[7] His gift to them will be to honor them with the opportunity to signify, however inadequately, what he already possesses. This helps him go on despising them, which is as it should be.

A similar view appears in *Leviathan*, where, characteristically, Hobbes bares its fangs:

> To have received from one, to whom we think ourselves equal, greater benefits than there is hope to requite, disposeth to counterfeit love; but really secret hatred. . . . For benefits oblige, and obligation is thraldom; and unrequitable obligation perpetual thraldom; which is to one's equal, hateful. But to have received benefits from one, whom we acknowledge for superior, inclines to love; because the obligation is no new depression: and cheerful acceptation, which men call *gratitude*, is such an honor done to the obliger, as is taken generally for retribution.[8]

Hobbes seems to assume that hierarchy preconditions the different responses of equals and unequals, but if his language doesn't actually destabilize the assumption, it lends it a certain bite. *Retribution*, for example, is a strong term for the gratitude that is the honor *done to* the obliger; it is a power word, and he uses it again in chapter 15 in a punitive sense to denote justified revenge. Is the donee's repayment, his discharging of the debt, a form of requital? "The obligation is no new depression": the donee is already depressed, pressed down; this inferiority is what valorizes his gratitude; he isn't expected to make a more substantial repayment; the donation reaffirms his need and inferiority, as does the honor his cheerful acceptation pays the donor. Perhaps, then, generosity is the donor's revenge. But why should this be?

Hobbes suggests why this should be in his discussion of honor: "The *value*, or WORTH of a man, is . . . his price; that is to say, so much as would be given for the use of his power: and therefore is not absolute; but a thing dependent on the need and judgment of another. . . . And as in other things, so in men, not the seller, but the buyer determines the price. For let a man, as most men do, rate themselves at the highest value they can; yet their true value is no more than it is esteemed by others" (1.10). This is the theme that, as D. J. Gordon has shown, is central to *Coriolanus*.[9] If obeying and honoring confer power, those who obey and honor *have* power, which they both exercise and alienate when they obey and honor. It may be that in the terms of this master–slave dialectic, the more depressed they are, the more gratitude and honor they pay out, the more power they alienate, the more power they have. But what is the value of the honor one receives from those he considers his inferiors, those he relies on to reaffirm his superiority? It may be that in the overall scheme of *Leviathan* this dialectic promotes anxiety in the natural person who becomes the preeminent artificial person when authorized by his subjects to represent them as their sovereign.

Aristotle is no less political than Hobbes in his approach to honor, but Hobbes is more sensitive to the abstract and mediated forces of commodity exchange embedded in (but in his time much closer to the surface of) the concrete exchange systems of what may be called logocentric hierarchy. As C. B. Macpherson paraphrases Hobbes's view, honor, "regarded subjectively by the recipient, is the difference between his own estimate and the market estimate of his value. But honor, regarded objectively, corresponds to the market estimate that both establishes his actual power and is established by his actual or apparent power."[10] One buys power or protection by paying out honor, and, as Hobbes asserts, the problem for the hero is that it is a buyer's market. This is because honor can't be taken or stolen or produced for self-consumption. It has to be borrowed, sold, or won; lent, bought, or ceded. As Ulysses puts it in *Troilus and Cressida*, the honor-seeker "Cannot make boast to have that which he hath, / Nor feels not what he owes but by reflection," and the pun on *owes* has real bite to it.

Early in Part One of *Henry IV*, the king calls Hotspur "the theme of honor's tongue, / Amongst the grove the very straightest plant, / Who is sweet Fortune's minion and her pride" (1.1.80–82). All the dilemmas of Hotspur's version of the discourse of honor are inscribed in these words. Honor is the theme of Hotspur's tongue, but since the honor-seeker's discourse is necessarily incomplete and solicits others' tongues, Hotspur is perforce the theme of honor's tongue. This chiasmic predicament is complicated by the fact that there has always been a troubled relation between the honor-seeker's tongue and his valor. It was so in warlike Sparta, from which we get the word and concept *laconic*. It was so in the wild American West, whose soft-spoken six-shooting heroes enjoyed actions louder than words. Enshrined in the films of the 1930s in such oversized, tight-lipped, woolly-mouthed fantasies as Gary Cooper and Randolph Scott, they asserted their special virtue by responding to the demands of civil life and civil or uncivil women with the antirhetoric of *awshucksism*. Who can fail to imagine John Wayne nasally twanging out Mowbray's

> 'Tis not the trial of a woman's war,
> The bitter clamor of two eager tongues,
> Can arbitrate this cause betwixt us twain . . . ?

He would have warmed to this, but the eighteen lines of eager tonguework Mowbray follows it with would have made him nervously toe the hoof-imprinted dirt. Our heroes show themselves aware of the ancient tradition of the *miles gloriosus*. The counterfeit warrior is the one who talks too much; the real one proves his courage by letting his gun and other people do his talking for him.

Paul Jorgensen's study of "the theme of the misplaced soldier" in Shakespeare and his contemporaries throws a certain amount of light on the man of valor's chief problem: "it is only on the battlefield that he is thoroughly at ease."[11] So, if Hotspur says, "I profess not talking," and if Coriolanus says, "When blows have made me stay, I fled from words," Jorgensen thinks this must be because they lack the polish needed to cope with a wordy world run by courtly and lawyerlike operators. But this explanation fails to account for the copiousness of speech with which Hotspur professes not talking, and for the rhetorical power of Coriolanus's wordy flight from words. The story has to change as soon as we recognize that these warrior heroes run away, not from what they do poorly, but from what they do too well—and in Hotspur's case, from what he does so enthusiastically that, when he encounters someone like Glendower who reflects back to him an inflated version of his own bombast, he becomes irritable and embarrassed.

I would argue against Jorgensen, then, that Hotspur's courage (and, in a different way, Coriolanus's) is inseparable from his weakness, and that it is more than battle courage. It is the ability to endure situations of verbal encounter that continually threaten him with disclosure of the weakness he fears. The language that speaks through him is a minefield, because it represents him as both rhetorically self-indulgent and disdainful of rhetorical self-indulgence. He deserves the honor he wants if only for his courage in traveling over linguistic terrain he doesn't control or trust. That terrain is "overcharg'd with double cracks," so it's a good thing he is devoted to his horse. Deep fears and defenses wound the language that represents Hotspur. His speech both dramatizes and problematizes his cardinal virtue by treating it as the transformation of a latent desire of flight, and fear of weakness, into warlike valor and aggressiveness.

The outlines of the problem can be more firmly set by noting that in the tradition which made Aristotle's ethics influential, the sphere of action allocated to the virtue of courage is narrowly circumscribed, and circumscribed in such a way as to create difficulties for its representation in Shakespeare's version of theatrical drama. From a Shakespearean standpoint, Aristotle begins well when, after defining courage as the virtue that observes "the mean in respect of fear and confidence," he states that "the things we fear are . . . broadly speaking, evil things." But the notion of evil is then simplified by the following line of argument: courage is displayed in response to fearful things; the courageous man willingly faces the most fearful things; "the most terrible thing of all is death"; not every kind of death gives an opportunity for courage—drowning and disease, for example, don't qualify as appropriate occasions; the noblest test for courage is the noblest form of death, that is, death in battle. "And this conclusion is borne out by the principle on which honors are bestowed in republics and under monarchies." Hence, the courageous man "will be he who fearlessly confronts a noble death, or some sudden peril that threatens death; and the perils of war answer this description most fully."[12]

Aristotle's subsequent discussion of courage is entirely confined to warfare. Were Shakespeare interested in dramatizing this version of courage he would confront the obvious difficulty that battles are not the easiest things to stage, and that audiences would tend to be diverted from the hero's display of martial courage to the actor's display of acrobatic dexterity, thus from warfare to choreography. Jorgensen addresses this problem in the first chapter of *Shakespeare's Military World*, mounting an astute defense of what had previously been judged a dramaturgical weakness, Shakespeare's "physical staging of warfare." He argues that if Shakespeare differed from some of his contemporaries in his greater scorn of "stage realism" and his more "restricted battle display," it was from choice rather than from the limited "martial resources of the stage" (2–3). Shakespeare chose to appeal to the auditory rather than visual imagination "either through actual sound or through a stylized, connotative rendering of it in dialogue" (3). "With his actual military music" of drums, trumpets, and alarms as well as with his "rhetorical 'music,'" he sought to transport

> his audience from the immediate experience of battle—in which sounds, cannon, and blows have a precise, uncolored meaning—to a superior level of imaginative participation. On this level, not the mind's eye but the mind's ear is appealed to principally as a substitute for a full display of warfare. Remoteness . . . is an essential quality of both the martial discourse and the martial music. And the ear, more susceptible than the eye to the

suggestiveness of distant and imminent events, is impressed both by the "sad harmony" of rhetoric and by a skillfully connotative use of drum and trumpet. (34)

The evidence Jorgensen adduces suggests a different and to my mind better generalization than the one his first sentence articulates. For example, he shows how the "persistent 'Low alarums'" in the last scenes of *Julius Caesar* underscore "Caesar's Nemesis-like pursuit of Brutus—but with an ultimate clarification in terms of military function" when "the identity of the Nemesis becomes prosaically clear with the arrival of the victorious enemy, whose presence on stage is far less impressive than the suggestiveness of their distant drums" (32–33). Similarly, Jorgensen remarks the increasing tension produced in the last scenes of *Macbeth* "by the cumulative effect of drums . . . and . . . alarums," and observes that "Macduff, like Octavius Caesar, may be a prosaic instrument of Nemesis, but not so the relentless music with which— in a more than military sense—he encompasses his victim" (33–34). What both these examples suggest is that Shakespeare first elicited "a superior level of imaginary participation" by appealing to the ear, and that the subsequent stage appearance of the victors seemed anticlimactic by contrast. And this is a significant pattern, evident in many plays, including the *Henriad*: the visualization onstage of battles and other external moments of conflict resolution is *represented* as unsatisfactory, as the reductive displacement of inner self-division to outward circumstances.

From Jorgensen's discussion, then, I force this hypothesis: Shakespeare uses the power of auditory effects to arouse a sense of foreboding and premonition that makes the stage realization the effects anticipate seem inadequate as "objective correlatives." We could say, in fact, that "objective" in Eliot's phrase means "inadequate" in the value system of Shakespearean dramaturgy. This isn't only because in "the immediate experience of [staged] battle . . . sounds, cannon, and blows have a precise, uncolored meaning," whereas in "martial discourse" they are more distanced and suggestive—more seductive, as Othello and Desdemona found: "She'd come again, and with a greedy ear / Devour up my discourse" (1.3.149–50). The "precise, uncolored meaning" is itself a meaning. It signifies that insufficient and premature closure has been imposed on latent meaning ("some other grief) by the process of displacement that allows theatrical ending to coincide with dramatic judgment. The effect is not to dispel but, on the contrary, to intensify our bewilderment, skepticism, foreboding, sadness, or terror.

"The music at the close" only reanimates the fearful and mysterious power of Shakespearean speech so that Desdemona's tremulous question remains the auditor's: "what does your speech import? / I understand a fury in your words,

/ But not the words" (4.2.31–33). And this is the perplexity that Shakespearean language continually inscribes in the speakers it represents: "what does my
speech import? / I understand a fury in my words, / But not the words." When
the fury is channeled outward in physical violence, the perplexity continues
to vibrate. Shakespeare's final *Exeunts* order us out of the theater because the
unfinished business they leave us with cannot be transacted here. It is as if, after
all the buildup, physical battle *au fond* tests nothing more significant than skill
in fencing and counterfeiting; as if the represented violence is no more "serious"
an expression of the "inward wars" than the choreography that mimes it. That is
not where Shakespeare's heroes kill and die. They kill and die in their language,
and we have to follow the lethal traces down into its burrows and rhizomes.

What stage death offers the hero is an escape from this verbal dying
into the rest that is silence. What it offers the audience is something like a
critique of this commitment to stageable closure as an escape from meaning.
When the hero finally faces the test of battle and arrives at the wished-for
haven where he can find judgment and prove his truth; when he is on the
verge of escaping from his bondage to words, woman, civil life, and perhaps
life itself, his drive toward transcendence may be betrayed, diminished, by
the very convention of theatrical closure to which he has committed himself.
Having displaced his inward wars to swordplay, he becomes vulnerable to a
critique that may have arisen accidentally, as a by-product of theatrical constraints, but that offers thematic possibilities to a writer who wants to raise
questions about such a displacement. The critique occurs when presentation
overpowers and interprets representation, that is, when the agility of actors
putting on a fencing exhibition preempts the mind's eye and occludes the
symbolic valency of the fictional conflict.

This critique speaks to the ethical limits of such notions as Aristotle's
circumscribed concept of courage, the courage that thinks to prove itself by facing death in battle as "the most terrible thing of all." What that notion fails to
consider may be suggested by glancing at the following qualification, in which
Aristotle limits the range of the term according to the doctrine of the mean: "to
seek death in order to escape from poverty, or the pangs of love, or from pain
or sorrow, is not the act of a courageous man, but rather of a coward; for it is
weakness to fly from troubles, and the suicide does not endure death because it
is noble to do so, but to escape evil."[13] But the interest, pathos, and poignancy
of Shakespeare's warrior-heroes is produced by ignoring this distinction.

* * *

In the language of *1 Henry IV* the politics of honor, the politics of speech,
and the politics of gender are closely interrelated. To begin with some

textualized representations of woman, consider the passage in which Gadshill boasts that he is the accomplice of those who

> pray continually to their saint the commonwealth, or rather not
> pray to her, but prey on her, for they ride up and down on her,
> and make her their boots.
> CHAM.
>   What, the commonwealth their boots? Will she hold out water
> in foul way?
> GADS.
>   She will, she will, justice hath liquored her: we steal as in a castle,
> cock-sure: we have the receipt of fern-seed, we walk invisible.
>   (2.1.79–86)

In this pathologically overstated piece of irreverence, the thrills of political, legal, and religious violation are reduced to that of sexual violation.
The commonwealth is feminized and canonized in the mode of Petrarchan
parody—as the idealized object of erotic worship who is simultaneously the
source, enemy, and target of sexual desire. Manly power and risk-taking
are exaggerated in a phallic fantasy the rhetoric of which centers on the
victimization of a woman and on the idea of preying on one's very source
of protection. Gadshill's idyllic society of thieves is held together homoso-
cially by what is imaged as a gang rape. The victim is not only violated but
also "liquored"—corrupted either by bribery or by drink—and thus easier
to penetrate.

An earlier analogue to this passage appears in Falstaff's famous play on
body/bawdy/beauty/booty:

> Marry then sweet wag, when thou art king let not us that are
> squires of the night's body be called thieves of the day's beauty:
> let us be Diana's foresters, gentlemen of the shade, minions of
> the moon; and let men say we be men of good government, being
> governed as the sea is, by our noble and chaste mistress the moon,
> under whose countenance we steal. (1.2.23–29)

The paradox in the last phrase is that those who steal under Diana's syl-
van authority also steal under her face; they are thieves as well as squires
of the night's body, beauty, and booty.[14] Manhood and male bonding are
defined in terms of the conventional strategy, first idealizing and then
violating the power, authority, or body of woman. Falstaff's idealization is
itself motivated by the Prince's equally one-sided derogation: "clocks the

tongues of bawds, and dials the signs of leaping-houses, and the blessed sun himself a fair hot wench in flame-colored taffeta" (1.2.8–10). When Falstaff replies, "we that take purses go by the moon" (13–14), he is not exactly changing the subject from prostitution to robbery, since purse-taking is an image that accommodates robbery to the metaphor of sexual violation. The point of Harry's insult to Falstaff is his susceptibility to the lusts of the flesh that make him an easy mark for women. Falstaff gets the point, and parries it a few speeches later: "is not my hostess of the tavern a most sweet wench?" (39–40). But his Diana speech is also a riposte: "when you are king, let my immersion in the life of sack, whores, and thievery to which you (so righteously) consign me be romantically mystified as a form of service to the goddess to whose chaste countenance these very things are anathema. And let you be that goddess."

This is "pretty daring" talk, as Dover Wilson observes, because it glances at the Virgin Queen.[15] The speech is also daring because Falstaff offers Harry the role of Diana. And it is even more daring because of the double pun in the last phrase: (1) "we *steal* (a) under her authority but also (b) right under her nose"; (2) "we *go stealthily* not only (a) under her authority but also (b) under her face." Meaning 2b is the most outrageous because it is sexual, and because it places Falstaff in the position of Actaeon. If Diana's foresters are men, they must be hunters *of* as well as *for* the goddess.[16] As Falstaff's five repetitions of "when thou art king" in this scene indicate, he is dogging his Diana now: laying bare the real project behind Harry's madcap role and goading Harry into exposing it himself, but also—and more compellingly—daring Harry to turn the verbal dogs back on their fat master.

The Actaeon myth figures explicitly and importantly in *Twelfth Night*, *A Midsummer Night's Dream*, and *The Merry Wives of Windsor*. Leonard Barkan has shown how *Merry Wives* articulates the comic aspects of the theme: the attempt to overmaster woman results in being mastered by woman; phallic aggression produces emasculation.[17] In this direct form, the Actaeon theme does not enter into the concerns of *1 Henry IV*. Its comic and farcical reduc-tion in *Merry Wives* is a consequence of full detextualization, which transfers the dispersed nodes of textual meaning to the dramatic and theatrical surface, where the dangers are explicit and controlled. In *1 Henry IV*, however, the traces of the myth produce a more sinister network of resonances. From his first words to his final rejection, Falstaff knowingly presents himself to Harry as a target, persistently probes beneath the madcap role to lay bare aggres-sive motives that Harry tries to conceal even from himself. In doing this, of course, he is asking for punishment and eliciting the gestures of negation or rebuttal that will add up to the ultimate rejection.

* * *

> By heaven, methinks it were an easy leap
> To pluck bright honor from the pale-fac'd moon . . .
>   (1.3.199–200)

With these lines Hotspur declares his candidacy for membership in Falstaff's Actaeon Club. The assault on the moon draws some of its energy not only from its echo of Falstaff's passage but also from a hunting image Hotspur has just unleashed:

> O, the blood more stirs
> To rouse a lion than to start a hare!
> NORTH.
> Imagination of some great exploit
> Drives him beyond the bounds of patience.
>   (1.3.195–98)

Some light on Hotspur's heroic frenzy and its Actaeonic implications is thrown by Barkan's comments on *Gl' Eroici Furori*:

> From the dedication to Sir Philip Sidney to all Bruno's sonnets which his dialogues analyze, it becomes clear that the conventional behavior and attitudes of the romantic lover are requisite for the visionary experience, *even if the true enthusiast must purge the purely sexual aspect of his love. The enthusiast is first a lover, and Bruno builds his visionary structure upon the foundation of Neoplatonic amorous furor.*[18]

It is the repression and displacement indicated by the italicized phrases that strike me as relevant to the Hotspurian discourse of honor. Erotic desire for woman is transformed into aggressive desire for honor. The linking term, *purge*, encodes a process in which the source of the "sexual aspect" is displaced outward to woman, and woman is violated either by the hero's direct assault or by his flight. The return and triumph of the repressed, which is inscribed in the fate of Actaeon, is also inscribed in Hotspur's language, and the consequent anxiety this language betrays is evident in his very first speech.

Henry's curt dismissal of Worcester at the beginning of 1.3, and his unbending attitude about Hotspur's prisoners, could not but be calculated to incense the Percys. The end of the play's first scene makes it clear that he looks forward to this confrontation, and that he had arranged it *before* his crusade speech. If he assumes that Hotspur is already infected by "his uncle's teaching," as Westmoreland claims (1.1.95), what he does in 1.3 can only be expected to aggravate the infection and strengthen Worcester's hand. We judge Henry's contribution to be even greater when we realize, early in 1.3, that Hotspur is not yet infected, and that although Worcester has clearly been up to something, Hotspur hears for the first time that Richard had proclaimed his brother-in-law, Mortimer, heir to the throne.

Against this background the emphasis in Hotspur's long speech explaining his denial of prisoners becomes more interesting for what it reveals about the speaker's basic motivation. He is chiefly concerned to document the source of his irritation in the behavior of the foppish messenger sent by the king. His caricature of a supercilious court butterfly conflates effeminacy with squeamishness, as in "neat and trimly dress'd, / Fresh as a bride-groom," "perfumed like a milliner," "With many holiday and lady terms," "a popinjay," "talk so like a waiting gentlewoman" (1.3.32–54). G. R. Hibbard sums it up thus: "Scorn and impatience ring through the entire passage. The images are precise, reductive, and, some of them, *admirably designed* to bring out the womanish qualities the soldier sees in the courtier. . . . Brusque, impetuous, impatient, direct, and courageous, Hotspur makes all this side of his nature evident in his first speech."[19] The italicized phrase betrays a certain diffuseness of reference that is no doubt occasioned by Hibbard's titular theme, the making of *Shakespeare's* dramatic poetry. Presumably the praise is directed toward the author rather than his character. But what if we ask whether the images are designed for the stated purpose by Hotspur: is he to be admired along with Shakespeare? Why? Hibbard's general objective often leads him to ignore crucial issues of motivation that would lend his judgments more weight.

Paul Jorgensen comes closer to the problem when he notes that Henry's accusation places Hotspur "in the defensive position habitual to the Elizabethan soldier," and that his apology reflects stereotypical features of the debate between the soldier and the courtier.[20] Hotspur is indeed apologetic, but not quite in the sense intended by Jorgensen. His speech is no less finicky than the finickiness he contemns. Judging by the extravagance of his rhetoric, the dandy whose "womanish qualities" irritated him on the battlefield continues to irritate him now. It is as if he is still compelled to decontaminate himself by a speech act that aims primarily at contrastive self-definition. Hence I think the verb in Hibbard's last clause should be taken more forcefully than he apparently intends it: "Hotspur *makes* all this side of his nature evident," that is, with self-dramatizing emphasis.

There are specific reasons for this emphasis. Hotspur enters the play already on the defense. His utterance is a response to Henry's demand for the prisoners taken at Holmedon, but far from being an aggressive refusal, it is conciliatory, even apologetic. "My liege, I did deny no prisoners," Hotspur begins, and then goes into a long diatribe against the messenger who carried the king's demand to the battlefield. His "bald unjointed chat" so irritated Hotspur that he answered inattentively ("I answer'd indirectly"), and he begs the king not to let the messenger's "report / come current for an accusation / Betwixt my love and your high majesty" (1.3.64–68). This conciliatory tone is not at all what we had been led to expect at the end of 1.1, where Henry and Westmoreland complained of "young Percy's pride" and of Worcester's bad influence, which makes Hotspur "prune himself, and bristle up / The crest of youth against your dignity" (91, 97–98). Hotspur's response is even more surprising in view of the law of arms mentioned in editorial footnotes, which is that Hotspur was entitled to keep all the prisoners he took except those of royal blood. If we suppose this is something Shakespeare not only knew but expected his audience to know, it is still not clear whether it is something they are expected to take note of as a motivational factor. There seems to have been no law that gives the king the right to the prisoners, so even if we ignored the other convention and the question remained moot, we could still see Henry's demand as an aggressive act, and perhaps as a challenge to Hotspur's honor. Why, then, shouldn't Hotspur treat it as such? A closer glance at the circumstances preceding and surrounding his speech will bring out the difficulty of his position.

Taking note of the law-of-arms convention about prisoners sharpens our sense of what motivates Henry's aggression. It reinforces a particular reading of the strategies he pursues in the first and third scenes of the play. His sending a messenger to Holmedon to make an issue of the prisoners; his setting up and eagerly awaiting the confrontation that, as the end of the first scene makes clear, he had arranged well *before* making his crusade speech (so that his frustration at having to call the crusade off is patently a pretense); his dismissal of Worcester and his angry deportment thereafter—these moves seem intended to provoke the Percys into an uprising that he can later be in the position to blame them for, as at the end of 1.1 when he implies that Hotspur is responsible for his having to cancel the crusade that he proposed primarily in order to be able to blame the cancellation on Hotspur. In all this he is deploying the tactics of the language game—the victim's discourse— various forms of which dominate the *Henriad*: stirring up trouble, disclaiming responsibility for it, targeting oneself as its victim.[21]

Hotspur does not make an issue of the denial of prisoners. But why does he downplay it? The reason is suggested at 1.3.76–79, when Henry accuses him of having at some point denied his prisoners,

But with proviso and exception,
That we at our own charge shall ransom straight
His brother-in-law, the foolish Mortimer.

Since Hotspur never disputes this allegation, it suggests that he has come
into the scene aware of several things that may well be disquieting to the
theme of honor's tongue, especially if one assumes (as I do) that Hotspur is
genuinely devoted to this theme.

First, Hotspur could not deny prisoners unless they had previously been
demanded, and Henry's aggressiveness by itself constitutes a challenge that
must be met. But the possibility of a clean and honorable response has already
been severely jeopardized. For, second, even if his initial words in the play
("My liege I did deny no prisoners") are true, at some moment between his
encounter with the messenger and the uttering of those words he decided to
deny prisoners. Hence the utterance is evasive, and the narrative that follows
it may be felt as a diversionary tactic. Third, since that encounter took place
he acquired a not fully determinable amount of information about what happened to Mortimer, and we can imagine that this affected his decision. That
is, it may not have been on principle that he decided to withhold prisoners
but in order to have some leverage in forcing Mortimer's ransom. Fourth,
however much or little he knows about Mortimer's defeat, the information he
gets from Henry is enough to suggest that it has already weakened Hotspur's
position. For he's come to his meeting with Henry prepared to do something
he may consider shameful in order to save his wife's brother. To say "I did deny
no prisoners" in this situation could be construed as an anticipatory gesture of
placation by someone preparing to breach the code—yield up prisoners that
were his by right—in order to bargain for his brother-in-law's release.

This helps us contextualize the gender-coded weakness he displaces to
the messenger. I read it as representing the sense of weakness aroused in the
speaker himself by the utterance of this speech. Isn't there the slightest taint
of cowardice and courtly sycophancy in his willingness to appease the king
and prepare for the exchange? Doesn't the very function of this speech—what
motivates it—subvert its rhetorical emphasis and reawaken the apprehension
of moral and political impotence it fends off?

From this standpoint, the figure of the messenger becomes the locus
at which two opposed yet cooperating vectors of symbolic power collide: he
represents the king's aggressive attempt to insult Hotspur, but he also represents Hotspur's repressed acknowledgment that—in making this elaborate
apology—he may be insulting and compromising himself. All this renders
more important and problematical Hotspur's relation to the shadowy figure of Mortimer. Having engaged his honor in Mortimer's behalf, he has

ceded partial control of it to someone on whose behavior his reputation now depends. And the apparent reason for this commitment can only increase his vulnerability: he is bound to Mortimer through Lady Percy. I shall return to this dilemma after considering one more feature of Hotspur's first speech.

The messenger offends Hotspur not only by his appearance and style, his disdainful comments, and his demand for prisoners, but also by something else. Hotspur complains that as he listened "Breathless and faint, leaning upon my sword" (31), the messenger rattled on about "guns, and drums, and wounds," and finally about what a pity it was that

> This villainous saltpeter should be digg'd
> Out of the bowels of the harmless earth,
> Which many a good tall fellow had destroy'd
> So cowardly, and but for these vile guns
> He would himself have been a soldier.
> This bald unjointed chat of his, my lord,
> I answer'd indirectly . . .
>   (59–65)

Why should this complaint disturb Hotspur? Shouldn't we expect him to agree with the messenger about "these vile guns" that might well diminish the military value of the sword he leans on?

The messenger's point, Kittredge writes, "was that warfare is no longer a glorious thing, as it was in the old days of hand-to-hand fighting before gunpowder was invented."[22] There are enough references to guns in the play (pistols, calivers, heavy-ordnance, powder) to remind us of the wishful archaism of Hotspur's attachment to the golden age of chivalry prior to the violation of mother earth. The clean heroics of single encounter is by no means obsolete, for example, the possibility that "Harry to Harry shall, hot horse to horse, / meet and ne'er part till one drop down a corse" (4.1.122–23). But it is circumscribed by the presence of more effective and less personal forms of warfare and instruments of death. Perhaps Hotspur's sympathy with the messenger's complaint is another reason for his irritation and decontamination. He never speaks of guns in his waking hours—only in his dreams (2.3.64).

The issue I am raising here is not, however, the familiar historical topic of the influence of technological change on sociopolitical change. I am not directly concerned with the way the decline of chivalry, the crisis of the aristocracy, may be represented in the portrayal of Hotspur's commitment to a threatened discourse of honor. Rather my emphasis is on another theme intrinsic to that discourse and to the ideal of manhood it expresses: the hero's need to have power over and to die his own death; to invent or choose it, to aim all his actions toward that consummation; to meet and stage his death in a public ritual that will inscribe it on the future and thus triumph over it.

Against this ideal, the play opposes two ignominious forms of death that are, appropriately, most often mentioned by Falstaff: the scaffold and "molten lead." In their different ways, both are threats to manhood. The fear of hanging, the image of an elevated body that suddenly drops toward mother earth (sometimes from a horse) and goes limp, gives focus to the pervasive anxiety that nourishes the villain's bravado. Hanging, in addition, suggests emasculation in a pointedly ironic form, since it produces—as an exception to the limpness of the rest of the corpse—an erect penis, which, like the supplementarity of a Priapean dildo, symbolizes the power it wants. The erection represents the power of another. To be hanged is to lose one's power over one's death, to be made the helpless site and spectacle of another's power. The other ignominious death is produced by a similar shift of phallic potency from the manly hero and his sword: death by firepower—basilisk, cannon, or culverin—is the wholesale anonymous death that is the fate of "pitiful rascals . . . good enough to toss, food for powder . . . they'll fill a pit as well as better" (4.2.64–66).

Although Hotspur does not mention guns again, there is a passage in 3.1 that testifies by its hyperbolic distortion to his abiding respect for the destructive force imprisoned in earth's bowels. It's true that in the following speech he is only chiding Glendower by attributing the shaking of the earth not to fear of the Welsh blowhard but to a bad case of gas. Nevertheless, his retort is itself shaken by fascination for the constrained violence that erupts from the image:

> O, then the earth shook to see the heavens on fire,
> And not in fear of your nativity.
> Diseased nature oftentimes breaks forth
> In strange eruptions, oft the teeming earth
> Is with a kind of colic pinch'd and vex'd
> By the imprisoning of unruly wind
> Within her womb, which for enlargement striving
> Shakes the old beldam earth, and topples down
> Steeples and moss-grown towers.
>   (3.1.22–30)

The energy with which Hotspur depicts the grotesque body is carnivaiesque. I imagine these lines fired off with the tart and testy exhilaration of a speaker who enjoys sending up the seismic flatulence of his interlocutor's rhetoric. But the caricature, like everything else about Hotspur, is overcharged with double cracks. Glendower embarrasses him because, however inflated his rhetoric and however absurd his pretensions, *they* caricature *Hotspur's*, as in a distorting mirror. He combines the excesses of the *miles gloriosus* with the musico-magical aspirations of a comic Prospero in so bizarre a fantasy of power as to betray the lack of self-mastery that makes him an easy mark. Yet the flatus Hotspur criticizes is a flatus that shakes his own language. The speech is itself a scapegoating violation of the maternal principle, to which it displaces vulnerability and impotence, incontinence and imminent rupture, the threat of having one's body possessed, concussed, by aliens that blow it apart—all the dangers that produce the fears that make the courage worthy of the honor the hero desires.

Glendower is good for laughs, but his role in the play's economy of honor gives him a special kind of power, the power of weakness. The most seductive appeal to erotic desire as well as the most direct gesture of emasculation both come from Wales. The seduction is conveyed in a form that accentuates its alienation from and by the rigid, self-protective warrior ethos: it is uttered in a foreign tongue by Glendower's daughter. As a doting father, he fears her grief and at first wants the warriors to sneak away to battle in order to avoid "a world of water shed" (3.1.90). But he then submits to her desire and translates her invitation in lilting cadences:

> She bids you on the wanton rushes lay you down,
> And rest your gentle head upon her lap,
> And she will sing the song that pleaseth you,
> And on your eyelids crown the god of sleep,
> Charming your blood with pleasing heaviness.
>   (207–11)

A truly Spenserian enticement, evoking the helpless Cymochles in Phaedria's lap, the helpless Verdant in Acrasia's, and also Shakespeare's more skittish Adonis with Venus. Glendower mobilizes cosmic harmonies and heavenly steeds in the service of a languor the dangerous allure of which even Hotspur grudgingly acknowledges, and resists with awkward jokes. It is entirely consistent with the uncompromising claims made by the Welsh *other* that, as Westmoreland reported in 1.1, after Glendower captured Mortimer and "butchered" a thousand of his soldiers, the Welshwomen mutilated the soldiers' corpses in "beastly shameless transformation" (44). Seductive enervation and violent dismemberment: these Cymochlean and Pyrochlean extremes represent the twin threats to manly autonomy inscribed in the male fantasy of feminine power. The reported maenadic explosion suggests not only an externalization of the male nightmare but also a futile gesture of revenge on the worse "part of valor" by those who momentarily overcame their discretion, those whom the homoerotic flight to the battlefield has marginalized and dispossessed. In this warrior community Welsh is "the discourse of the other." The extremes over which Glendower presides—the extremes that he himself exemplifies in his grotesque doubleness as a cosmic braggadocio and his daughter's pliable advocate—have the same symbolic force. They speak to fears that male fantasy tries to dispel by blaming them on the power of the frailty named Woman. And that frailty sometimes tries to strike back. Westmoreland's report can serve as a brief reminder that war between men is a form of war against woman. It is a perverse and futile expression of the desire, the lack, attending the more permanent state of bereavement of which Hotspur's banished wife complains in 2.3.

* * *

Hotspur's problematic relation to firepower is suggested in the first mention of his name, when Westmoreland describes his fight with the Douglas:

> On Holy-rood day, the gallant Hotspur there,
> Young Harry Percy, and brave Archibald,
> That ever valiant and approved Scot,
> At Holmedon met, where they did spend
> A sad and bloody hour;
> As by discharge of their artillery,
> And shape of likelihood, the news was told.
>   (1.1.52–58)

The first five lines imply single combat, but the sixth line renders that uncertain. Although Humphreys notes that *artillery* formerly referred to "any missiles in war"—arrows, for example—and was "not confined to gunfire," the messenger's remarks about guns at Holmedon render this gloss gratuitous. The line allows us to wonder whether Westmoreland's previous statement refers literally to single combat or synecdochically to two armies. When we subsequently learn that Douglas has been "discomfited" and that "Ten thousand bold Scots, two and twenty knights" lie "Balk'd in their own blood" (67–69), we may also wonder about the nature of the artillery responsible for such mayhem.[23] The issue is somewhat clouded by the earlier reference to the barbaric Glendower's butchery of a thousand of Mortimer's soldiers: *butchered* (42) could well suggest manual warfare, though it does not have to (mention of Glendower's "rude hands" in the previous line prompts the suggestion), but at any rate the "beastly shameless transformation" wrought by the Welshwomen may comment on the meaning of the wholesale slaughter of anonymous men.

These issues are reawakened when Hotspur, in 1.3, defends Mortimer against Henry's charge that the latter "wilfully betray'd / The lives of those that he did lead to fight" against Glendower, "Whose daughter, as we hear, the Earl of March / Hath lately marry'd" (80–84). Hotspur's response is marked by the same impulse to decontamination that shaped his account of the messenger. The claim that Mortimer was seduced into treason by the offer of marriage—a claim at least partly borne out by subsequent disclosures—touches off another apology, and one that further betrays the speaker's anxiety:

> He never did fall off, my sovereign liege,
> But by the chance of war: to prove that true
> Needs no more but one tongue for all those wounds,
> Those mouthed wounds, which valiantly he took,
> When on the gentle Severn's sedgy bank,
> In single opposition hand to hand,
> He did confound the best part of an hour
> In changing hardiment with great Glendower.
> Three times they breath'd, and three times did they drink
> Upon agreement of swift Severn's flood,
> Who then affrighted with their bloody looks
> Ran fearfully among the trembling reeds,
> And hid his crisp head in the hollow bank,
> Bloodstained with these valiant combatants.
> Never did bare and rotten policy
> Color her working with such deadly wounds,
> Nor never could the noble Mortimer
> Receive so many, and all willingly:
> Then let him not be slander'd with revolt.
>   (1.3.93–111)

The speech is extraordinary because Hotspur is describing an encounter he had not seen—and one that may not even have taken place. This fantasy, in which Mortimer becomes the heroic Hotspurian loser, may well be an imaginative replay of Hotspur's own "sad and bloody hour" of battle with Douglas, and if it is, it isolates that conflict by framing it as single encounter and pushing the rest of the fray—the "artillery" and the ten thousand victims—into the background. What prompts this suggestion is the analogy to Hotspur's ignoring the "thousand . . . people butchered" by Glendower. Such conspicuous exclusion renders his account more problematic.

It is already problematic because he uses it to protect himself, along
with Mortimer, from the stigma of shameful fear, effeminate cowardice, that
Henry tries to mark him with by association. His language continues to be
nagged by the rhetoric of decontamination, and the continuity is marked by
the echo of the foppish messenger in the figure of the Severn as crisp-headed
coward. Hotspur sends "him" cringing to the sheltering lap ("hollow bank")
of blood-stained mother earth, and goes on to feminize "bare and rotten policy" by way of parrying the charge that Mortimer "fell off for the sake of a
woman and succumbed to the base condition of which the messenger's "fresh"
appearance had reminded Hotspur: "a bridegroom." Henry's first reference to
Mortimer had clearly put Hotspur on the defensive: "His brother-in-law, the
foolish Mortimer" (1.3.79). Since it is Hotspur's marriage that links him to
Mortimer and exposes him to the vagaries of Mortimer's behavior, Mortimer's purported vulnerability and folly reflect his own.

This is partly why Mortimer's wounds *do* speak with Hotspur's tongue,
and why that odd revision, "those mouthed wounds," is so telling. The wounds
are mouthed because they eat—or are penetrated by—the sword and because
they would speak of honor if they had tongues. But because honor's tongue
is the tongue of another, the hero's wounds are mute and their mouths mutilated. The defeated hero is doubly emasculated, his heroic autonomy twice
breached. The implications of the figure are more explicit in *Coriolanus* and
Julius Caesar. The Third Citizen says that if Coriolanus "show us his wounds
and tell us his deeds, we are to put our tongues into those wounds and speak
for them" (2.3.5–8). The metaphor associates stabbing, sexual penetration,
licking (to eat or heal), and a surgical probe or *tent* with the giving of voices/
votes that affirms Coriolanus's right to the consular honor. In *Julius Caesar*,
Antony describes Caesar's wounds in a figure that reminds one of Lavinia's—
or any well-behaved woman's—mouth: "like dumb mouths, [they] do ope
their ruby lips / To beg the voice and utterance of my tongue" (3.1.260–61).
Honor's phallic tongue is what wounds, like women, lack and long for.

Hotspur is more comfortable with the idea of eating swords fed by an
enemy than with the idea of feeding "on cates" served up by a friend (3.1.157).
The friend happens to be Glendower, whom he finds as tedious as "a railing
wife" (154), and "cates"—delicacies—happens to echo the name of his wife.
Yet the appetite for swords makes the hero dependent on and vulnerable to
the enemy who feeds him. If he finds the prospect of violation and dismemberment by the sword nourishing, it is because "the voice and utterance" of
honor can be begged only by exposing oneself to the risk of the ultimate
emasculation: the loss of life and speech. Thus Hotspur, dying, grieves that
Harry has "*robb'd*" him of his youth and "proud titles," and that "the earthly
and cold hand of death" lying on his tongue cuts him off before he can

"prophesy"—which means, perhaps, before he can put his own tongue into his wounds (5.4.76–84). The word *robb'd* briefly discharges into this moment the meanings generated in earlier episodes by the incessant play on threats to manhood—cowardice, victimization, the ignominy of hanging—inscribed in the activities of purse-snatching and pocket-picking. Even the noblest death may be no better than the casual by-product of robbery unless redeemed by honor's tongue. Since winner and loser are equally affected by this logic, Harry redeems both their honors by finishing Hotspur's sentence and letting "my favors hide thy mangled face" (5.4.95). Perhaps it is because he is doing himself a favor that he then somewhat oddly says, "I'll thank myself / For doing these fair rites of tenderness" (96–97).

The discourse of honor allows the hero to enjoy the foretaste and reiterate the promise of whatever may be redeeming in that death. It is a continuous incantation soliciting the tongue that can heal the final wound, and for these reasons the hero loves the talk that defers it. But talk is cheap, incurs debts, and the more the hero talks the greater will be the need to discharge the obligation not by victory but by death. The way of Tamburlaine must be avoided, the way of Sarpedon espoused. Hotspur keeps talking to the end, and at the last moment starts a new sentence that he won't be able to finish in order to leave space in the wound for Harry's tongue. The rationale behind this heroic *ars moriendi* was inadvertently prefigured in an earlier utterance: "I thank him that he cuts me from my tale, / For I profess not talking" (5.2.90–91). Later, it finds its way into Falstaff's mouth: "The better part of valor is discretion" (5.4.119); one meaning of *discretion* is "cutting off."[24]

Returning to the Hotspur/Mortimer relation, we have no information on the basis of which to ascertain what happened (or why it happened) before Mortimer "Was by the rude hands of that Welshman taken" (1.1.41), nor can we ascertain under what conditions he accepted a wife from the same hands. The latter fact is expressed by Henry as hearsay (1.3.83), and since Hotspur doesn't challenge the statement it must be assumed that he is fully aware of it even as he insists that Mortimer "never did fall off . . . / But by the chance of war," and goes on to elaborate a chivalric fantasy "to prove that true." Yet the links between these two events remain mysterious. We needn't assume that Hotspur knows more about those links than we do and is therefore lying. Much more interesting is the assumption that he doesn't know and that what he says is what he would like to believe. But if that is the case, if he knows only as much as Henry knows, then we are entitled to feel that his chivalric defense against Henry's interpretation may be breached by doubt—and it will be well to remember this later, when Mortimer fails to show up at Shrewsbury. Hotspur's own honor would be threatened if Henry's interpretation were true and Mortimer proved to be a traitor for love. More immediately, the honorableness of his discourse is threatened for the same reason. The defense of Mortimer is a reckless move, and puts Hotspur at a disadvantage. He commits himself with high-rhetorical ardor to an interpretation that may be false. Henry directly challenges his account: "Thou dost belie him, Percy, thou dost belie him, / He never did encounter with Glendower," and thrusts home with "Art thou not asham'd?" (1.3.112–16). After he storms out and Worcester returns, Hotspur's report of the heated interchange is evasive:

> He will forsooth have all my prisoners,
> And when I urg'd the ransom once again
> Of my wife's brother, then his cheek look'd pale,
> And on my face he turn'd an eye of death,
> Trembling even at the name of Mortimer.
>   (138–42)

This is not at all how the conversation went: Hotspur's account of the battle is deleted and replaced by the second clause above, which reports something he did not explicitly say. The deletion argues a kind of willed forgetfulness of the extravagant claims he made on Mortimer's behalf, claims he is as yet powerless to verify. The extravagance may be read as an anxious reaction to his powerlessness, and his choleric response to Henry's exit speech seems all the more defensive in the light of the evasive report that follows it. "Art thou not asham'd?": perhaps he is, or fears to be; Henry seems to have more success managing Hotspur's sense of shame than he does in his parallel project of managing Harry's. Here he may have opened up a wound.

When Worcester returns, however, he pours balm into that wound by mentioning Mortimer's claim to the crown. We should expect this news to relieve Hotspur because it legitimizes his political and verbal activity on behalf of someone who, it now turns out, defected not only for love but also for reasons of state. And indeed, he seizes this opportunity to regain his equilibrium. Relief pours out in the form of a long speech devoted primarily to heaping shame on "you" who helped the usurper to the throne. Worcester had given him the cue: for Richard's deposition and murder "we in the world's wide mouth / Live scandaliz'd and foully spoken of (151–52)—slander as mastication; the blatant beast; another source of mouthed wounds. Worcester appeals to Hotspur's sense of shame—his *we* reaches out toward his nephew—but in his long response Hotspur gradually narrows the referential focus of his offsetting *you* and evades Worcester's reach by himself assuming the role of appellant. The last half of his speech is directed specifically to his father and uncle, as the parenthetical line below (172) makes clear:

O, pardon me, that I descend so low,
To show the line and the predicament
Wherein you range under this subtle King!
Shall it for shame be spoken in these days,
Or fill up chronicles in time to come,
That men of your nobility and power
Did gage them both in an unjust behalf
(As both of you, God pardon it, have done)
To put down Richard, that sweet lovely rose,
And plant this thorn, this canker Bolingbroke?
And shall it in more shame be further spoken,
That you are fool'd, discarded, and shook off
By him for whom these shames ye underwent?
No, time yet serves wherein you may redeem
Your banish'd honors, and restore yourselves
Into the good thoughts of the world again:
Revenge the jeering and disdain'd contempt
Of this proud King, who studies day and night
To answer all the debt he owes to you,
Even with the bloody payment of your deaths:
Therefore, I say—

WOR.
Peace, cousin, say no more.
(1.3.165–85)

Hotspur's last eight lines trigger a vivid recollection of the end of Harry's "I know you all" soliloquy in the previous scene. The effect of superimposing the two passages, and their respective scenarios, is to increase our sense that Hotspur, like Harry, is selectively emphasizing a not fully justifiable line of argument by way of fending off another that is more reprehensible. In other words, he situates his appeal entirely within the discourse of honor and says nothing about the dishonor that would attend another insurrection against a ruler who—however dubiously he won the crown—was formally invested: "that same greatness," as Worcester had said, "which our own hands / Have holp to make so portly" (1.3.12–13). In doing this, Hotspur joins both Henry and Harry in playing the familiar game of disclaiming responsibility and pleading victimization. He unpacks this argument from the hints conspiratorially dropped by Worcester and Northumberland (143–52) and gives it back to them as a justifying spur to rebellious action—a spur, really, to revenge for the shames doubly heaped on them. But at the same time, by insisting that the responsibility and dishonor are theirs, not his, he directs the argument *against them.*

As my previous discussion has suggested, Hotspur's opposition to the king is rooted in a sense of personal affront which is exacerbated by the suspicion that he may be complicit in compromising his own honor. Here that opposition is inseparably bound to a new one: his competition with his senior kinsmen. He uses this speech event not merely to begin to "redeem" his banished honor, but to do so by dissociating himself from their shame. The force of this move is increased by its reverberation of the more familiar analogue that the verbal echoes of the "I know you all" soliloquy evoke: Harry's dissociating himself from his father. And as the soliloquy looks forward to the Great Day of his glittering reformation, so Hotspur begins his race along the *cursus honoris* with the express intention of wearing "Without corrival all her dignities" (205).

On the other side, Worcester and Northumberland are obviously less interested in honor than in power and safety (in the power that will make them safe). Worcester's "Peace, cousin, say no more" is comical in part because he has already laid plans for the redemption of honors, and in part because having deliberately set Hotspur's discourse machine in motion he has a hard time shutting it off. The elder Percys need Hotspur to "face" their uprising, and if we bear this in mind we may be curious about their employment of Mortimer's claim, which had never been mentioned before, either in this play or in *Richard II.* Whether it is genuine or not—and we may as well assume that it is—is less important than the use they are putting it to as a political appeal to the legitimacy of the cause and a personal appeal to Mortimer's brother-in-law. The conspiratorial manner in which they broach the topic gives it an unpleasant smell, and the question is whether there is any indication that the smell reaches Hotspur's nose. They are using Mortimer to line their own enterprise, and using Hotspur to line Mortimer's. Does his language reveal any awareness of this?

The phrase I just used is borrowed from Lady Percy who, in 2.3, after expressing concern over Hotspur's recent behavior, says, "I fear my brother Mortimer doth stir / About his title, and hath sent for you / To line his enterprise" (82–84). This is hardly a complimentary way to put it: she fears Mortimer has sent for him as for his factor or tailor. In the words Hotspur uses to show his kinsmen their "line and predicament," she fears he is being sent for as one of "the agents, or base second means" (1.3.163). Lady Percy's phrasing expresses a hint of disapproval directed at Mortimer for being the possible cause of Hotspur's anxiety, but if we hear it with Hotspur's ears we may feel that it only increases his anxiety at the position he finds himself in. For it is possible that he is aware of lining his wife's brother's enterprise at some cost to his own chivalric autonomy and self-respect, and his responses to Lady Percy in 2.3, which I discuss below, play back over his performance in 1.3. Mortimer's subsequent behavior, which suggests that uxoriousness (and perhaps cowardice?) may have caused his failure to show up at Shrewsbury, puts the whole of the enterprise in a bad light, and revives the questions that may have disturbed Hotspur in the early part of 1.3.

Taking all this into consideration, one can't but wonder about the variety of dubious circumstances that hedge Hotspur in from the beginning and wound his sense of honor. From the moment he opens his mouth he appears trapped, like Mowbray, in "chains of bondage" to political, psychological, and social circumstances, not to mention the military specter of "vile guns." They jeopardize his honor, his manhood, and his chivalric autonomy. He tries by his speech to silence these truths, defend against them, and preserve the discourse of honor in its purity. But his language, inscribed within truth's "quiet breast," continues to disclose them. Even his castigation of Worcester and Northumberland betrays an attempt to ignore the more reprehensible aspects of the action to which he commits himself, as well as a self-defeating attempt to compete with his allies in the race for honor. During the remainder of the scene, these doubts about his own condition give themselves away both in compensatory outbursts of bravado and in deliberately irritating behavior, which—with a wry and self-mocking awareness—he displays as if asking his kinsmen to rebuke him.

After Hotspur's rhetoric arcs excitedly up toward the moon, it comes back down to earth with a set of figures whose idiomatic vividness has a peculiar effect:

> But I will find him when he lies asleep,
> And in his ear I'll holla "Mortimer!"
> Nay, I'll have a starling shall be taught to speak
> Nothing but "Mortimer" . . .
> All studies here I solemnly defy,
> Save how to gall and pinch this Bolingbroke:
> And that same sword-and-buckler prince of Wales,
>
> . . . . .
> I would have him poison'd with a pot of ale!
> NORTH.
> Why, what a wasp-stung and impatient fool
> Art thou to break into this woman's mood,
> Tying thine ear to no tongue but thine own!
> HOT.
> Why, look you, I am whipp'd and scourg'd with rods,

> Nettled, and stung with pismires, when I hear
> of this vile politician Bolingbroke.
> (1.3.219–22, 225–30, 233–38)

Hotspur at his most winning playfully vents and deflates his anger. There is self-mockery in the kind and level of punishment he devises—in the threat to turn starling teacher and pester Henry like a popinjay (cf. 3.1.253–54 and 1.3.49), and in the tonal drop from "solemnly defy" to "gall and pinch." It is not so much that he is charming as that he is being charming, begging his auditors' indulgence and apologizing for his own so that he can go on indulging himself, can go on savoring his minor grievances and revenges like a small boy who has been shamed and is bent on getting even. Yet his language acknowledges both his low tolerance for such grievances and his high tolerance for the speech they enable. To scale them down to the level of galls, pinches, beatings, and stings is to admit he has been making more of them than he should. But even as he apologizes to his auditors for his performance, and even if it is an enabling apology, he seems willfully, perversely, to give them—and here I borrow Portia's phrase—a vantage to exclaim on him.

In the speech action of this scene, as in the battle action later, Hotspur (like Harry) stacks the odds against himself and maximizes his commitment to the role of underdog. This relation of interlocutory disadvantage dramatizes one of the self-subverting aspects of the discourse of honor. He presents himself to his uncle and father, his paternal "corrivals," as a naughty headstrong boy who in effect resigns to them the responsibility of tolerating him, checking him, and guiding him, just as he leaves it up to them to find the battlefield he longs for and to aim him toward it. His dependence on them, his obligation to them, and his consequent lack of self-sufficiency are immediately present and active in the conversational protocol he establishes. To assume such a position is to enhance the authority of the fathers he intends to surpass in the race for honor. He relies on his corrivals to help him achieve the goal of wearing honor's dignities without corrival. The irony of Northumberland's subsequent defection is that it gives Hotspur what he wants. Does it give Northumberland what he wants?

The question may not be answerable, yet it is reasonable to ask it in a tetralogy centered on a set of father–son conflicts that reverberate, overlap, and speak to each other. Weak fathers like Gaunt, York, Henry, and Northumberland may be forgiven for flinching from their sons, and from the shame or guilt of small and great betrayals. But of course the plays don't ask us to get into the business of forgiving, as if we had any right to the voyeuristic power of divine judgment. All they ask us to look into is whether the fathers can forgive themselves.

A good case can be made that in *Richard II* Gaunt's manhood and honor are threatened both by his son's behavior and by his response to it. What about Northumberland? There isn't much to go on. His brief responses to Hotspur reveal only irritation. But if we listen to Hotspur with *Northumberland*'s ears, or lend him *ours*, we may feel that he is being upstaged, challenged, by the son who speaks of plucking all honor for himself while using his father as a factor. The final replies of father and son to Worcester's instructions poignantly drive home the contrast between them:

> NORTH.
> Farewell, good brother; we shall thrive, I trust.
> HOT.
> Uncle, adieu: O, let the hours be short,
> Till fields, and blows, and groans applaud our sport.
> (1.3.294–96)

Hotspur looks forward eagerly to the crowds cheering him on the day of the big game. But his father's "I trust," the last words he speaks in the play, hangs weakly and indecisively at the end of a line whose faltering rhythm prepares us for his absence from the future scene of his son's heroics. The father who began the scene interceding for his son, ends it edging away from him.

Until fields and blows and groans applaud his sport, Hotspur finds a substitute outlet in words. His speech drives to an aggressive climax in his violent assault on the moon, a passage that reverbs Falstaff's stealthier attack on "our noble and chaste mistress" and is echoed in Gadshill's attack on Saint Commonwealth. These passages reinforce each other and are all the more significant for being merely incidental to what seems to occupy their speakers' attention. Here, at line 199, is what Hotspur says:

> By heaven methinks it were an easy leap
> To pluck bright honor from the pale-fac'd moon,
> Or dive into the bottom of the deep,
> Where fathom-line could never touch the ground,
> And pluck up drowned honor by the locks,
> So he that doth redeem her thence might wear
> Without corrival all her dignities:
> But out upon this half-fac'd fellowship!

"An oration in Ercles' vein," says the Arden editor: a touch of heroic frenzy. But there is more to it than rant, and it is more than a conventionally hyperbolic expression of chivalric ardors. Several of Hotspur's previous phrases in the scene are echoed: the pale-cheeked king "high in the air," "the downtrod Mortimer," the redemption of "banish'd honors," and the threat of drowning all converge, and some are transsexualized, in the chaste mistress of the moon who rules the deep. They discharge into that figure the value of the Enemy who threatens and challenges, and who provides honor with its occasion because she withholds it as if to "wear / Without corrival all her dignities."

What the figure virtually says is that to desire and pursue honor is to dishonor a woman and a goddess—to violate her, to cause her to drown, to make her pale with fear and anger. (However irrelevant it may be, an image of the drowned Ophelia crosses briefly over my sense of this passage.) The rude force of "pluck up ... by the locks" casts a dim light on "redeem," especially since what will be redeemed is a corpse. Honor, the ultimate prey of the desire for honor, is identified with, expressed in, the perpetration of dishonor and shame on its possessor. If to receive honor as a gift from others is to be diminished, emasculated, reduced to a minion, then the gift must be refused so that honor may be taken by force.

Hotspur's imagined violation is also a self-violation. There is a suggestion of transvestism in the image of honor's redeemer wearing *her* dignities. It is as if his language refuses to let him defeminize himself, as if the woman who withholds honor stubbornly resists his violence. Honor as the lunar goddess is the ultimate figure of *danger* in the romance sense—the Spenserian *daunger*. Like Belphoebe, she protects the rights of women against the assaults of their male corrivals. Hotspur clearly means *corrival* to refer to his male peers, but in the figure, *corrival* refers to "her." "Half-fac'd" echoes "pale-fac'd" and can describe the figure of the moon, which, whether half or full, is flat, like the image stamped on a coin. So long as Hotspur shares honor with "her," so long as her pale face is partnered to his half-face, he remains impure, incomplete, merely half a man. To castigate and destroy the "noble and chaste mistress" within is the precondition for surpassing other males in honor.

* * *

Act 2, scene 3, is a short scene, running to only about 120 lines. It begins with a prose soliloquy in which Hotspur testily responds aloud to the letter of an anonymous correspondent who writes that he is going to pass up the invitation to join the uprising against the king. Hotspur's wife then walks in and spends 27 lines of blank verse complaining about how she has been ignored by her husband and worrying about the obsession with warfare that makes him talk in his sleep. The remaining interchanges between them feature his affectionate but nervous diffidence and her frustrated demands for more love and information. I conclude with some comments on this scene because in it is distilled the essential warfare between the claims of honor and those of gender within Hotspur's language.

The opening soliloquy reads so like a dialogue carried on by the speaker with himself as well as with his correspondent that it has been interpreted by Robert Merrix and Arthur Palacas as an unsuccessful effort at self-reassurance. They attribute the "signs of inner conflict" revealed by his language to his "doubts about the rebellion," doubts which they think he silences "with a combination of argument, exhausting wordiness, and irrational tirade. Even in the face of the possibility that the letter's author will 'to the King and lay open all our proceedings,' Hotspur finally concludes, 'Hang him, let him to the King! we are prepared. I will set forward tonight.'"[25] But is this his only fear, or doesn't he also worry that the rebels' enterprise may succeed? Recall his impatience with "half-fac'd fellowship" in 1.3 and the irritability projected from his expressions of concern for honor. The impatience extended to the details of plotting, which he had wanted to leave up to his elders; they would work out the logistics and he would then ride off and reap the rewards:

HOT.
  I smell it. Upon my life it will do well!
NORTH.
  Before the game is afoot thou still let'st slip.
HOT.
  Why, it cannot choose but be a noble plot;
            . . . . .
In faith it is exceedingly well aim'd.
    (1.3.271–76)

He is now aware that he may have proved his father right by "letting slip" when he exposed the plot to the correspondent whose "fear and cold heart" might lead him to turn informer. What is interesting about this is that although he blames himself for his folly, his words hardly betray any depth of guilt: "O, I could divide myself, and go to buffets, for moving such a dish of skim milk with so honorable an action" (2.3.32–34). The self-accusation is lightheartedly irritable, and it is implicitly affirmative insofar as his own discretion proceeds from a rash willingness to take chances (in divulging the plot to potential allies—or informers?) that is more honorable than the correspondent's cautious scruples. The same pattern of contrastive definition is at work here as was evident in his fulminations against the effeminate courtier. If, as Merrix and Palacas observe, the very anonymity of the correspondent "demonstrates dramatically that Hotspur's ravings and defenses are ... the unsolicited product of his own turmoil,"[26] then the charge of effeminate cowardice may conceivably displace the fear—the fear of fear—inscribed in the discourse that speaks through him.

It is thus questionable that Hotspur's anxiety is to be attributed solely to his "doubts about the rebellion," or that those doubts are silenced by the end of the soliloquy. Yet he anticipates new danger in an oddly positive tone of conviction: "You shall see now in the very sincerity of fear and cold heart will he to the King. . . ." This could be read as the utterance of the naughty "lackbrain" boy who has acted as his father suspected he might, and who expects—not without satisfaction—to get what he deserves. But it could also—if more obscurely—be read as another expression of the wish to be an underdog: to give the secret away will increase the danger and hence the excitement and honorableness of the action. It is as if the soundness of the plot detracts from honor. His anger at the writer's cowardice may well conflict with a touch of fretfulness over the careful plotting that allies him with so many corrivals, and threatens to diminish his share in "so honorable an action."

The impatience of "Hang him, let him to the King, we are prepared: I will set forward tonight" is thus the product of an unresolved clash of motives; it is given a competitive edge by his previous statement that some of his corrivals have "set forward already" (2.3.28–29). But as a way of concluding the soliloquy it is also another gesture of escape to the enfranchisement of "fields, and blows, and groans"—escape from the tug of conflicting motives and from such logistical nettles or pismires as the precautions of plotting. The situation I analyzed in my reading of 1.3 suggests to me that in addition to the contradictions internal to the discourse of honor, Hotspur's behavior in the circumstances entangling him in Mortimer's affairs could only intensify his uneasiness. Thus I deduce that in the soliloquy he summons up and welcomes the politico-military doubts Merrix and Palacas describe—summons them up to provide the trifling galls and pinches with which he diverts himself from other fears. "*Enter* Hotspur *solus, reading a letter*": the soliloquy is itself a single encounter against an absent foe whose "craven scruple" reflects those fears in conveniently parodic and displaced form. Having routed the foe in speech he can rush off to the battlefield before being attacked by second thoughts.

Before dwelling with too long a face on Hotspur's uneasiness I think it is important to appreciate the keenness with which the soliloquist enjoys this verbal encounter. The rhythms of the language make it easy for actors performing the soliloquy to move audiences to laugh not merely at the speaker's expense but in sympathetic enjoyment of his rhetorical exuberance. By the very vivacity of his utterance the actor can secure our approval of, for example, the scornful common sense of "'tis dangerous to take a cold, to sleep, to drink," and can induce us to applaud the memorable riposte that counters it, "but I tell you, my lord fool, out of this nettle, danger, we pluck this flower, safety" (2.3.8–10). The speaker means to distinguish the ultimate risk-taking Danger from quotidian sources of vulnerability, and the gallantry of the sentiment combines with its aphoristic form to elicit our assent. Nevertheless, the language resists this meaning. The syntax confuses the two kinds of danger because "nettle" is another minimizing figure, and "pluck this flower"—which recalls "pluck bright honor"—is a self-defeating image of the fragile, transient safety sought by fleeing from dangers to Danger. This resistance uncovers something deeper and more abiding in Hotspur's language, something engendered not simply by his uncertainty about the rebellion but by a fundamental ambivalence in the discourse of honor to which he commits himself. Merrix and Palacas make good use of the trope of proleptic parody to show how Hotspur's uncertainty is foregrounded by comparison with the prior performance of Gadshill in 1.2: "Whereas Gadshill's defensiveness arises from an attempt to set his challenger [the Chamberlain] straight, Hotspur's much more intense disputations, voiced on a stage empty of everyone but himself, are directed against himself."[27] I imagine Hotspur trying to set himself straight but not fully persuading himself—imagine an edge of self-parody in his romantic posturing, a sense of being trapped in, embattled by, the bravery of a discourse he loves but has doubts about. If it is dangerous to sleep and drink, it is also dangerous to speak.

And it is indeed dangerous to sleep, as we learn when Lady Percy enters:

O my good lord, why are you thus alone?
For what offence have I this fortnight been
A banish'd woman from my Harry's bed?
Tell me, sweet lord, what is't that takes from thee
Thy stomach, pleasure, and thy golden sleep?
Why dost thou bend thine eyes upon the earth,
And start so often when thou sit'st alone?
Why hast thou lost the fresh blood in thy cheeks,
And given my treasures and my rights of thee
To thick-ey'd musing, and curst melancholy?
In thy faint slumbers I by thee have watch'd,
And heard thee murmur tales of iron wars,
Speak terms of manage to thy bounding steed,
Cry "Courage! To the field!" And thou hast talk'd

> Of sallies, and retires, of trenches, tents,
> Of palisadoes, frontiers, parapets,
> Of basilisks, of cannon, culverin,
> Of prisoners' ransom, and of soldiers slain,
> And all the currents of a heady fight.
> Thy spirit within thee hath been so at war,
> And thus hath so bestirr'd thee in thy sleep,
> That beads of sweat have stood upon thy brow
> Like bubbles in a late-disturbed stream,
> And in thy face strange motions have appear'd,
> Such as we see when men restrain their breath
> On some great sudden hest, O, what portents are these?
> Some heavy business hath my lord in hand,
> And I must know it, else he loves me not.
>   (2.3.38–65)

The first thing we learn from this is that whatever bothers Hotspur ante-dates the reception of the letter (unless he is imagined to have spent fifteen days talking back to it), and we can assume that it affected the response expressed in his soliloquy. Perhaps wounded honor is part of the problem: the word *banish'd* works like a mnemonic trigger connecting the violation of his wife's rights to the violent effect on him of his concern to "redeem / . . . banish'd honors." When she refigures "beads of sweat" to "bubbles in a late-disturbed stream," the image matches and recalls Hotspur's "drowned honor" (1.3.203), and it also recalls his fantasy of the disturbance that "affrighted" the Severn (1.3.103). These echoes filter back into "currents of a heady fight" and trigger another recall, Worcester's "current roaring loud" along with Hotspur's "If he fall in, good night, or sink, or swim" (1.3.185–94). In this context of recollective allusion, "prisoners' ransom" and "soldiers slain" evoke not only Hotspur's generic martial anticipations but also specific backward references to Henry's demand and to the carnage in Wales for which his wife's brother may have been responsible.

To read Lady Hotspur's speech this way is to go beyond the information available to the speaker, to see that the "portents" are also retrospects, and to place a different construction on "heavy business." At the same time it is also to validate the interpretive intuitions displayed in her two comparisons in lines 59–63. Above all it is to listen with Hotspur's ears, not hers, for she knows less than he does. Doubtless this befits a woman's place, and the very accuracy of her woman's intuition might well motivate him to keep her in it. Her insight may cut too deep, her mirror reflect back to him a true image of the heavy business that he may want *not* to know as much as she wants to know it. She reveals the intimacy and demands the rights of a second self, and perhaps the demand itself has the force of "some great sudden hest," since to share in half-faced partnership with a wifely corrival could only widen the breach in his honor and manhood. He can't redeem "drowned honor" or pluck honor from the pale-faced king without at the same time banishing—plucking honor from—his wife. Yet this might confront him with another problem.

"And I must know it, else he loves me not": that importunate "hest" could be bothersome just because he does love her—there can be no other way to read the playful affection and banter that mark their two scenes together. She speaks to him with the frankness, sympathy, and confidence of one assured in his love and therefore perplexed by his recent transformation. If we respond to this, it complicates our sense of the "heavy business" that besets him. For the business comes to include the demands she makes on him not only generally as his wife but also here and now, in this speech, and this adds a more immediate source to those that keep the spirit within him "so at war." Her questions mingle anxiety for his welfare with anxiety over her own frustrated claims on him, while her description mingles the marks of the distraught lover with the marks of fear. But what love, and what fear? Is it the love and fear of "iron wars" that rob him of his "golden sleep" and her of her "treasures" and "rights"? That bend him "thick-ey'd" toward Henry's "thirsty . . . soil," the man-eating mother (1.1.5–6), or toward the "lean earth" the sweating Falstaff lards (2.2.103–4)? And what does the cry she reports mean? Is it only the leader's cry to his soldiers, or is it self-directed? And if self-directed, does it mean that he has to summon up courage to go to the field, or that going to the field—seeking the solace of "all the currents of a heady fight"—will give him the courage he needs? But courage, then, to defend against what fear if not that of "Thy stomach, pleasure, and thy golden sleep," if not that of "my treasures and my rights of thee"? Or is there another fear, another reason why he would feel threatened by the words with which the watcher at his bed anxiously reflects his anxiety back to him?

The first of the "tales of iron wars" she reports fits comfortably within the chivalric paradigm: lines 50–51 suggest the clean heroics of single encounter, of "Harry to Harry, hot horse to horse." But she then goes on to report his tale of the messier warfare "Of basilisks, of cannon, culverin." It is as if, once the dreamer galloped into the field, he was confronted not by another Harry but by the hungry mouths of heavy ordnance and by the ultimate impotence, the prospect of a death he has no power to make his own—more pointedly, the prospect articulated by the fop who so irritated him on the battlefield with talk of "these vile guns" that "many a good tall fellow had destroy'd" (1.3.62–63), and whose connection with Henry and the question of prisoners is marked by Lady Hotspur's linking the sleeper's talk of guns to his talk "Of

prisoners' ransom, and of soldiers slain." Behind this veil of references lurks
the problematic figure of Mortimer and thus the even more problematic bond
to Mortimer through Lady Hotspur, whose subsequent expression of concern
("I fear my brother Mortimer ... / ... hath sent for you / To line his enterprise," 82–84) touches on the network of constraints and accommodations
that have compromised Hotspur's honor from the start.

As a bearer of messages from Hotspur's troubled dreamland, this messenger can only add to the anxieties and vulnerabilities her account reflects.
We can imagine why he would be eager neither to have her know what he
betrays in his sleep nor to have the betrayal mirrored back to him so that he
is forced to recognize fears and terrors his waking words never acknowledge.
Doesn't all this give a more poignant edge and urgency to the self-defeating
impulse to flight inscribed in "out of this nettle, danger, we pluck this flower,
safety"? Poignant, I mean, for both of them, for her as well as for him. His
response is powerfully evasive. He says nothing to her in reply but instead
turns away and calls a servant:

> What ho!
> Is Gilliams with the packet gone?
> SERV.
> He is, my lord, an hour ago.
> HOT.
> Hath Butler brought those horses from the sheriff?
> SERV.
> One horse, my lord, he brought even now.
> HOT.
> What horse? A roan, a crop-ear is it not?
> SERV.
> It is, my lord.
> HOT.
> That roan shall be my throne.
> Well, I will back him straight. O Esperance!
> Bid Butler lead him forth into the park.
> (1.3.66–73)

He has betrayed his fear to his wife in his sleep, he flinches both from her
reflecting it back to him and from her claims on him, and he begins to move
rapidly away from that surveillance and self-dividing confrontation toward
Esperance. The Percy motto, "Esperance ma comforte," seems reducible here
to "Horse is my stay," especially the horse that carries him away from his
wife. Is there any reason why the text contains that apparently gratuitous

epithet, "crop-ear"? Animal ears are cropped as a sign of identification, human ears as a sign of punishment. Hotspur's expression becomes less gratuitous when we situate it in the set of references that include a horse named Cut (2.1.5) and Gadshill's gelding (2.1.33, 94). "Cut" signifies either a curtal or a gelding, a horse that has been symbolically or literally castrated. If horses can represent their masters, then perhaps "Cut" speaks to the sense of powerlessness and apprehensiveness expressed by the Carriers who, in 2.1, utter a version of the victim's discourse, and perhaps Gadshill's gelding comments on what lies underneath and bears up the aggressive machismo of his rhetoric in that scene. Applying the same logic to Hotspur, "crop-ear" may conceivably suggest something about his wounded mode of audition, his diffident response to the articulateness of the claims, the sympathy, the careful observation, that threaten to make his wife his loving corrival. His affection for her is apparent in all their exchanges, hence if the crop-eared horse on which he plans to escape from her is identified as his, it may hint at a motive of self-punishment in his flight. But to admit this symbolism is to trot out a telling inconsistency: why should the equine instrument of his flight from the fear of emasculation itself be marked as a symbol of what he flees from?

* * *

"What is it carries you away?" Hotspur's wife asks, and when he answers, "my horse, my love, my horse" (2.3.76–77), it may occur to us that his horse performs the same function as his galloping speech, a perpetually unfinished rush of self-representation interrupted only by the death it dooms him to. If there is an Icarian and also an Actaeonic futility inscribed in Hotspur's speech it is because this scene as a whole reveals that from the moment Hotspur opens his mouth he appears trapped in "chains of bondage" to political, psychological, and social circumstances that jeopardize his honor, his manhood, and his chivalric autonomy. He tries by his speech to silence these truths, defend against them, and preserve the discourse of honor in its Artemisian purity. But his language continues to defeat him. "That roan shall be my throne": his only throne will be his crop-eared roan. There is as much desperation and futility as there is determination in this utterance. He is king over himself only when he rides the horse that carries him away from his wife toward "golden"—or leaden—"uncontroll'd enfranchisement." Although the discourse of honor carries him away from the weakness he fears, it continually reproduces the weakness in the rhetorical transports that seduce his tongue. When he claims "I profess not talking," when he shows uneasiness about poetry, singing, and lovemaking, he is in flight from his own vulnerabilities. Behind this obvious point is a more significant one: the language assigned to Hotspur is shot through with the awareness that the accents of honor are inseparable from those of the weakness and uncontrol that the discourse of honor marks as dishonorable or shameful. The hero loves and fears what Mowbray dismissively calls "the trial of a woman's war" as much as he loves and fears the only fate that will justify it and put an end to it.

Notes

1. All quotations from *1 Henry IV* in this and subsequent chapters are from *The First Part of King Henry IV*, ed. A. R. Humphreys, The Arden Shakespeare, 6th ed. (1960; repr. London: Methuen, 1974).

2. Pierre Bourdieu, *Outline of a Theory of Practice*, trans. Richard Nice (Cambridge: Cambridge University Press, 1977), 4–15; Marcel Mauss, *The Gift: Forms and Functions of Exchange in Archaic Societies*, trans. Ian Cunnison (New York: Norton, 1967), 72–73, 63.

3. Bourdieu, *Outline*, 10ff.

4. Ibid., 12, 11.

5. Aristotle, *Nichomachean Ethics* 1.5.4 (1095b), trans. H. Rackham, Loeb Classical Library (London: Heinemann, 1945), 14–15.

6. Aristotle, *Rhetoric* 1.5.9 (1361a), trans. J. H. Freese, in *The "Art" of Rhetoric*, Loeb Classical Library (London: Heinemann, 1947), 53; *Nichomachean Ethics* 4.3.22, 24 (1124b), pp. 221–23.

7. *Nichomachean Ethics* 4.3.17 (1124a), p. 219.

8. Thomas Hobbes, *Leviathan*, ed. Michael Oakeshott (Oxford: Basic Blackwell, 1960), 65 (1.11).

9. D. J. Gordon, "Name and Fame: Shakespeare's *Coriolanus*," in *The Renaissance Imagination: Essays and Lectures by D. J. Gordon*, ed. Stephen J. Orgel (Berkeley: University of California Press, 1980), 20319, esp. 210–13.

10. C. B. Macpherson, *The Political Theory of Possessive Individualism* (Oxford: Clarendon Press, 1962), 38.

11. Paul A. Jorgensen, *Shakespeare's Military World* (Berkeley: University of California Press, 1956), 240, 296.

12. *Nichomachean Ethics* 3.6.6 (1115a27), p. 155.

13. Ibid., 3.7.13 (1116a13–15), pp. 161–63.

14. The filaments of the Actaeon myth curling about this cluster are too wispy and discontinuous to nurture into a thesis. They nevertheless have a certain interest. At 3.3.155–56, Harry calls Diana's fat forester an "embossed rascal," and this denotes a young lean deer as well as a fat swollen rogue (Arden notes). See also Harry's "Death hath not struck so fat a deer today" at 5.4.106. The first passage is connected with the pocket-picking episode, while the second is shortly followed by Falstaff's stabbing the dead Hotspur in the thigh. Both, then, are connected with castration symbolism. The "rascal" as both rogue and victim, predator and prey, man and deer, puts forth a tenuous trailer toward the chaste mistress of the pale-faced moon when Hotspur's threat to pluck bright honor from that figure places him in Actaeon's position. For a wonderful discussion of the implications of this theme, see

Leonard Barkan, "Diana and Actaeon: The Myth as Synthesis," *English Literary Renaissance* 10 (1980): 317–59, esp. 349ff.

15. J. Dover Wilson, ed., *The First Part of the History of Henry IV* (Cambridge: Cambridge University Press, 1958), 120.

16. That Diana should have men as companions is itself outrageous. Is Diana a man in drag? Are her foresters dressed as women? Is Diana secretly "a fair hot wench"?

17. Barkan, "Diana and Actaeon," 351–52.

18. Ibid., 343; my italics.

19. G. R. Hibbard, *The Making of Shakespeare's Dramatic Poetry* (Toronto: University of Toronto Press, 1981), 175–76; my italics.

20. Jorgensen, *Shakespeare's Military World*, 240–41.

21. The game appears frequently in Shakespeare. It is the game played by Prospero and by Lear and Gloucester and by the Duke of Vienna as well as by Richard II, Henry, and Harry.

22. The First Part of "King Henry the Fourth," ed. George Lyman Kittredge (Boston: Ginn, 1940), 117. See also Ullrich Langer, "Gunpowder as Transgressive Invention in Ronsard," in *Literary Theory/Renaissance Texts*, ed. Patricia Parker and David Quint (Baltimore: Johns Hopkins University Press), 96–114; pp. 104–6 are especially relevant to this discussion.

23. We may also wonder about the disproportion between 10,000 "bold Scots" and 22 knights. Does Henry mean to imply an equitable distribution—22 aristocrats = 10,000 commoners?

24. See Paul A. Jorgensen, "Valor's Better Parts: Backgrounds and Meanings of Shakespeare's Most Difficult Proverb," *Shakespeare Studies* 9 (1976): 152. Jorgensen comments on the relation of this pun to "the defense of threatened manhood in the passage and in Falstaff's entire career" (153), and one need only add that Falstaff, the source of the pun, is making a similar comment about himself.

25. Robert P. Merrix and Arthur Palacas, "Gadshill, Hotspur, and the Design of Proleptic Parody," *Comparative Drama* 14 (1980–81): 303.

26. Ibid., 302–3.

27. Ibid., 303.

A . D . N U T T A L L

The Major Histories

"Be yourself": *Richard II*

Shakespeare began his writing career with histories and then branched out into comedy and tragedy. In the first part of *Henry VI* he probed the nature of historical causation. He presented the origin of the Wars of the Roses as mysterious. Starting in an inchoate sense of genealogical wrong the play progresses swiftly and incrementally; the mere fact of taking sides, the adoption of badges, adds irrationally to the momentum. If this is psychology entering historiography it is very much a psychology socially conceived, in terms of the interaction of persons and groups. In *Richard III* the strongest psychological interest was in the isolated individual, in a king who seems to become two persons when he introspects. In *The Comedy of Errors* the idea of a doubled self is allowed to dance free from individual psychology into a fairyland of twins, objectively coexisting doubles. If *The Comedy of Errors* is earlier than *Richard III* we must say that Shakespeare played with the idea of split identity before he worked with it, in the history play. Psychological tension, as we saw, did get into *The Comedy of Errors*, but the play was primarily social. The comedic interest in the tension between same-sex solidarity and heterosexual love may be called psychological but is, again, social in its reference. The characters in the four comedies, *The Comedy of Errors, Two Gentlemen of Verona, The Taming of the Shrew,* and *A Midsummer Night's Dream,* are in comparison with those in the history plays slight and

From *Shakespeare the Thinker*, pp. 133–70. © 2007 by A.D. Nuttall.

schematic. Lysander and Demetrius are hard to keep distinct in the mind, but no one ever forgets Richard III, alone at the end. At the same time, however, comedy allowed an excursion from concrete into abstract thinking, from "What caused what in the history of England?" to metaphysical questions: "What is real? What is imagination? What is role-playing?"

In *Richard II* Shakespeare marries the comedic worry about role-playing and pretence to the analysis of introspection begun in *Richard III*. Richard II, as everyone knows, is Shakespeare's player-king—at least until Act V, where he turns into the poet-king. Like Jean-Paul Sartre's waiter in *L'Être et le néant* who can be watched playing the part of a waiter, Richard histrionically struts as—what he in fact is—king.

At the beginning of the play Richard has to deal with a dangerous dispute between two noblemen. Bullingbrook accuses Mowbray of murdering the Duke of Gloucester. Mowbray was involved in the murder but cannot allude openly to the fact that King Richard himself had wanted Gloucester dead. Mowbray can claim truthfully that his hand did not actually kill the Duke, but he is in a difficult position because of the obligation to observe secrecy. As he proclaims his innocence to his accuser, he tries as it were to catch the King's eye and to apologize, preposterously enough, for not having moved more swiftly against Gloucester. Hence the curious, choking speech:

> For Gloucester's death,
> I slew him not, but to my own disgrace
> Neglected my sworn duty in that case.
>   (I.i.132–34)

How is the audience to understand this? There was an anonymous play, *Thomas of Woodstock*, that told the story of Gloucester's murder, and A. P. Rossiter thought that Shakespeare was relying on the fact that the audience had seen this recently,[1] but it is by no means clear that *Woodstock* was staged before *Richard II*. Mowbray's speech is best explained by the account given in Holinshed's Chronicles. There we are told that Richard secretly ordered the death of Gloucester and Mowbray temporized. But Shakespeare could not assume knowledge of Holinshed in his audience. There was no such thing as "program notes" in the Elizabethan theatre. In the following scene, however, Richard's complicity in the murder is made explicit. John of Gaunt says,

> God's is the quarrel, for God's substitute,
> His deputy appointed in His sight,
> Hath caus'd his death, the which if wrongfully,

Let heaven revenge, for I may never lift
An angry arm against His minister.
     (I.ii.37–41)

This, however, leaves us still with the question, "How did the audience understand Mowbray's earlier speech, *before* they had the information now provided by Gaunt?" It is likely that the first audience of the play, as it listened to Mowbray's contorted sentence, was sharp enough to see that something lay in the background, that Mowbray was for some reason unable to speak directly. No film of archaism was imposed for them, as it is for us, between thought and expression. Also, they were attuned, in a general way, to the manner in which significant political moves are made in a monarchy; the courtier rises by gambling; he guesses that the king (who cannot speak openly) desires that a certain thing be done, so the courtier does it, as a speculation; if the king is pleased, the courtier rises; if the king disowns the action, the courtier must remain silent. In the case of Gloucester's death, it turns out, Richard did rather more than express a vague wish. Perhaps, then, Shakespeare could trust his audience to keep the puzzle about Mowbray simmering at the back of the mind long enough for it to be resolved by Gaunt's explanation in the following scene.

We may remember *1 Henry VI*, in which we saw the medieval simplicity of embattled armies on either side of the stage played against an extraordinary intuition of latency and mystery at the level of causes. So here in Act I, Scene iii, Bullingbrook and Mowbray, horns locked, are medieval, about to fight to the death by the laws of chivalry. That makes the brightly painted surface of the play. What is latent, behind the surface, is the King's involvement. By the time we reach the actual trial by combat, Gaunt has enlightened the audience, but within the scene itself the explanation still cannot be spoken aloud. Silence on this point remains crucial. As soon as the latent dimension is admitted, however, chivalric conflict becomes a complex political problem, with implications. Richard rises to the public occasion. At the last moment he throws his warder down (I.iii.118). This stops the fight, and the King banishes both parties. It is done with flair, and it is easy to think that we are watching a politician of genius. He has defused the situation and got both of the dangerous antagonists out of the way. But flair is one thing, real political prudence another. Richard's performance is good theatre not just for us but for those watching within the play. As the scene unfolds, however, we sense a tremor in the governing hand (Richard's use of the phrase "with some unwillingness" at line 149 gives much away); the King first sentences Bullingbrook to ten years' banishment and then commutes it to six (I.iii.219–11). Mowbray is banished for life (I.iii.150–53). The cleansing symmetry of the

King's original action has now gone. The audience wonders why the King is being kinder to Bullingbrook than to Mowbray. To be sure, Bullingbrook is the accuser, Mowbray the accused, and it might seem reasonable to punish the accused more severely. At the same time Mowbray is technically innocent of a crime the King himself had ordered. We wonder if Mowbray has been sent away for life not because of his crime but because of what he might tell people. Also, although the main charges are laid by Bullingbrook against Mowbray, Mowbray accuses Bullingbrook of treachery to the King and prophecies, correctly, that the King will come to see that Bullingbrook is his enemy (I.iii.24, 205).

Here perhaps we move to a latency deeper still. If Bullingbrook knows how Gloucester died, his motives could be deep indeed and might include embarrassing the King. He gives no sign, however, of any such awareness. In terms of plot and known history he is in any case the real threat to Richard, and this makes him like the Duke of York, in relation to the King in *1 Henry VI*. Shakespeare's play about Henry VI is early, but Henry VI himself belongs of course to a later phase of English history. The analogy nevertheless holds: two unstable kings, each threatened. In *1 Henry VI* the House of Lancaster is threatened by the House of York on the ground of the frailty of the Lancastrian claim to the throne. In *Richard II* we are taken back to the time when that dubious Lancastrian grip on the throne was first obtained. Bullingbrook's father is John of Gaunt, Duke of Lancaster. As the drama proceeds Bullingbrook will demolish Richard. Yet he bears with him no discernable consciousness of any such overarching design. He moves one step at a time, each taken, apparently, for a small-scale reason, until he finds himself on a great, unstoppable slide into usurpation. Tania Demetriou said the origin of the Wars of the Roses was silence and that the conflict grew to a sudden violence through a series of trivial physical actions. Of course Bullingbrook could be a Machiavel, playing his cards close to his chest, knowing very well what he is about, but Shakespeare never presents him to us as a Machiavel. All the *consciousness* of revolution is on Richard's side. Bullingbrook seems merely to move, mutely, into spaces vacated for him, with bitterly ironic courtesy, by Richard. The aetiological silence of the rose-picking scene in *1 Henry VI* is in this play confined to Bullingbrook. He is a walking (fighting, killing) absence of motive—or seems so. Of course he is not literally silent. The part is one of the longer ones in Shakespeare. Bullingbrook has much to say, of a stolid, un-illuminating kind. Richard's part is longer, indeed, but number of words is not the point. Richard, in any case, says much more than Bullingbrook in the same number of lines. Those who believe that plain English is loaded with meaning while poetry is short on meaning may be surprised by this, for Bullingbrook's style is plain where Richard's is poetic. A moment's reflection should show, however, that the richly figurative character of poetic utterance allows simultaneous meaning—and that means more meaning in the same space. The obstinate nonappearance of any explanation, from Bullingbrook himself, of why he overturned the kingdom becomes palpable as the play develops.

Richard, meanwhile, is commonly seen as hopelessly detached from reality. As "the player king" he gives the court good theatre when what is required is good government. Yet it is Richard who sees the real meaning of Bullingbrook's return from banishment. "I just want my rights," says Bullingbrook, in effect (III.iii.112–16). "It means rebellion," says Richard. Richard is right, so does that make him the realist? No, because he remains detached from the truth he perceives. He knows everything about his situation except, somehow, the fact that it is actually happening. He responds to the crisis by suggesting a session of story-telling:

> For God's sake let us sit upon the ground
> And tell sad stories of the death of kings:
> How some have been depos'd, some slain in war,
> Some haunted by the ghosts they have deposed,
> Some poisoned by their wives, some sleeping kill'd,
> All murthered—for within the hollow crown
> That rounds the mortal temples of a king
> Keeps Death his court, and there the antic sits,
> Scoffing his state and grinning at his pomp,
> Allowing him a breath, a little scene,
> To monarchize, be fear'd, and kill with looks,
> Infusing him with self and vain conceit
> As if this flesh which walls about our life
> Were brass impregnable; and humour'd thus,
> Comes at the last and with a little pin
> Bores thorough his castle wall, and farewell king!
>   (III.ii.155–70)

The speech is simultaneously a truancy from crisis, a flight into legend and imagination, and an uncannily accurate perception of what is really coming. Richard, with disquieting, faintly schizophrenic gaiety, expatiates in what is technically known as the *de casibus* tradition, stories of the falls of princes as set out in the immensely popular *Mirror for Magistrates* (editions in 1555, 1559, 1563, 1574, 1575, 1578, 1587, and 1609). Richard turns his own imminent peril into a multiple narrative retrospect. Within the speech he even anticipates the analysis I have just offered and diagnoses his own theatricality, on the words "scene," "monarchize," and "conceit." This degree of awareness might seem to save him from the charge of escapist fantasy, but the relishing love of language betrayed in every line means that the speech comes over, finally, as a shimmering screen of painted images. Anyone who was there, listening to the King talking in this way, would be embarrassed, would smell hysteria, would *not* say, "This man has grip."

The aetiological silence and the roses taken as badges in *1 Henry VI* are rethought and redeployed in *Richard II*. The silence on the origin of the movement that would topple Henry becomes the reticence of Bullingbrook, who will topple Richard. The scarlet and white of the flowers picked in the Temple Garden turn into the garish bravura of Richard's language. In *1 Henry VI* the flowers crystallized the reasons for war. It may be that Richard's fertility in imagery crystallizes his own destruction. If Bullingbrook is from the start a Machiavel, this idea cannot stand. But, as we have seen, Shakespeare consistently refuses to present him in that way. If his motives are genuinely inchoate, the possibility arises that Richard is not just foreseeing his own destruction but may be contributing to it.

There is an old maxim of school-teachers: "Don't say 'Don't.'" Don't say, "Don't draw on the walls," to children who, until that moment, had never thought of doing so. Richard's seemingly extravagant speeches may reengage the real world by assuming a causal force. His escape from the immediate situation into vivid hypothesis can free the *behaviour* of a less imaginative, more practical listener. This once more is shrewd as historiography. Violent political movements grow not only with the adoption of badges of allegiance but also in response to beckoning images, especially when these are offered by the potential victim. Shakespeare is substituting a multilinear causation for the easier unilinear model. Using the unilinear model we would say, "Ambitious York collected supporters and took action accordingly." By the multilinear model we would say, "York began to move in a certain direction, and his supporters took fire and accelerated the process." In the multilinear version the supposedly passive context is allowed causal input.

Richard is therefore both a fantasist and a realist. Sometimes, indeed, one can begin to feel that he is not one man but two. For example, he is both an unpleasingly "modern" figure, tainted by dodgy financial schemes, and a sacral king, anointed by God, above the laws that bind his subjects, bearing the mystique of a hallowed past. When people remember the play after an interval of time, the sacral figure is usually dominant in their minds (this is partly because of the way the play ends). John of Gaunt's speech about "this other Eden" (II.i.40–66) is remembered as a celebration of Richard's England, as it was before the usurper brought in an age of grey *Realpolitik*. But most of the speech is not about the England of Richard. It is elegiac, saved from vulgar jingoism by its infinite sadness. Gaunt, a dying man, speaks of an England lost, as Eden was lost:

> This land of such dear souls, this dear dear land,
> Dear for her reputation through the world,
> Is now leas'd out—I die pronouncing it—
> Like to a tenement or pelting farm.
> England, bound in with the triumphant sea,
> Whose rocky shore beats back the envious siege
> Of wat'ry Neptune, is now bound in with shame,
> With inky blots and rotten parchment bonds.
>   (II.i.57–64)

Who has done this to England? The King. "Landlord of England art thou now, not king" (II.i.113). We are made to feel that the old aristocracy, men whose names are the names of English counties, are rooted in the earth. "Earth," used twice, and "plot" are key words in the speech. But the King is by contrast a modern figure, having to survive by "farming the realm" (I.iv.45), taking out leases, confiscating property. "Farming the realm" means granting certain areas to tax collectors who, on payment of a fee, are free to collect whatever they can get. It is as if the King's possession of all England is merely notional. Because the soil is divided among the barons he is forced to fund his lavish lifestyle by financial ingenuity. We seem to have in Richard a glowing retrospective ideal and a chilling forward-looking possibility. Gaunt is clear that the country he loves, the England that is like a moated manor house, has been destroyed by Richard. There is, however, a latent oddity in all of this.

It is commonly supposed that the further back one goes in time the more unconfined is the power of the ruler. In fact the sixteenth century, the century in which Shakespeare wrote *Richard II*, saw a remarkable shift *towards* monarchical absolutism. In the great medieval treatise of Henry de Bracton the king is under the law because the law makes him king.[2] Where Bracton backs the power of the king, he supports an executive rather than a legislative power (though there are places where Roman law breaks in with confusing effect). Thomas Aquinas is clear that the subject is not obliged to obey a wicked king. Indeed, such kings are tyrants and ought to be deposed (*Summa theologiae*, za 2ae, 60.5).[3] This conception of kingship is sustained in the sixteenth century by the profoundly traditional Richard Hooker: "Where the lawe doth give dominion, who doubteth that the King who receiveth it is under the lawe," and "The King is *major singulis universis minor*, greater than any but less than all."[4] The medieval poet William Langland says of the king,

"Might of the communes made hym to regne" (*Piers Plowman*, B Text, Prologue, 113). George Buchanan argued similarly in his *De jure regni* of 1571 for a form of monarchy in which kings could be legitimately deposed, but we are now in the sixteenth century; Buchanan's book was condemned by act of Parliament in 1584. Medieval theorists repeatedly asserted the priority of the people to the king. Of course, in practice medieval kings ordered everyone about. This is partly because no one had any idea how to set up a general election. Yet theoretically elective monarchies are common in the period, and there is often a rudimentary election, a throwing up of hats and cheering in the main square. In William Tyndale's *Obedience of a Christian Man* (1528) we suddenly hear a different voice: "The kinge is in this worlde without lawe and maye at his owne lust doo right and wronge and shall geve acomptes but to God only."[5] The idea took hold rapidly. *The Homilie against Disobedience and Wylful Rebellion* (1571?) requires unqualified submission by the subject to the prince, even if that prince be an evil tyrant, like Nero. Any rebel is worse, the Homilist observes, than the worst tyrant.[6]

Of course, as Hooker was Bractonian in the Renaissance, so there were medieval absolutists. Continental theories formed to protect the Holy Roman Empire from papal encroachment contain many pre-echoes of what became "the divine right of kings" in seventeenth-century England. The emperor Frederick II who so dazzled Dante was startlingly absolutist. But the general direction in the sixteenth century is towards rather than away from absolutism. The trend continued after Shakespeare's death until we reach the full divine right of kings promulgated by Charles I and the consequent explosion, the English Civil War.

So Richard's blazing claim to be, as God's anointed, above the petty rules and regulations that restrain his subjects ought to sound as "modern" as his queasy financial dealing.

> Not all the water in the rough rude sea
> Can wash the balm off from an anointed king;
> The breath of worldly men cannot depose
> The deputy elected by the Lord;
> For every man that Bullingbrook hath press'd
> To lift shrewd steel against our golden crown,
> God for his Richard hath in heavenly pay
> A glorious angel.
>   (III.ii.54–61)

This is the new doctrine, but it does not sound new. The speech is like a stained-glass window. Moreover Gaunt, who represents the old England against tax-raising Richard, backs the new absolutism when he says that he could never lift an angry arm against the Lord's anointed (I.ii.40–44).

There is, however, a tremor in the thought later. Gaunt says, "Thy state of law is bondslave to the law" (II.i.113). He means that Richard, properly above the law, has forfeited that status by his behaviour, has fallen from grace and is now as subject to rules and regulations as his meanest subjects. We are now very close indeed to the medieval doctrine that a tyrant need not be obeyed. But the words of Gaunt still suggest that absolutism is something immemorial, now suddenly threatened, rather than a novel idea. When Richard is speaking, his use of biblical imagery has the effect of a hallowing antiquity.

Is this a conjuring trick? Well, not exactly. To make matters still more complex it turns out that the real Richard II did claim to be above the law, back in the fourteenth century. Historians differ as to how far this was a curious anticipation of later events or how far it was a momentary rhetorical aberration (Richard posing as superman while continuing to operate within the existing legal arrangements, judges, parliaments, royal indentured servants, and so on—he never actually attempted to raise an unparliamentary tax). He is, interestingly, the first English king to require that he be addressed as "Your Majesty." One begins to wonder whether Shakespeare has brought off not so much a conjuring trick as a cunning coup on behalf of "the Tudor Myth" of absolutism. He has taken the disquieting novelty out of Tyndale's doctrine by successfully grounding it in a real medieval absolutist (or one plausibly presentable as such). This complex account assumes that Shakespeare knew that absolutism was a novel doctrine rather than immemorial orthodoxy. Is it not possible, however, that Shakespeare simply believed in the doctrine of sacred supra-legal monarchy and was completely unaware that it was not the usual medieval view? This line is a little like the view that the Reformation fails to register in the comedies because Shakespeare was so innocent as to be unaware that it had actually happened.

In fact, neither view is tenable. Even if Shakespeare had somehow remained unaware of the movement in political theory, he certainly read Holinshed with close attention. Holinshed gives a vivid picture not only of the appalling behaviour of the king but also of what counted most heavily against him when his record was scrutinized. Holinshed quotes from the articles of deposition, where much is made of the fact that Richard had said that the laws of the realm were in his head (and sometimes "in his breast"). This is described as a "fantastical opinion."[7] After Shakespeare has put his Holinshed to one side and returned to his manuscript, he makes others apart from Richard support the idea of a sacred, legally untouchable king (Gaunt at I.ii.37–41, York at III.iii.9). This does look, so far, like an attempt to doctor history in the interests of the Tudors. Queen Elizabeth, we may think, could hardly have had a better or more obsequious spin doctor. Oddly enough, we have a glimpse of what the queen thought in the story of the courtier William Lambarde. On an August day in 1601 Lambarde was going through miscellaneous records with the queen when they came to the reign of Richard II. The queen said, enigmatically, "I am Richard II, know ye not that?" Lambarde's mind flew at once to the Essex rebellion against Elizabeth's authority. Elizabeth then spoke of Shakespeare's "tragedie, played forty times in open streets and houses."[8] As we read these words the political import of Shakespeare's play flips inside out. Elizabeth, it seems, was far from seeing the play as astute propaganda on behalf of the Tudors. She sees a play that shows that a monarch can be deposed, predictably used by subversives. At last we notice what Shakespeare's contemporaries would surely have seen at once. This God-defended king who calls on angels to beat back the soldiers of Bullingbrook finds in the event that the angels cannot help him. The deposition scene was cut by the censor from early quarto editions of the play because of its dangerous audacity. In 1601 Robert Devereux, the second Earl of Essex, commissioned a revival of what, almost certainly, was Shakespeare's *Richard II*, to be performed the day before he led an uprising against the queen.[9]

Richard's notion of undefeatable angels is indeed a primitive, magical version of absolutism. He is a little like the Lady's brother in Milton's *A Masque* who held that chastity was an armour of complete steel, so that no chaste girl could ever in fact be raped (line 421). We all know that this is false. Since Richard gave us the long account of princes who were successfully removed, we may surmise that he actually knew the angels weren't a safe bet. If we suppose the power of the king to be divinely given *de jure* rather than *de facto*, we find as we shift to the ideal realm that kingship is after all genuinely indestructible. If the present incumbent is struck down, the power simply slides to the next in line, according to the rules of inheritance.

Shakespeare has made the frailty of anointed kings, on the ground, vivid for all to see. So is Shakespeare after all covertly satirizing the Tudor myth? I think not. Two stories run concurrently in *Richard II*. There is a supernatural story of a divinely ordained line, broken by the deposition of Richard (not righted until after the death of Richard III). This is the Tudor myth of Edward Hall's Chronicle and E. M. W. Tillyard's *Shakespeare's History Plays*. That story is clearly there, un-satirized, in the drama. Then there is a naturalist story of a clever but not entirely competent wheeler-dealer, an immoral king in difficulties, who is plainly finding psychological refuge in the sacral role he has inherited. At this level we feel the unreality of the image more than we feel its truth. A play univocally committed to presenting the Tudor myth with maximum power would have shown us a gravely dignified, suffering king (think how royalist writers presented Charles I after his death). But everyone knows that Richard is somehow fooling around; everyone feels that he should take a deep breath and calm down. Richard compares himself with Christ ("Some of you, with Pilate, wash your hands," IV.i.239), but few are less Christ-like than he. Christ loved the world; Richard loves Richard. Have we not heard those words before?[10] We receive the impression of a deep instability, a man with ideals but no convictions, a walking congeries of images, poses, pretences, who, because he is intelligent, ironically perceives what is afoot, but from the side, in narrative profile. This contemplative observer is really at the heart of the action, is its sacrificial victim.

Richard, then, is a complex figure. His self-consciousness leads him into convulsive introspection, and introspection as we saw leads to a splitting of identity. This division creates in its turn a wholly internal field of conflicting forces. We saw how Richard III, left alone, became two, "I and I" (V.iii.183, Quarto). Shakespeare now pushes the idea further, joining it to his first essay on comedic identity in *A Comedy of Errors*. There nature divided herself, producing, in the two sets of twins, objective mirror images. In the happy story of that play the mirroring twins, united at the end, heal the wound of lost identity imagined by Antipholus of Syracuse as water lost in water. If any one had said to Richard before his deposition, "Who are you?" he would have answered, "I am the king." Stripped by Bullingbrook of his social, relational identity he is, like Richard III, thrown back upon himself and now, like Antipholus, seeks his mirror image. In the middle of the deposition scene he abruptly calls for a glass:

> Give me that glass, and therein will I read.
> No deeper wrinkles yet? Hath sorrow struck
> So many blows upon this face of mine,
> And made no deeper wounds? O flatt'ring glass,
> Like to my followers in prosperity,
> Thou dost beguile me! Was this face the face
> That every day under his household roof
> Did keep ten thousand men? Was this the face
> That like the sun, did make beholders wink?
> Is this the face which fac'd so many follies,
> That was at last out-fac'd by Bullingbrook?
> A brittle glory shineth in this face,
> As brittle as the glory is the face,
>   [*Dashes the glass against the ground.*]
> For there it is, crack'd in a hundred shivers.
> Mark, silent king, the moral of this sport,
> How soon my sorrow hath destroy'd my face.
>   (IV.i.276–91)

Richard needs to double himself, as was done so happily at the level of plot in *The Comedy of Errors*, in order to see himself. Or rather, to watch himself. For Richard is enjoying this.

What is happening here is a profound shift in the scope of drama, nothing less than the discovery of human interiority. It happened before, but only once, in the oddly separate history of Greek drama. Euripides' Hippolytus is strangely like Shakespeare's Richard, excitable, narcissistic, doomed. Near the end Euripides gives his protagonist an enigmatic speech (I will translate the Greek as literally as English will bear): "Would it were possible for me, having stood opposite myself, to look at myself, at the evils we are suffering" (1078–79). Hippolytus and Richard both wish to look at themselves and, simultaneously, to watch a great show. In Richard's speech the word "face" recurs with great power. The repeated "Was this ... ?" must carry a memory of Marlowe's *Doctor Faustus*: "Was this the face that launch'd a thousand ships / And burnt the topless towers of Ilium?" (1604, V.i.91–92), with its burden, the heart-wrenching beauty of Helen, catastrophic destruction, falling towers, Troy in flames. "Face" as Richard uses it is emblematic of the sacral king, but at the same time it suggests "surface," or even "mask." The King, whose fertility in imagery may have accelerated the usurpation, now conducts what Walter Pater rightly saw as an inverted coronation ceremony.[11] Bullingbrook, who in the chronicles overthrew Richard by violence, is here strangely passive, the "silent king." Richard is in charge: "mark me how I will undo myself" (IV.i.203).

When Richard looks in the glass, his first reaction is disappointment: "No deeper wrinkles yet?" In the middle of his splendid tragedy he wishes to check on the appearance of the protagonist and finds, instead of the required countenance ravaged by suffering, a perfectly healthy, youthful face. He smashes the incompetent image in a fit of pique bordering on hysteria. With part of his mind he may even know that the situation could be seen as funny. He turns to Bullingbrook and, with his usual facility in imaginative anticipation (for Bullingbrook has not yet ascended the throne), addresses him as "silent *king*." "Mark," he says, "how soon my sorrow hath destroy'd my face." Bullingbrook answers sturdily, "The shadow of your sorrow hath destroy'd / The shadow of your face" (IV.i.291–92). It is the answer of a literalist whose patience is wearing thin. Bullingbrook means, "*Of course* sorrow hasn't destroyed your face! What lies broken on the ground is a mere image, and your 'sorrow' too is play-acting." This sounds like good sense. But Richard is not silenced:

> Say that again.
> The shadow of my sorrow! Ha, let's see.
> 'Tis very true, my grief lies all within.
> (IV.i.293–95)

"Say that again" is aesthetically appreciative. But Richard knocks back the charge that his grief is outward posturing by first accepting it and then denying the implication. He has been posturing, he grants, but meanwhile the true grief is there, tongueless, within him. He has been acting, as if it were a fiction, the person he really is. Bullingbrook, the supposed realist of the pair, is disabled by a kind of tunnel vision. He speaks as if Richard were exaggerating, as if nothing terrible were happening. But a great objective tragedy is going forward before our eyes. A king is being cast down from his throne. The fancy figurative language of Richard is more *accurate* than the plain language of the usurper.

Shakespeare's mind refuses rest. Having broken through to the notion that introspection in so far as it entails an observer and an observed requires the generation of a second self, he goes on to ask what is involved in this generation. In the background, always, stands Ovid's Narcissus, who saw himself in a pool and fell hopelessly in love with what he saw. Richard III is anti-Ovidian; he, as ugly as Narcissus was beautiful, immediately detests the self he tries to love. Richard II is closer to Ovid's myth. He loves his own face; that is why he uses the word so often. But at this point in the action "face" carries the further meaning "sacral king," and he is thrown by the fact that the "observed self," the face seen in the glass, fails to match the idea of royalty disfigured that has been forming in his imagination. The suggestion is planted that all introspection, because it has to rely on an imagined second self, is systematically imperfect, unreliable. Yet rich interiority of character is dependent on introspection.

To this point in the action the play has been all about the simultaneity of fictive irresponsibility, practical insight, and causal efficacy in Richard. These tensions are given a special force by the prior existence of what E. H. Kantorowicz called "the King's two bodies," the king's physical body as a man and his office as king.[12] After the stripping away of his public identity Richard's verbal behaviour changes. The Richard we see awaiting death in prison is another man in more ways than one. He no longer pirouettes as he did when he had the court for his audience. He always knew that he was playing but somehow could not stop—another case of the spinning wheel that the mind's eye is powerless to arrest. But now the wheel has ceased to turn, apparently of its own accord. He looks steadily at the sad, histrionic sequence through which he has passed:

Thus play I in one person many people,
And none contented. Sometimes am I king;
Then treasons make me wish myself a beggar,
And so I am. Then crushing penury

> Persuades me I was better when a king;
> Then am I king'd again, and by and by
> Think that I am unking'd by Bullingbrook,
> And straight am nothing. But what e'er I be,
> Nor I, nor any man that but man is,
> With nothing shall be pleas'd, till he be eas'd
> With being nothing.
>   (V.v.31–41)

The stories multiply and nest one within another. The reversion to being king after his time as a beggar precedes the "unkinging" at the hands of Bullingbrook, as if the deposition were just another pretence. It is here, however, that the catalogue of fantasies passes into real history—but with no mark of discontinuity. "*Think* that I am unking'd" catches exactly the way it all was for Richard at the time; it felt like a dream; actuality still eluded his grasp, even as he was being, actually, overthrown. But Richard pauses abruptly after the confident phrase, "straight am nothing." This is still the easy hyperbole of what I have called the pirouetting style. It is also in the present tense and announces non-existence. The hyperbole is shrill, uncomfortable. So far the Richard we have come to know is still there. When he continues, however, the voice is suddenly quite different, graver, all trace of lingering hysteria now gone.

> Nor I, nor any man that but man is,
> With nothing shall be pleas'd till he be eas'd
> With being nothing.

The nervous tic of stylistic ingenuity (remember Berowne in *Love's Labour's Lost*) is still there in the chiming of "pleas'd" and "eas'd," but the thought is suddenly straight and serious. Richard has disengaged himself from the figurative phantasmagoria in which he has been trapped. He means, "I, like other human beings, can never rest until I am *really* nothing, that is, dead." Richard has found his "core identity": a sentient, thinking physical body, and it is entirely different from the "selves" conjured in play-acting or by self-projective introspection.

It is in this scene that Shakespeare turns his protagonist from player-king to poet-king:

> I have been studying how I may compare
> This prison where I live unto the world;
> And for because the world is populous,

And here is not a creature but myself,
I cannot do it.
    (V.v.1–5)

He is reacting to the falling away of that scaffolding of relation and comparison that enables us in normal circumstances to know who we are, what is what. At the same time he is discovering a central identity.

We have been concerned so far with various models of non-linear causation. First we saw how an irrationally expanding circumambient excitement moved the Wars of the Roses from possibility to actuality. Then, in *Richard II*, garishly coloured imagery of sacral majesty and fallen kings created a field of momentum *around* the taciturn rebel, Bullingbrook (again suggesting that context may be more causally potent than we normally assume). Finally, the question, "Who is Richard?" seems best answered, for long stretches of the play, by "He is the image he creates; he fashions himself in his creative performance." This answer is philosophically congenial to twentieth-century thought and is perhaps still seductive. The Existentialists argued that we play the parts by which we are known in the world and the Structuralists delighted in resolving identity into relation. But Shakespeare will not rest in these thoughts. He will never say, "And that is that."

There is perhaps a fault in *Richard II*. It is hard to reconcile the cold, greedy, *thin* personality that says, before visiting the dying Gaunt, "Pray God we may make haste and come too late!" (I.iv.64) with the figure who dies so bravely at the end. It may be said that this is the live, developing characterization for which Shakespeare is famous; Richard has grown up, matured to the point of full *anagnorisis*, in the sense in which that term applies to Sophocles' Oedipus, self-understanding. Perhaps the trauma of usurpation is itself enough to account for the change. But we do not see enough of the transition. The movement at the end is so profound that it engages the audience entirely. We have no mental leisure to wonder any more how such a thing could happen. Suddenly we love Richard. But I am not sure that we should.

Invisible Acting: *Henry IV*, Parts 1 and 2, *Henry V*
We all think of Richard II as a brilliant actor, and this seems to be in line with the way he speaks of himself. But Shakespeare also shows us Richard through another person's eyes, where, curiously, he appears as a bad actor. York, describing the triumphal entry into London of Bullingbrook, says that Richard in comparison with Henry Bullingbrook seemed like an inept player who somehow manages to lose the audience as soon as he steps on stage:

As in a theatre the eyes of men,
After a well-grac'd actor leaves the stage,
Are idly bent on him that enters next,
Thinking his prattle to be tedious,
Even so, or with much more contempt, men's eyes
Did scowl on gentle Richard.
(V.ii.23–28)

Teachers of literature who have been instructing their pupils that Richard is the dazzler, Bullingbrook the dull dog, tend to avert their eyes from this passage. For York, Bullingbrook with his warm "I thank you, countrymen," is the skilled performer, Richard the unskilled. Doubts about the quality of Richard's acting may have been sown earlier. "Over the top," "camping it up," and "ham" are terms of abuse, and they all apply to Richard well before the fifth act.

Setting aside Bullingbrook, is there another player-king in Shakespeare who is truly "well-grac'd"? There is, and his name is Henry V. Henry V appears in the two parts of *Henry IV* as Prince Hal. Hal, no less than Richard, is engaged in systematic pretence, but where Richard's style is high-fantastical, Hal's is naturalistic. Hal plays the good fellow, the boon companion, the pub regular, warm-hearted, spontaneous, never standoffish. I have said that we should set aside Bullingbrook, but it may be that in making Bullingbrook the good actor in York's speech Shakespeare was preparing the way for the great study of invisible acting that was to follow in *1* and *2 Henry IV* and *Henry V*. Bullingbrook's matey, notably un-Ricardian way of addressing his subjects as "countrymen" is not simple reality succeeding false pretence; it is itself a style. Mark Antony, the supreme Shakespearean orator, addresses the Roman citizens as "countrymen" in the speech he delivers over the body of the slain Caesar (*Julius Caesar*, III.ii.13, 73).

Our own age has a taste for formalism and likes to credit earlier artistically successful periods with similar tastes. The Elizabethans, we are told, loved rhetoric, exalted lyricism, schematic images, vivid histrionics. The truth is that rhetoricians long before Shakespeare discovered the efficacy of antirhetorical rhetoric. Mark Antony says, "I am no orator, as Brutus is" (III. ii.217). The notion that *ars est celare artem*, "art lies in concealing art," predates Shakespeare by many centuries.[13] The end of *Richard II* caused Shakespeare's mind to swing back from "outside-in" versions of causation to the idea of a surviving core self. This then operates as the central engine of *1* and *2 Henry IV* and *Henry V*. I refer now not to the civil wars of Henry IV's reign but to the inexorable rise from humiliation to glory of Prince Hal. The structure, terminating in *Henry V*, is comedic, not tragic. It has a happy ending. Hal's artful performance does not precipitate events inadvertently in the manner of the over-imaginative Richard, because Hal is completely in charge. The key fact about Hal is that this jovial drinking companion is utterly isolated. But isolation in Hal's case does not lead to introspection and doubling of identity as it did with Richard III and Richard II. It issues at once in action. It is as if (perhaps because of the dubiety of his father's claim to the throne) Hal dare not ask, "Who am I?" What dominates his mind is self-dedication, to maintaining the crown and the kingdom.

In the service of this good end he is a kind of Machiavel.[14] W. H. Auden was the first to notice how in soliloquy he can sound like Iago.[15] Although the dramatic conception of *invisible* rhetorical or histrionic potency begins with Bullingbrook and may seem naturally to imply Machiavellian cunning, I do not believe that Bullingbrook is a Machiavel. We wonder at times if his rise to power was planned in detail from the beginning, but the dominant impression remains one of unarticulated motive (Richard does all the articulation). But the slow rise of Prince Hal clearly is planned from the start. The idea of the invisible actor is now not emergent but fully formed. A mode of Machiavellianism—"white Machiavellianism"—is explicitly entailed. Certainly in his isolation he needs a usable image, but the image he builds is entirely subservient to the plan of gradual but surprising domination. It is utterly practical, and because this player-king produces major effects by design, not accident, he actually is a *central*, unified cause. He, not a fortuitous combination of circumstances, recovers England's greatness. This means that we are now leaving the philosophy I described as congenial to the present age. For Shakespeare the dissolution of central agency into a nexus of relations is an early phase only. In suddenly heading due north, for central substance, he is not in fact contradicting himself. In *1 Henry VI* he never came near to saying anything so metaphysically absolute—so foolish—as "There is no core self." Instead, more modestly, less vulnerably, he says, "Historical causation *can be*" (not "is always") "contextually driven."

We know that Hal is acting because of the important soliloquy placed very near the beginning of the play, in which he takes a long look at the jovial company of the Boar's Head:

> I know you all and will a while uphold
> The unyok'd humor of your idleness,
> Yet herein will I imitate the sun,
> Who doth permit the base contagious clouds
> To smother up his beauty from the world,

That when he please again to be himself,
Being wanted, he may be more wonder'd at
By breaking through the foul and ugly mists
Of vapors that did seem to strangle him.

So when this loose behaviour I throw off
And pay the debt I never promised,
By how much better than my word I am,
By so much shall I falsify men's hopes,
And like bright metal on a sullen ground,
My reformation, glitt'ring o'er my fault,
Shall show more goodly and attract more eyes
Than that which hath no foil to set it off.
I'll so offend, to make offense a skill,
Redeeming time when men think least I will.
    (I.ii.195–203, 208–17)

It was once fashionable to argue that this speech tells us nothing about the Prince's character, that it is simply a program note, transposed to the stage, pure information, to allay anxiety in the audience: "The Prince is keeping dubious company but—don't worry—later he will change and amaze everyone." This reading founders on the little words "that" and "to" in lines 200 and 216. These words connote conscious purpose. Even if we stick to the "program note" reading and insist that the speech is pure information, the information includes the fact that the whole sequence is deliberately designed by Hal. The note does not read, "The Prince will change." It reads, "He knows what he's doing; he's using this phase in his career as the base for a surprise initiative, later." It follows that in so far as the Prince leads Falstaff and the rest to believe that he loves them for themselves alone he is deceiving them by a performance.

Everyone is faintly shocked by the coldness of the speech—even, I suspect, those very Elizabethans who, with another part of their minds, were eager to be assured that the Prince was no low-lifer. The sentimentalist is not pleased by the speech. But, we may think for a moment, Machiavelli might not have been too pleased either, from an opposite perspective; the scheme looks crazy if considered as practical politics. Can one really found a successful political career on a carefully contrived early reputation for drinking and keeping wild company followed by sudden seriousness? Surely the plan could easily misfire? It may be that this doubt is conditioned by the democratic conventions of the twenty-first century. If Hal knew that he would have to seek election later he would perhaps be less inclined to burn so many boats ahead of time. But he can be confident, as the heir apparent, that all eyes will be on him and no one else at the moment of transformation. Indeed I was wrong to suggest that Machiavelli would scorn the plan. The idea is Machiavellian—quite literally. The Italian theorist devotes a whole chapter of the *Discorsi* to the proposition "that it is a Very Good Notion at times to pretend to be a Fool," and backs it up with the example of the Roman Junius Brutus.[16] At the same time the scheme Hal sets out smells strongly of the theatre. The muffled figure who suddenly unmasks is immediately familiar to playgoers.

When I say that Hal's friendship with Falstaff and the rest is a pretence, I do not wish to insist that he has no affection at all for the fat knight. Hal's stratagem involves naturalistic acting, and naturalistic actors are often "method actors." That is to say, they work by inducing or finding real emotions in themselves and building on these. I would go so far as to say that Hal is naturally convivial, humorous, and playful. He will, after all, become "the king with the common touch," though that phrase will remind us of the political usefulness of such a character. When Hal thinks that Falstaff is dead on the field of Shrewsbury he says, "I could have better spar'd a better man" (*1 Henry IV*, V.iv.104). This is to confess ethical division. He loves Falstaff better than he should. But the tone still conveys cold separation more vividly than it conveys love. In the famous rejection of Falstaff—the moment when the sun appears from behind the clouds—Hal, now King Henry, momentarily slips back into the old ragging on the line, "know the grave doth gape / For thee thrice wider than for other men" (*2 Henry IV*, V.v.53–54). We know that Falstaff spots the crack in the new royal façade (jokes on Falstaff's fatness came thick and fast in the good old times) and that his eye brightens, by the next words of the King: "Reply not to me with a fool-born jest, / Presume not that I am the thing I was" (V.v.55–56). The King slaps down Falstaff, but at the same time he is slapping down something in himself. When at the end of the speech the King rules that Falstaff is not to come within ten miles of his person, we sense that he *fears* the attraction of Falstaff, a truly cold manipulator would not need to make any such provision, would simply forget Falstaff at this point. Despite these moments, the speech of rejection rolls forward unstoppably. It breaks Falstaff's heart and does the trick, politically. We hate Henry as we watch, but then we have to think, if we are English, "He is doing this for us."

Prince Hal knows from the first that he has an enormous responsibility and a very difficult job to do. If he fails, thousands of his subjects, people he will never meet, does not know, will suffer horribly. Civil war, in which father kills son, brother brother, is the worst thing of all. We have already seen how Henry VI, Hal's successor in the tainted Lancastrian line, was unable to prevent these horrors. Although *Richard II*, *1* and *2 Henry IV*, and *Henry V* do not really form a tetralogy (a single work of art having four parts) as the Oresteian plays of Aeschylus form a trilogy, they are nevertheless closely linked. It may be that *1* and *2 Henry IV* can properly be termed a "dylogy," if that is the right word. Moreover, Prince Hal at the beginning of *1 Henry IV* is the man we see later, older and somewhat changed, at the end of *Henry V.*

Here we find him proposing marriage to the French Princess. He is still acting, naturalistically, brilliantly. The tone, as we have learned to expect, is jolly. "Here am I, a simple chap," he seems to say, "How about it?" By happy accident the Princess has the same name as the lady in *The Taming of the Shrew*, Katherine, so that Henry can sound, as he modulates from the formal version of her name; like a gentler, sweeter Petruchio: "Do you like me, Kate?" (*Henry V*, V.ii.107). This is followed by a long, immensely persuasive speech by Henry (V.ii.132–68) all about his being no good at smooth talking, more familiar with boxing and horses than with courtly ways but straight as a die—"a plain soldier." Just before the end Henry half-discloses the subtext: "Take a soldier; take a soldier, take a king." Katherine instantly picks up on the word "king" and shatters the atmosphere: "Is it possible dat I sould love de ennemie of France?" (V.ii.169–70). The agreeable oaf addressing her has just altered the disposition of whole kingdoms by slaughtering thousands of her countrymen on the field of Agincourt. These two have never met before. Henry has not fallen in love with Katherine. He is working, as hard as he can, to put together a political alliance. Again, we have to say, his motive is good. It is time to make friends with France. He does an excellent job. If, wildly, we imagine Shakespeare, long before he has put pen to paper, auditioning actors and being confronted by Richard II and Henry V, both hungry for work, one can perhaps begin to see how Henry would get the part (if, that is, the part required conviction—but most parts do). Henry wooing the French Princess is so convincing that we do not notice that he is acting. But he must be.

In the two parts of *Henry IV* the rising star of Prince Hal is played against the setting star of Falstaff. I wrote about Falstaff more than twenty years ago in *A New Mimesis* and think now as I thought then. Falstaff is an astonishing compound of gargantuan appetite (for drink, not food) and sharp intelligence. His love for Hal is deep, his selfishness complete. He can be childlike: "I would 'twere bed-time, Hal, and all well" (*1 Henry IV*, V.i.125). He dies smiling on his finger's end like a baby (*Henry V*, II.iii.15) and tells us how he "was born about three of the clock in the afternoon, with a white head and something a round belly" (*2 Henry IV*, I.ii.187–88), which is pretty much how he looks now. "Something" is a stroke of genius: "Not really *fat* you understand." He is given lyrically beautiful English linking him to saints' days and King Arthur (*2 Henry IV*, II.iv.33, III.ii.280–81). He is the old England.

Shakespeare changed his name to Falstaff from Oldcastle, and the original Oldcastle was a Lollard, a sort of pre-Reformation Protestant. I see no trace of Protestantism in the figure we have in the plays. Tom McAlindon has accurately picked up Puritan expressions used by Falstaff but has in my opinion misunderstood their tone and paid too little heed to context.[17] McAlindon suggests that Falstaff is presented by Shakespeare as a Puritan hypocrite, exposed as a coward when the fighting begins. When Falstaff says, "Would I were a weaver, I could sing psalms" (*1 Henry IV*, II.iv.133), Shakespeare counts on his audience knowing that many East Anglian weavers were Protestant refugees from Holland, but the humour turns on the unbridgeable distance between Falstaff and any such persons. Falstaff certainly uses the language of Puritan preachers (for example, "Pharaoh's lean kine," *1 Henry IV*, II.iv.473), but he does so because he thinks it is funny, much as a consciously low-minded, reactionary humorist might use "politically correct" language today. And it is a coarse criticism that is content to say, without qualification, that Falstaff is exposed as a hypocritical coward. Of course he is "found out" when he boasts about fighting off enormous odds in the Gadshill episode, but the "finding out" does not matter. When the Prince explains that he was there and that he and Poins were the only adversaries Falstaff had to face, Falstaff happily wriggles free at once with the brilliant "Was it for me to kill the heir-apparent?" (*1 Henry IV*, II.iv.268–69). Some even think that the entire "finding out" was planned by Falstaff. This claim is based on the fact that in *2 Henry IV* Hal says to Falstaff, "You knew me, as you did when you ran away by Gadshill" (II.iv.306–7). But the Prince is probably speaking sarcastically, remembering Falstaff's bare-faced "By the Lord, I knew ye as well as he that made ye" at *1 Henry IV*, II.iv.267–68. What is clear is that Falstaff thrives on such moments. True hypocrites never enjoy being unmasked. As Maurice Morgann saw 250 years ago,[18] the stage direction at the crisis of the Gadshill episode is all-important. It reads, "As they are sharing, the Prince and Poins set upon them; they all run away, and Falstaff, after a blow or two, runs away too, leaving the booty behind them." Falstaff is differentiated from Bardolph and Peto by the words, "after a blow or two." It is enough to show that he is not the simple comedy coward too many take him for. The others instantly panic; Falstaff, redeemed as always by intelligence, takes a second to make sure that he can't win and *then* runs. To be sure he is no warrior. We may laugh at him because he is physically unfit, but he is himself quite aware that he is too fat to fight. Our primitive derision is defused and changed by the anticipatory intelligence of the "butt."

In fact Falstaff is the first person we meet in Shakespeare to have a "philosophy" in the technical sense of the word. He explains it in his speech on honour:

Can honor set to a leg? No. Or an arm? No. Or take away the grief
of a wound? No. Honor hath no skill in surgery then? No. What is
honor? A word. What is in that word honor? What is that honor?
Air. A trim reckoning! Who hath it? He that died a' Wednesday.
Doth he feel it? No. 'Tis insensible then? Yea, to the dead. But
will't not live with the living? No. Why? Detraction will not suffer
it. Therefore I'll none of it, honor is a mere scutcheon. So ends my
catechism. (*1 Henry IV*, V.i.131–41)

Medieval philosophy saw a debate between two parties, the Realists and
the Nominalists. "Realist" has a technical sense that can surprise modern
readers. The Realists believed that universal terms such as "beauty" refer to
something that exists in its own right. They are a little like Platonists. The
Nominalists on the contrary held that only particulars exist; there may be
beautiful things, but there is no such thing as beauty, existing separately
from those things. This, note, is the philosophy I thought I could detect
behind current Historicist criticism.[19] Nominalism can be traced back to
the ninth century A.D., to Eric of Auxerre. Falstaff shows himself to be a
card-carrying Nominalist when he uses the word "air" ("What is that honor?
Air"). The idea that universals were mere words and those words, in their
turn, mere breath, *flatus vocis*,[20] became a commonplace of Nominalism.
The word "air," with the same hidden Nominalist force, gets into Duke
Theseus's speech about the lunatic, the lover, and the poet in *A Midsummer
Night's Dream* (V.i.7–22). Imagination, he says, "gives to *aery* nothing / A
local habitation and a name," and adds that the poet cannot think of joy, say,
without turning it into a concrete "bringer of that joy." Theseus, the materialist, does not rejoice at this materializing tendency in poetry, because of its
lawless misapplication of terms. Clearly, he says, abstractions like "joy" are
airy nothings, *flatus vocis*, and only confusion can result if we pretend that
they are things.

It is a perfectly proper exercise of hindsight to see in Nominalism the
seed-bed of modern scientific materialism. There is a line that runs from William of Ockham through the materialist philosophy of Thomas Hobbes to
the scientific revolution. Moreover, scepticism about universals has a political
dimension. The communist inhabitants of Thomas More's Utopia are unre-
flective Nominalists who can make no sense of "humanity" but agree at once
that there are human beings.[21] For many years this gambit was the rhetorical
property of the radical left. Then Margaret Thatcher dished the Labour Party
(making *them* appear old-fashioned) by stealing the gambit; she declared that
there was "no society," only people (but she recanted later). In general the
Nominalist line is felt as a threat to the high-minded ethical—sometimes as

revolutionary. Falstaff, though he may be termed a communist in so far as he has absolutely no sense of the sanctity of private property, is no revolutionary. The real revolutionary of the play is Prince Hal, and his revolution is as invisible as his acting.

The Prince's real revolution is not his switch from wild young man to ruler but his turning inside out of English history. The transformation of Hal is indeed made very visible in the play, but at the same time Shakespeare teaches us, gently, that there may never have been any change at all in Hal himself. Hal was never a wild young man. That was all part of the act! Inheriting a throne tainted by his father's act of usurpation, he redirects the aggression of his countrymen from baronial in-fighting to a consolidated assault on a foreign power, France, thereby achieving glory. This is radical. Henry IV thought he would perish in Jerusalem but died instead in the Jerusalem chamber, on his native soil, never winning through to the great imagined crusade. His son never got to Jerusalem either, but he contrives the true simulacrum of a crusade in the defeat of France.

It is sometimes said that political leaders require a "demonised Other" to retain control of their citizens. If the people are to be ruled they must first be scared. This is very nearly the situation at the beginning of *Henry V*. The King desperately needs a war with France if he is to control such as Scroop and Grey. So far, so cynical. Richard II lost control of Mowbray and Bullingbrook; Henry VI will lose control of Yorkist and Lancastrian nobles. If civil war really is the worst thing of all, and if picking a fight with France is the only way to avoid civil war, we may have moved from cynical power politics to an obscure, unlovable duty. Even so, however, Henry will not move until it is clear that his claim on France is legally well founded.

The long scene near the beginning of *Henry V* (I. ii) in which the Archbishop of Canterbury sets out the case in tedious detail is often misunderstood. Directors, embarrassed by the grinding technicalities, often tell the actor to play it for laughs—"If you're going to bore them, play it *as* a comic bore—then it will look as if you did it all on purpose." The trouble with this line is that it is the result of tunnel vision. It is always important to attend to everyone present in a Shakespearean scene, not just to the person who happens to be speaking. It is very probable that most of those on stage are bored by the Archbishop's speech, but there is one exception. Henry is on the edge of his seat as he listens. This is enough to impart a strand of latent excitement to the scene by way of group dynamics. The good director will not need to invent a comic apology for the Archbishop if he makes sure that the audience is simultaneously aware, throughout, of Henry's tense figure. The tension is itself morally complex. At one level he is straining at the leash to go to war (for an ethical reason, to bind up the wounds of England); at another he is genuinely constrained by the sense that he must show a true *casus belli*. When Henry, close to desperation, says, "May I with right and conscience make this claim?" (I.ii.96), many today hear only the contained aggression, but "right" and "conscience" are serious words. The King cannot move if he does not receive an affirmative answer.

The ethical drama is intense. The scene in which Henry listens to the legal justification of his act of war is preceded by a scene in which the church-men—the party that will lay on the required justification—are shown talk-ing in private. It is made clear that they have an interest in coming up with what, they know, the King wants. They are threatened by a bill that would deprive them of the income from temporal lands donated by devout benefac-tors; if they give the desired legal advice, the effect of the bill may be softened. Shakespeare has planted a presumption of doubt, ahead of the big speech of justification—the speech Henry is relieved to accept. The legal justification they provide could still be good; we just don't know. Similarly, we do not know whether the King has actually promised money if they say what he needs or whether they are simply counting on a reward, given afterwards, more inno-cently, by a grateful sovereign. The first alternative—that Henry has bought the justification he needs, will, I suppose, be absolutely unacceptable to most twenty-first-century persons. Yet even this might itself be ethically justified, for Shakespeare, by the good gained, the averting of (a far worse) civil war. But the way Act I, Scene ii, is written suggests that the King is not so far the "white Machiavel" that he would go to war without real legal grounds. As the elaborate justification is expounded there is no sign that the King is anxious to rush the business through. Rather he is simply anxious that it be clear that there is a legal case. The King has indeed made the claim before consulting the Archbishop, but, manifestly, he makes it clear that the ruling is just that, a pronouncement by which he will be bound. Far more disquieting is the behaviour that follows. Once the war machine is in motion it is obvious that Henry will do nothing to arrest it. The incident of the Dolphin's (Dauphin's) insult, the present of tennis balls (I.ii.258), is joyfully seized, as if it were a *casus belli* in itself. In Act II, Scene iv, we see the King of France shaken by the approach of the English and apparently ready to negotiate. After Henry's demands have been communicated to him, he asks for time (II.iv.140). We are told by the Chorus that opens Act III that the King of France has offered Henry his daughter's hand in marriage and certain territories (but apparently less than Henry demanded). Henry's army rolls forward, and the French King is forced, it might be said, into a posture of defiance. The scene of justification is indeed the place in the play where the modern audience is alienated from Henry. Certainly, Shakespeare has laced this scene with anxiety and uncer-tainty. The dramatist, I suspect, loves and pities Henry here.

Falstaff's sceptical Nominalism is the real *philosophical* opposition to Henry's strangely ethical *Realpolitik*, his white Machiavellianism. The conflict is much subtler than the usual collision between high-flown martial rhetoric and cynical self-interest. The Prince is saying, "I must involve thousands in bloodshed to prevent worse happening." Falstaff is saying, "I don't believe any of that; war is war; men die and all the grand language is sheer illusion."

Just as the Prince's eagerness for war with France is subject to facile condemnation from readers and auditors, so Falstaff's behaviour in the matter of recruiting is unintelligently condemned. Falstaff turns down two reasonably robust men, Mouldy and Bullcalf, because he gets three pounds apiece by doing so. He then heartlessly signs up Wart, Feeble, and Shadow, pathetic scarecrows. What possible justification can there conceivably be for this? Falstaff has given the justification in the words, "Food for powder; they'll fill a pit as well as better. Tush, man, mortal men, mortal men" (*1 Henry IV*, IV.ii.66–67). This is callous, but at the same time it is intellectually challenging. Would it really have been so much better to send strong young men to their deaths instead of these? In the bleak democracy of death why not take the odd kickback and spend the proceeds on a cheering drink? The words "mortal men, mortal men" are suddenly resonant. The standard syllogism of the Schools, "All men are mortal; Socrates is a man; therefore Socrates is mortal," collapses into an intuition of the blankly undifferentiated, undifferentiating character of that death that awaits us all, a radical truth that may make nonsense of the Prince's conscientious policy. As Maurice Morgann said, "Falstaff was a kind of military freethinker, and has accordingly incurred the obloquy of his condition."[22]

Falstaff is sceptical about the martial mystique of honour. The Prince, perhaps surprisingly, is not clearly against him. Falstaff's clear anti-type is the wild northerner, Hotspur, who despises poetry, loves fighting, and is caught up into a kind of ecstasy by the word "honor":

> methinks it were an easy leap,
> To pluck bright honor from the pale-fac'd moon,
> Or dive into the bottom of the deep,
> Where fadom-line could never touch the ground,
> And pluck up drowned honour by the locks.
> (*1 Henry IV*, I.iii.201–5)

The dizzy verticality of this, dropping from the moon, as it swims high above us in the night sky, down to the ocean floor, cuts across the complex horizontals of the play's political action. Hotspur, who will never grow old, is unimpeded by thoughts of means and ends, by worries about precedent and consequence. When Henry speaks of honour, we are in a different, more difficult world: "If it be a sin to covet honor, / I am the most offending soul alive" (*Henry V*, IV.iii.28–29). The context is one of mounting excitement before a battle. Henry is saying that he does not share Westmorland's wish that they had more men—the fewer the men, the greater the glory. This is stirring, but we seem to hear also a bat-squeak of doubt. Something in us wants to say, "Is he crazy?" That the speaker and the dramatist are conscious of this element is shown by the convoluted character of the sentence. The question, "Is it a sin?" is allowed to arise in the mind before it is firmly crushed. And we can scent in the self-deprecating confession, "I am the most offending soul alive" (= "I must plead guilty on that one!"), an attempt to manipulate the listener in a manner that would never occur to Hotspur. Henry is counting on the response, "Nonsense! Good for you!" but the "plain man" voice that we have learned to distrust here masks a far from plain engagement with the ethics of war. In detecting this troubling subtext I do not mean to erase the dominant, martial force of the speech.

> We few, we happy few, we band of brothers;
> . . . .
> And gentlemen in England, now a-bed,
> Will think themselves accurs'd they were not here.
>   (IV.iii.60, 64–65)

Words like these, from one facing likely death, still work with an amazing power that has survived all the anti-war poetry of the twentieth century. The thrill is real, and huge. It is also (more quietly) moving, because this is pure courage. But the speaker, unlike Hotspur, inhabits a clouded world. It is nonsense to say that Henry represents the Aristotelean mean between the extreme views of honour put forward by Falstaff and Hotspur. His position is much less clear than that. Two scenes earlier it has been made abundantly plain, both to Henry and to us, that it is just not true that every English soldier is happy to be there. Not all are buoyed by the honour of the enterprise. This is what emerged when the King, emotional eavesdropper that he is, was rash enough to go in disguise among the common soldiers.

The revealing accent of conciliation, the anxiety to be liked that can be heard as an implicit plea in "I am the most offending soul alive," is fully articulated in the nocturnal debate with the soldiers. Stephen Greenblatt argued that authority figures in Shakespeare operate by instilling anxiety in their subjects.[23] In fact, it is the kings who are anxious. They are the ones who cannot sleep at night. *Henry IV* opens with the King's insomnia. This is handed down, a sick inheritance, to the supremely successful Henry V. Henry moves unknown among his men and hungrily engages them in conversation. He falls in with John Bates, Alexander Court, and Michael Williams. This is the first time we have seen him talking on apparently equal terms with working-class persons. Students writing essays on the history plays often refer to the drinkers at the Boar's Head as "low company," and the expression is not wrong—but they are not as low as all that. Falstaff is a knight. Bardolph and the rest are hard to place socially, but they are not of the working class. They are alcoholic, decayed military men, a little like Captain Grimes in Evelyn Waugh's *Decline and Fall*. One can begin to feel, in the Boar's Head scenes, that the social divisions are indeed unbridgeable and that it is simply inconceivable that the Prince could ever talk to an ostler or a tapster otherwise than as to a servant. But now disguise makes a path for truth.

The first thing Henry says in an eagerly preemptive response to the sentry's challenge, is that he is their *friend* (IV.i.92). He then gambles (as it turns out, rashly) on their goodwill by suggesting that they are all in for a crushing defeat. He adds, with serpentine indirection, that it might be better not to communicate such fears to the King, who is after all only human and could in his turn dishearten the army. This is dangerous stuff. Obviously Henry has fears, wishes to have them exorcised, cannot obtain exorcism without explaining them, cannot explain them without a risk of—precisely—disheartening the army. In Shakespearean drama figures of authority sometimes pretend that terrible things are happening in order to bring out the glowing loyalty of the temporarily deceived subject. All ends happily with an "I did this but to try thee." Thus in *Macbeth* Malcolm pretends to be vicious in order to bring out the essential goodness of his (briefly horrified) servant, Macduff (IV.iii.1–137). Henry's talk of likely defeat looks like an "I did this but to try thee" that goes horribly wrong. When the disguised sovereign says, as he says here, "The King is but a man, as I am" (IV.i.101–2), there is a joke for the audience to pick up ("But this is the King; in saying 'a man, as I am' he isn't really asserting equality at all!") and, at the same time, an eager confession of real frail humanity ("I am just like you, really"). Bates says that although the King may put on a show of courage, he is sure that he would rather be up to his neck in the cold London river than where he is at present. The image of immersion in cold water, independent of the logic of the sentence, reinforces the idea of fear. The King answers with evident sincerity that he is sure the King would not wish to be anywhere but where he is. We believe him, but the exalted "happy band of brothers" tone of the St. Crispin's Day speech is implicitly subjected to an intense strain—before it has been delivered! Bates, who is not in any way presented as other than a good man, refuses to rise to the rhetorical bait: "Then I would he were here alone; so should he be sure to be ransomed, and a many poor men's lives saved" (IV.i.121–23). Henry, clearly shaken, says he is sure Bates cannot mean that. In an eerie moment of evasive self-projection he suggests that Bates must be talking in this way in order to "feel other men's minds," which is of course exactly what he, the King, is doing. He then stakes all, with the words, "Methinks I could not die any where so contented as in the King's company, his cause being just and his quarrel honorable" (IV.i.126–28). Honour again! Michael Williams's reply is utterly bleak: "That's more than we know." It is a rich man's war and a poor man's fight. Falstaff on the theme of honour exhibited what could be described as reductive philosophic wit. Williams and Bates have none of that. But their position is similarly sceptical. Bates's talk of the King being ransomed is wide of the mark in this case, but the assumption was reasonable. Bates and Williams agree, however, that, if the cause is not good, at least the King will bear the responsibility. It is here that Williams conjures a nightmare image, like something out of Grimmelshausen: a monstrous composite of maimed body parts, growing together and rising up to accuse the King at the latter day, "some swearing, some crying for a surgeon" (V.i.138). It is a hideously distorted pre-echo of the famous title page of Hobbes's *Leviathan*—no co-operative commonwealth, this. The reference to the surgeon, implicitly horrific in an age before anaesthetics, takes us back to Falstaff's dry observation that honour has no skill in surgery (*1 Henry IV*, V.i.133).

Henry replies casuistically: If a father sends his son on a voyage connected with the family business and the ship happens to sink, should we blame the father? The argument is not strong. The shipwreck was not foreseeable, and this absolves the father in the King's analogy. But when a ruler declares war on a large scale, death and maiming are not just foreseeable, they are virtual certainties. The soldiers are so far persuaded as to admit that they too carry a burden of possible sin in this war—not quite the happy bonding Henry had been working for. Of course the soldiers are not entirely fair to Henry, simply because they are imperfectly informed. Unable to bear the misconstruction of his motives, Henry says he is sure that the King would not be ransomed, adding that, if he were to be, then he'd never trust the King again. He is prevented by his disguise from swearing on the Bible that he will do no such thing, but nevertheless he is now engaged, as by a promise. Williams, entirely understandably, dismisses the proposition as claptrap: How could a common soldier ever challenge, on such a point? The ordinary soldiers will all be dead anyway. Henry is now very near the edge. He cannot argue openly. He declares that he has a quarrel with Williams and will wear a certain favour so that Williams can recognize him and challenge him later. Williams genially agrees to box his ears when the time comes. Bates has the last word. He tells them not to quarrel because they need now to be united against the common enemy. Bates, and only Bates, talks like a king.

Afterwards the real king, left alone, expostulates:

Upon the King! let us our lives, our souls,
Our debts, our careful wives,
Our children, and our sins lay on the King!
    (IV.i.230–32)

He did not win the argument, and now he sounds almost pettish. He knows that really they were not wrong. All does indeed rest on his shoulders: "We must bear all."

Once more I would guess that the dominant feeling in the dramatist is pity for the King at this point. Henry, the best actor of them all, was always the man with the common touch, the man who, while remaining at the deepest level utterly alone, could always create a warm bond with others. I have suggested that the "outside-in" causality of the earlier *Henry VI* plays is now replaced by a centrist causality, located in a single figure who can, alone, modify history. To be sure, while the *Henry VI* plays are earlier in composition, Shakespeare and his audience would have been conscious throughout of the fact that, historically, Henry V is the remoter, Henry VI the more recent figure. Perhaps the claims of "non-centrist" causality become stronger as the historical material is less remote from current political experience. But the figure of Henry V is not simple. It is itself doubled to meet the needs of the time. The rhetorically accelerating momentum of a group dynamic is now supplied by the outward, expertly put together aspect of Henry himself, the public societal self. He creates an apparent field of warmly co-operating persons, yet all this is exerted, with cold control, from a single originative subject. But now it is not working. Falstaffian scepticism rises up in other places to subvert the grand Henrician program. Falstaff, who loves Henry so much that his heart is broken by the final rejection, remains the fundamental, philosophical antagonist.

There is a wonderful postscript to the debate by night. Later in the play Williams and the King meet again, and Williams realizes that it was the King whose ears he had promised to box. It must be understood that according to the common usage of the time this alone is enough to doom him. Williams comports himself with steady courage. He never intended any offence, he says, to the King's majesty. The King replies witlessly, saying, in effect, "But you offended *me*." Williams answers, with obvious festering resentment, "Your Majesty came not like yourself. You appear'd to me but as a common man; . . . I beseech you take it for your own fault and not mine" (IV.viii.50–54). The audience holds its breath. But the King, instead of striking him, smiles broadly and gives him a glove full of money.

Anne Barton in an admirable essay sets this moment beside comparable episodes in Robert Greene's (?) *George a Greene, the Pinner of Wakefield*, George Peele's *Edward I*, and Thomas Heywood's *The First Part of King Edward IV*.[24] The general pattern, fed by Robin Hood legends, is that the King, incognito, falls in with social inferiors and is grossly insulted but reveals all and is jovially united at last with the accidentally delinquent party. What is distinctive about *Henry V*, as Barton saw, is that the jovial conclusion fails to materialize. Williams at the precise point at which his heart should be bursting with gratitude and loyalty, says, amazingly, "I will none of your money" (IV.viii.67).

All this works together to compose a sceptical counterpoint to the heroic theme of the play. But the dominant martial theme is still there, still the principal thing. Agincourt is certainly felt as a glorious triumph, against the odds. The King has succeeded and is a good king. Yet Shakespeare has allowed these subtle fault-lines to develop in the majestic structure. Indeed he insists on them. The exchange with Williams shows how even Henrician acting can go wrong, as Richard II's very different style of acting went wrong, so many years before.

I have called Henry "cold" and have stressed his status as a central agent, but there are strange oscillations and weakenings within that central agency. We have seen how real affection for Falstaff could break through at moments in the prolonged white-Machiavellian performance. Henry's need to be reassured on the night before the battle is nakedly, emotionally human. It is right that he be shown as vulnerable at this point. Machiavelli himself enjoyed debating the old question, whether it is better to be loved or to be feared (deciding, perhaps predictably, that fear is the safer bet).[25] Henry evidently wants to be loved, and to most of us this will seem more a redeeming feature than a weakness. One is tempted to say, paraphrasing Aristotle on the unsocial man, that the person who does not want to be loved is either a god or a beast.[26]

The *salus populi suprema lex*[27] argument that justified (?) the war on France could, if stretched to the limit, lead us into darker regions still. The behaviour of Prince John at Gaultree is such a region. Prince John promises solemnly that he will redress all the grievances of the rebels (*2 Henry IV*, IV.ii.59–60). The insurgents scatter:

> Like youthful steers unyok'd, they take their courses
> East, west, north, south, or, like a school broke up,
> Each hurries towards his home and sporting-place.
>   (IV.ii.103–5)

The familiar imagery expresses pure happiness. Prince John moves at once, coldly, to sentence the now defenceless rebels to death. Once more the talk is of honour. A rebel asks, "Is this proceeding just and honorable?" West-merland answers for the Prince, "Is your assembly so?" (IV.ii.110–11). The reply seems to concede, formally, that both sides have acted dishonourably. Hotspur's shining ideal is no longer available, to anyone now on the stage. Prince John meanwhile insists that he has not broken faith at all. He promised to redress the grievances and will do just that; he never promised to spare the lives of the insurgents themselves. The moral is clear: when you negotiate with Prince John, have your lawyer go through the small print (and when you sup with him, use a long spoon). Would the Elizabethans have been shocked by this? Portia in *The Merchant of Venice* shows a cast of mind not unlike Prince John's: "The contract allows you a pound of flesh but allows no blood." Portia's legal quibble draws warm assent, perhaps actual applause from the audience, but the matter is complicated by the fact that Shylock is here caught, deliciously, by his own legalism. A. R. Humphreys observed that the story of Cleomenes (who first agreed to a seven-day truce and then attacked swiftly by night, alleging that the agreement had mentioned days but not nights) was seen in the sixteenth century as a tale of dishonourable behaviour.[28] Samuel Johnson and A. C. Bradley both found the Gaultree episode horrifying.[29] But Utilitarian ethics, the principle of the greatest happiness of the greatest number, can perhaps save Prince John as a moral agent. The rebellion was potentially disastrous, in terms of the likely suffering it would cause, far worse, Jeremy Bentham would point out, than a broken promise or a misleading statement. If Shakespeare had wished to ram home the logic of white Machiavellianism in the person of Hal/Henry he would have placed him, not Prince John, behind this unlovable act. But the plot allows a displacement: let the younger brother do this one. Of course, "Delegate odious offices" is itself a Machiavellian injunction. But now Shakespeare is doing the delegating.

The great worry about formalism has vanished, notice, with the death of Richard II. That special horror of consciousness with its fatal capacity to arrest attention at the level of the word, of style, so that a glass wall is erected between the subject and reality, has now gone. Although Henry is an actor, because he plays not "the anointed King" but "the plain man" we do not *see* the acting, and in a way he doesn't see it either. The words uttered in *1* and *2 Henry IV* and *Henry V* are in consequence curiously free from that dramaturgical neurosis, formal self-consciousness. In the earlier work isolation caused the persons of the plays to introspect and to generate the reduplicative images of the self needed by introspection. Yet Henry, though he is both a player-king and more horribly alone than anyone else in Shakespeare except, perhaps, Hamlet,[30] has no leisure for radical introspection. He is after all a player-king only in that he is both a player and a king; he is not playing *at* being a king. His chosen role of affable humanity immediately involves him not only in relationships but in action. When he is in soliloquy we learn his frailty, his anxiety, his hesitation, but he never gazes at himself, in separation from action. It is all oddly practical.

A whole book could be written on the way the word "dream" is used by Shakespeare. Perhaps the strangest instance of the word is in the rejection of Falstaff. The new-made king says,

> I have long dreamt of such a kind of man,
> So surfeit-swell'd, so old, and so profane;
> But being awak'd, I do despise my dream.
> (*2 Henry IV*, V.v.49–51)

We shall come later to the place where Cleopatra, looking back, describes her love-vision of Antony as a dream inwardly stronger than common experience. The dream of the moonstruck lovers in a wood near Athens lies behind. Henry V is using—or thinks he is using—the word "dream" as a term of contempt. Regally (a little like Duke Theseus) he consigns Falstaff to a realm of unreality. Yet we can see Falstaff, whose heart is breaking as the King speaks. As in the earlier comedy the word "dream" has resonances unintended by the dismissive speaker. Savagely, the King insists that this "dream" was a nightmare (dreams are naturally nightmares for Hamlet—"In that sleep of death what dreams may come?" III.i.65): a vision of hideous greed, of physical and moral decay. But the audience knows that Falstaff is a figure of enchantment. He too is one who belongs to moonlit nights rather than to sour, political days: "Let us be Diana's foresters, gentlemen of the shade, minions of the moon" (*1 Henry IV*, I.ii.25–26). There is also about him the glow—one can almost say the glory—that will later invest Cleopatra's Antony. "His delights / Were dolphin-like" (*Antony and Cleopatra*, V.ii.88–89) describes Falstaff as well as it describes the rather better-looking Roman lover. The King is not wrong when he says that Falstaff is an aging, profane alcoholic, but it is one half of a reality the other half of which is stored with immense emotional power. Where the King is straightforwardly—almost absurdly—wrong is when he says that Falstaff was never real at all. It may be said that Henry is merely employing a figure of speech and is therefore not "wrong" in any meaningful sense of the word. But the King is at this moment erasing Falstaff, from his love, from the practical universe he has suddenly entered. Street beggars say the thing they cannot bear is to be treated by passers-by as if they did not exist, to be "looked through." The imposing sovereign who grandly consigns his old drinking companion to the category of illusion is, we cannot help noticing, at another level, "in denial."

There was a time in history when chivalry was unknown, when men were perhaps harder and more brutally practical than at any time before or since. Within a year or two of completing the two parts of *Henry IV*, perhaps while he was still working on *Henry V*, Shakespeare turned to the Roman world, and wrote *Julius Caesar*.

NOTES

1. A. P. Rossiter, *Angel with Horns* (London, 1961), 29ff.

2. Henry de Bracton, "Rex . . . sub Deo et sub lege, quia lex facit regem," *On the Laws and Customs of England* [*De legibus et consuetudinibus Angliae*], ed. and trans. Samuel E. Thorne, 4 vols. (Cambridge, Mass., 1968–77), 2:33. Scholars now think that Bracton was more the editor than the author of this work.

3. Thomas Aquinas, in the Blackfriars edition of the *Summa theologiae*, 61 vols. (London, 1953–80), 36:78–82.

4. Richard Hooker, *Ecclesiastical Polity*, VIII.ii.3, VIII.iii.1, in the Folger edition of *The Works of Richard Hooker*, ed. W. Speed Hill, 7 vols. in 8 (Cambridge, Mass., 1977–93), 3:332, 337.

5. William Tyndale, *Obedience of a Christian Man*, Scolar Press facsimile (Menston, 1970) of the 1528 edition (described as having been printed at "Malborowe" but really Antwerp), fol. 32v.

6. *The Two Books of Homilies* (Oxford, 1859), 557, 555.

7. See *Holinshed's Chronicles, R II, 1398–1400, H IV and H V* (Oxford, 1923), 33.

8. See Peter Ure's Arden edition of *Richard II* (London, 1966), lix.

9. Sir Gelly Merrick testified under examination that "the play was of King Henry the Fourth, and of the killing of Richard the Second." It is overwhelmingly probable (but not certain) that the play performed was Shakespeare's *Richard II*. *See Calendar of State Papers (Domestic Series) Reign of Elizabeth, 1598–1601*, ed. M. A. E. Green, the Kraus Reprint (Nendeln, Liechtenstein, 1967), 575. For Devereux's identifying with Bullingbrook, see ibid., 555, 567. See also Andrew Gurr's updated edition of *Richard II* (Cambridge, 2003), 7.

10. *Richard III*, V.iii.183.

11. Walter Pater, *Appreciations* (London, 1910), 198.

12. E. H. Kantorowicz, *The King's Two Bodies: A Study in Mediaeval Political Theology* (Princeton, N.J., 1957)

13. Cf. Ovid, *Ars amatoria*, ii.313, *Si latet ars, prodest*.

14. I called him a "white Machiavel" in *A New Mimesis* (London, 1983), 147.

15. W. H. Auden, *The Dyer's Hand and Other Essays* (London, 1963), 205–6.

16. Niccolò Machiavelli, *Discorsi*, III.i, trans. Leslie J. Walker (Harmondsworth, 1970), 390–92. Near the end of *The Rape of Lucrece* Shakespeare tells how Brutus, at a crucial moment, threw off "the shallow habit / . . . wherein deep policy did him disguise" (lines 1814–15).

17. Tom McAlindon, "Perfect Answers: Religious Inquisition, Falstaffian Wit," *Shakespeare Survey*, 54 (2001), 100–107.

18. Maurice Morgann, *Essay on the Dramatic Character of Sir John Falstaff*, in Daniel A. Fineman, ed., *Maurice Morgann: Shakespearean Criticism* (Oxford; 1972), 192.

19. See pp. 9–10, above.

20. See Anselm's reply to Roscelin, canon of Compiègne, in J.-P. Migne, ed., *Patrologiae cursus completus; Series Latina*, 221 vols. (Paris, 1844–64), 158:col. 265.

21. Thomas More, *Utopia*, Book ii, in the edition by Edward Surtz and J. H. Hexter (New Haven, 1965), 158.

22. Morgann, *Essay on the Dramatic Character of Sir John Falstaff*, 182.

23. Stephen Greenblatt, *Shakespearean Negotiations: The Circulation of Social Energy in Renaissance England* (Oxford, 1988), 135ff.

24. Anne Barton, "The King Disguised," in Barton, *Essays, Mainly Shakespearean* (Cambridge, 1994), 207–33.

25. Niccolò Machiavelli, *The Prince*, trans. Harvey C. Mansfield (Chicago, 1998), 66.

26. Aristotle, *Politics*, 1253a.

27. "The well-being of the people is the highest law."

28. See B. de Locque, *Discourses of Warre and Single Combat*, trans. John Eliot (London, 1591), 33, and A. R. Humphreys's Arden edition of *2 Henry IV* (London, 1966), 33.

29. See Samuel Johnson's note to *2 Henry IV*, IV.ii.122, and A. C. Bradley, *Oxford Lectures on Poetry* (London, 1965), 256.

30. Hamlet has company, but it is not unambiguously welcome. He is haunted by a dead king.

Chronology

1564	William Shakespeare christened at Stratford-on-Avon April 26.
1582	Marries Anne Hathaway in November.
1583	Daughter Susanna born, baptized on May 26.
1585	Twins Hamnet and Judith born, baptized on February 2.
1587	Shakespeare goes to London, without family.
1589–90	*Henry VI, Part 1* written.
1590–91	*Henry VI, Part 2* and *Henry VI, Part 3* written.
1592–93	*Richard III* and *The Two Gentlemen of Verona* written.
1593	Publication of *Venus and Adonis*, dedicated to the Earl of Southampton; the *Sonnets* probably begun.
1593	*The Comedy of Errors* written.
1593–94	Publication of *The Rape of Lucrece*, also dedicated to the Earl of Southampton. *Titus Andronicus* and *The Taming of the Shrew* written.
1594–95	*Love's Labour's Lost, King John*, and *Richard II* written.
1595–96	*Romeo and Juliet* and *A Midsummer Night's Dream* written.
1596	Son Hamnet dies.

1596–97	*The Merchant of Venice* and *Henry IV, Part 1* written; purchases New Place in Stratford.
1597–98	*The Merry Wives of Windsor* and *Henry IV, Part 2* written.
1598–99	*Much Ado About Nothing* written.
1599	*Henry V, Julius Caesar,* and *As You Like It* written.
1600–01	*Hamlet* written.
1601	*The Phoenix and the Turtle* written; father dies.
1601–02	*Twelfth Night* and *Troilus and Cressida* written.
1602–03	*All's Well That Ends Well* written.
1603	Shakespeare's company becomes the King's Men.
1604	*Measure for Measure* and *Othello* written.
1605	*King Lear* written.
1606	*Macbeth* and *Antony and Cleopatra* written.
1607	Marriage of daughter Susanna on June 5.
1607–08	*Coriolanus, Timon of Athens,* and *Pericles* written.
1608	Mother dies.
1609	Publication, probably unauthorized, of the quarto edition of the *Sonnets.*
1609–10	*Cymbeline* written.
1610–11	*The Winter's Tale* written.
1611	*The Tempest* written. Shakespeare returns to Stratford, where he will live until his death.
1612	*A Funeral Elegy* written.
1612–13	*Henry VIII* written; The Globe Theatre destroyed by fire.
1613	*The Two Noble Kinsmen* written (with John Fletcher).
1616	Daughter Judith marries on February 10; Shakespeare dies April 23.
1623	Publication of the First Folio edition of Shakespeare's plays.

Contributors

HAROLD BLOOM is Sterling Professor of the Humanities at Yale University. He is the author of 30 books, including *Shelley's Mythmaking, The Visionary Company, Blake's Apocalypse, Yeats, A Map of Misreading, Kabbalah and Criticism, Agon: Toward a Theory of Revisionism, The American Religion, The Western Canon,* and *Omens of Millennium: The Gnosis of Angels, Dreams, and Resurrection. The Anxiety of Influence* sets forth Professor Bloom's provocative theory of the literary relationships between the great writers and their predecessors. His most recent books include *Shakespeare: The Invention of the Human,* a 1998 National Book Award finalist, *How to Read and Why, Genius: A Mosaic of One Hundred Exemplary Creative Minds, Hamlet: Poem Unlimited, Where Shall Wisdom Be Found?,* and *Jesus and Yahweh: The Names Divine.* In 1999, Professor Bloom received the prestigious American Academy of Arts and Letters Gold Medal for Criticism. He has also received the International Prize of Catalonia, the Alfonso Reyes Prize of Mexico, and the Hans Christian Andersen Bicentennial Prize of Denmark.

NORTHROP FRYE was University Professor at the University of Toronto and also a professor of English in Victoria College at the University of Toronto for many years. He wrote numerous books, including the seminal work *Anatomy of Criticism.*

KIRBY FARRELL is a professor at the University of Massachusetts, Amherst. He is the author of *Play Death and Heroism in Shakespeare, Shakespeare's Creation,* and other early modern studies. He also has published several novels and is an editor of *English Literary Renaissance.*

217

SHERMAN HAWKINS is an emeritus professor of Wesleyan University. He is a Shakespeare scholar, the author of *Religious Patterning in Shakespeare's Major Tragedies*, editor of *Seven Princeton Poets*, and has also acted in Shakespeare plays.

MAURICE CHARNEY, emeritus professor at Rutgers University, teaches at the New School. He is former president of the Shakespeare Association of America and Academy of Literary Studies and author of *Shakespeare on Love & Lust, Shakespearean Comedy*, and other titles.

HARRY LEVIN was a professor of comparative literature at Harvard University and is considered one of the founders of the field of comparative literature in the United States. He wrote on such varied subjects as William Shakespeare, comedy, modernism, and the Renaissance. Some of his major works include *The Myth of the Golden Age in the Renaissance* and *Shakespeare and the Revolution of the Times*.

ALEXANDER LEGGATT retired from the University of Toronto as a professor of English. He has done much work on Shakespeare, including authoring *Shakespeare's Tragedies: Violation and Identity* and editing *The Cambridge Companion to Shakespearean Comedy*.

HARRY BERGER JR. is professor emeritus of literature and art history at the University of California, Santa Cruz, of which he also is a founding faculty member. He taught a variety of subjects under the general category of culture theory and Renaissance culture, including Renaissance drama and Shakespeare. He is the author of numerous books, among them *Imaginary Audition: Shakespeare on Stage and Page*.

A.D. NUTTALL was a professor of English at Oxford University. He was the author of numerous books, including *A New Mimesis: Shakespeare and the Representation of Reality* and *Two Concepts of Allegory: A Study of Shakespeare's* The Tempest.

Bibliography

Andrews, Michael Cameron. *This Action of Our Death: The Performance of Death in English Renaissance Drama*. Newark: University of Delaware Press; London and Toronto: Associated University Presses, 1989.

Ansari, A.A. "Political Man in Shakespeare's English History Plays." *Aligarh Journal of English Studies* 9, no. 1 (1984): 10–42.

Batson, Beatrice, ed. *Shakespeare's Second Historical Tetralogy: Some Christian Features*. West Cornwall, Conn.: Locust Hill Press, 2004.

Blanpied, John W. *Time and the Artist in Shakespeare's English Histories*. Newark: University of Delaware Press; London and Toronto: Associated University Presses, 1983.

Bloom, Harold. *Shakespeare: The Invention of the Human*. New York: Riverhead Books, 1998.

Bolton, W.F. *Shakespeare's English: Language in the History Plays*. Cambridge, Mass.: B. Blackwell, 1992.

Bradshaw, Graham. *Misrepresentations: Shakespeare and the Materialists*. Ithaca, N.Y.: Cornell University Press, 1993.

———. *Shakespeare's Scepticism*. New York: St. Martin's Press, 1987.

Candido, Joseph. "Once More into the Play: Beginning the Sequel in Shakespeare's History Plays." In *Entering the Maze: Shakespeare's Art of Beginning*, edited by Robert F. Willson Jr., pp. 55–73. New York: Peter Lang, 1995.

Cavanagh, Dermot, Stuart Hampton-Reeves, and Stephen Longstaffe, ed. *Shakespeare's Histories and Counter-Histories*. Manchester: Manchester University Press, 2006.

Chaudhury, Sarbani. "Public Relations and Persona Projection in Shakespeare's History Plays." *Journal of the Department of English* (Calcutta) 25, nos. 1–2 (1995–96): 31–7.

Cohen, Derek. *Shakespeare's Culture of Violence*. New York: St. Martin's Press, 1993.

Coursen, H.R. *The Leasing Out of England: Shakespeare's Second Henriad*. Washington, D.C.: University Press of America, 1982.

Cox, John D. "Shakespeare and Political Philosophy." *Philosophy and Literature* 26 (2002): 107–24.

Diede, Martha Kalnin. *Shakespeare's Knowledgeable Body*. New York; Frankfurt: Lang, 2008.

Empson, William. *Essays on Shakespeare*, edited by David B. Pirie. Cambridge [Cambridgeshire]; New York: Cambridge University Press, 1986.

Fischer, Sandra K. "'He means to pay': Value and Metaphor in the Lancastrian Tetralogy." *Shakespeare Quarterly* 40 (1989): 149–64.

Garber, Marjorie. "'What's Past Is Prologue': Temporality and Prophecy in Shakespeare's History Plays." In *Renaissance Genres: Essays on Theory, History, and Interpretation*, edited by Barbara Kiefer Lewalski, pp. 301–31. Cambridge: Harvard University Press, 1986.

———. *Shakespeare's Ghost Writers: Literature as Uncanny Causality*. New York: Methuen, 1987.

Grene, Nicholas. *Shakespeare's Serial History Plays*. Cambridge, U.K.; New York: Cambridge University Press, 2002.

Hawley, William M. *Critical Hermeneutics and Shakespeare's History Plays*. New York: Lang, 1992.

Hodgon, Barbara. *The End Crowns All: Closure and Contradiction in Shakespeare's History*. Princeton, N.J.: Princeton University Press, 1991.

Holderness, Graham. *Shakespeare's History*. Dublin: Gill and Macmillan; New York: St. Martin's Press, 1985.

Holderness, Graham, ed. *Shakespeare's History Plays: Richard II to Henry V*. New York: St. Martin's Press, 1992.

Holderness, Graham; Banks, Carol. "Bravehearts: Images of Masculinity in Shakespeare's History Plays." *Parergon*, new series, 15 (1997): 137–60.

Holstun, James. "Damned Commotion: Riot and Rebellion in Shakespeare's Histories." In *A Companion to Shakespeare's Works*, edited by Richard Dutton and Jean E. Howard, pp. 194–219. Malden, Mass.: Blackwell, 2003.

Honigmann, E.A.J. *British Academy Shakespeare Lectures 1980–89*. Oxford: Published for the British Academy by Oxford University Press, 1993.

Huang, Bikang. *Politics in Form: Imagery and Ideology in Shakespeare's History Plays*. Beijing: Peking University Press, 2000.

Hunt, Maurice. "The Conversion of Opposites and Tragedy in Shakespeare's *Richard II.*" *Explorations in Renaissance Culture* 25 (1999): 1–18.

———. "The Hybrid Reformations of Shakespeare's Second Henriad." *Comparative Drama* 32 (1998–99): 176–206.

———. "The Politics of Vision in Shakespeare's *1 Henry VI.*" *South Central Review* 19, no. 1 (2002): 76–101.

———. "Shakespeare's *King Richard III* and the Problematics of Tudor Bastardy." *Papers on Language and Literature* 33 (1997): 115–41.

———. "Unnaturalness in Shakespeare's *3 Henry VI.*" *English Studies* 80 (1999): 146–67.

Hutson, Lorna. *The Invention of Suspicion: Law and Mimesis in Shakespeare and Renaissance Drama.* Oxford, England: Oxford University Press, 2007.

Iser, Wolfgang. *Staging Politics: The Lasting Impact of Shakespeare's Histories,* translated from the German by David Henry Wilson. New York: Columbia University Press, 1993.

Jones, Robert C. *These Valiant Dead: Renewing the Past in Shakespeare's Histories.* Iowa City: University of Iowa Press, 1991.

Kermode, Frank. *Shakespeare's Language.* London: Allen Lane, 2007.

Leggatt, Alexander. *Shakespeare's Political Drama: The History Plays and the Roman Plays.* London; New York: Routledge, 1988.

Levin, Harry. *Scenes from Shakespeare,* edited by Gwynne B. Evans. New York: Garland, 2000.

———. "Two Tents on Bosworth Field: *Richard III,* V, iii, iv, v." *Canadian Review of Comparative Literature* 18 (1991): 199–216.

Marx, Steven. "Shakespeare's Pacifism." *Renaissance Quarterly* 45 (1992): 49–95.

Moseley, C.W.R.D. *Shakespeare's History Plays: Richard II to Henry V: The Making of a King.* London: Penguin, 1988.

Muir, Kenneth. *Shakespeare's Didactic Art.* St. John's, Newfoundland: Memorial University, 1984.

Norwich, John Julius. *Shakespeare's Kings: The Great Plays and the History of England in the Middle Ages, 1337–1485.* New York: Scribner, 1999.

Nuttall, A.D. *A New Mimesis: Shakespeare and the Representation of Reality.* New ed. New Haven, Conn.; London: Yale University Press, 2007.

Pearlman, E. *William Shakespeare: The History Plays.* New York: Twayne; Toronto: Maxwell Macmillan Canada, 1992.

Saccio, Peter. *Shakespeare's English Kings: History, Chronicle, and Drama.* 2nd ed. Oxford; New York: Oxford University Press, 2000.

Siegel, Paul N. *Shakespeare's English and Roman History Plays: A Marxist Approach.* Rutherford: Fairleigh Dickinson University Press, 1986.

Spiekerman, Tim. *Shakespeare's Political Realism: The English History Plays*. Albany: State University of New York Press, 2001.

Thayer, C.G. *Shakespearean Politics: Government and Misgovernment in the Great Histories*. Athens and London: Ohio University Press, 1983.

Watt, R.J.C., ed. *Shakespeare's History Plays*. London; New York: Longman, 2002.

Acknowledgments

Northrop Frye, "The Bolingbroke Plays (*Richard II, Henry IV*)." From *Northrop Frye on Shakespeare*, edited by Robert Sandler, published by Yale University Press. Copyright © 1986 by Northrop Frye. Reprinted by permission.

Kirby Farrell, "Prophetic Behavior in Shakespeare's Histories." From *Shakespeare Studies* 19 (1987): 17–40. Copyright © 1987 by Associated University Presses.

Sherman Hawkins, "Structural Pattern in Shakespeare's Histories." From *Studies in Philology* vol. 88, no. 1 (Winter 1991): 16–45. Copyright © 1991 by University of North Carolina Press. Used by permission of the publisher. www.uncpress.unc.edu

Maurice Charney, "*King John*." From *All of Shakespeare*. Copyright © 1993 by Columbia University Press. Reprinted with permission of the publisher.

Harry Levin, "Sitting upon the Ground (*Richard II*, IV, I)." From *Shakespeare's Universe: Renaissance Ideas and Conventions: Essays in Honour of W. R. Elton*, edited by John M. Mucciolo with the assistance of Steven J. Doloff and Edward A. Rauchut and published by Scolar Press. Copyright © 1996 by the contributors.

Alexander Leggatt, "The Death of John Talbot." Excerpt from *Shakespeare's English Histories: A Quest for Form and Genre*, edited by John W. Velz. Medieval & Renaissance Texts & Studies, volume 133, Tempe, AZ, 1997. Copyright Arizona Board of Regents for Arizona State University. Reprinted with permission.

Harry Berger Jr., "Food for Words: Hotspur and the Discourse of Honor." From *Making Trifles of Terrors: Redistributing Complicities in Shakespeare*, edited by Peter Erickson. Copyright © 1997 by the Board of Trustees of the Leland Stanford Jr. University. With the permission of Stanford University Press, www.sup.org

A.D. Nuttall, "The Major Histories." From *Shakespeare the Thinker*, published by Yale University Press. © 2007 by A.D. Nuttall. All rights reserved by the estate of A.D. Nuttall, c/o Writers Representatives LLC, New York, NY.

Index

Italic type is used for titles of plays (*Richard III)* to distinguish them from the actual persons in plain type (Henry (*Henry V*). Numbers in parenthesis indicate the part (*Henry IV* (1)).Characters are listed followed by the play in which they appear.

absolutism, 69, 87, 189–190
Actaeon theme, 152–153, 177–178
Agincourt, battle of, 108, 112, 200
Aquinas, Thomas, 187
Aristotle, on courage, 148, 150
Arthur (*King John)*, 93, 98–99
Auden, W.H., on Falstaff, 3
Aumerle (Edward, *Richard II*), 18, 22, 25–26, 30

Bastard (*King John)*
    final speech of, 94, 101
    Hubert and, 95, 98–100
    patriotism of, 96–98
    precursor to Falstaff, 4
    virtual abdication by John to, 94
    witty bravado of, 95–96, 101
Bloom, Harold, 1–15
    Falstaffiad, as center of
        Shakespeare's work, 1–2
    Henry IV (*1&2*), 1–8
    Richard II, 11–15
    Richard III, 8–11
    See also Falstaff, Sir John (*Henry IV 1&2)*
Bolingbroke. *See* Henry Bolingbroke

Bolingbroke plays, sequence of, 17
Bourdieu, Pierre, 143–144
Bracton, Henry de, 187
Bradley, A.C., on Falstaff, 2
Buchanan, George, 188
Bullingbrook. *See* Henry
    Bolingbroke

Cain, imagery of, 24–25, 26
Civil Wars (Daniel), 106
Comedy of Errors, The, 181, 191–192
Confessions (St. Augustine), 57–58
Constance of Brittany (*King John)*, 93, 98

Daniel, Samuel, 106
De jure regni (1571) (Buchanan), 188
death of John Talbot, 123–139
    as rite of passage, 127–128, 129
    death of John foreordained, 125–126
    division of Shakespeare's plays, 123–124
    father and son bound together, 125–126, 130–131, 137–138
    foreshadowing of death, 125

Joan and shepherd, 132–133
Joan rejected by John, 128
Orleans and, 128–129
paradox of, 126–127, 137
parent-child configuration and,
    134
Shakespeare's later work and,
    125, 129, 130
Talbot-John relationship
    variations, 134–136
Titus Andronicus and, 138–139
Towton allegory and, 137–138
See also *Henry VI* trilogy
*Defensative against the Poyson of
    Supposed Prophecies* (Howard), 53
Doctor Faustus (Marlowe), 192
Doll Tearsheet (*Henry IV (1&2)*), 40
dream, as used by Shakespeare, 212
dual myths of two tetralogies
    framework of, 103–104
    Henry VI versus *Richard II*, 70–71
    Henry VI versus *Richard III*,
        70–71
    Richard II versus *Henry V*, 70–71

Edmund, Duke of York, 18
Edward II (Marlowe), 14–15, 107
Elinor (*King John*), 98
Elizabeth I
    Richard II and, 189–190
    William Hacket and, 52
Empson, William, on ambiguity of
    Falstaff, 4–5
Evans, Maurice, 120–121
Exton (*Richard II*), 25, 118, 130–131

Fall of Princes (Lygate), 105
Falstaff, Sir John (*Henry IV 1&2*),
    200–201
    Actaeon Club and, 152–153
    ambiguity of, 4–5
    as parody father of Hal, 33
    as reason for *Part 2*, 40
    as time-blocking figure, 38
    complexity of, 35–36

demise foretold by Hal, 59–60
dualism of, 3
first remark on time, 38
Hamlet and, 3, 4, 7, 8
on honor, 201–202, 208
hopes of being King Henry's
    right-hand man, 41
immanence of, 3–4
Johnson on, 3
Lazarus and, 6
love for Prince Hal, 3, 4–5, 37,
    200–201, 209
originality of, 7–8
play on words by, 151–152
rejection of by Henry, 2, 6–7,
    40–41, 199, 209, 212
Shakespeare's histories and, 2
skepticism of war and, 205
weak spots in, 36–37
See also Bloom, Harold
*Famous Victories of Henry the Fifth,
    The*, 37
Faulconbridge (*King John*). See
    Bastard (*King John*)
food for words. See words, food for
fourteenth-century calamities,
    107–108

Gadshill (*Henry IV (1)*), 150–151,
    201
garden, imagery of, 112
Gaultree episode in *Henry IV (2)*, 24,
    40–42, 61–62, 210–211
Geoffrey (*King John*), 98
Gielgud, John, 120–121
gift, discourse on, 143
Goddard, Harold, 2

Hacket, William, 52
Harry Percy. See Hotspur
Hastings (*Richard III*), prediction of
    own death, 46, 58
"Henriad," 81–83
Henry (*Henry V*)
    "good king," 69–70

Henry VI and, 80–81
on honor, 69
marriage proposal of, 200
Henry *(Henry VI* trilogy)
compared to Henry IV, 80–81
Henry V and, 80–81
Richard II and, 70–71
Richard III and, 70–71
Henry Bolingbroke (later Henry IV)
(Richard II)
as usurper, 18, 22
central character in four plays, 17
closing lines of *Richard II*, 20
denouncement of, 22
expatriation of, 109
inscrutability and, 26–27, 38–39
motives of, 22, 107, 109, 184–185
sentencing of, 24–25
son of John of Gaunt, 18, 184
style of, 184–85
symmetricality of, 24, 25
triumphal entry of, 195–196
versus Mobray, 182–184
See also Henry IV (1&2)
Henry IV (1), act 2, scene 3
summary of scene, 170–171
Actaeonic futility in Hotspur's
speech, 177–178
Hotspur's evasive response to
wife, 176–177
Lady Percy's complaints, 173–176
opening soliloquy of, 171–173
Henry IV (1&2)
(1) act 2, scene 4, 39
(1) death of Henry, 41, 164
(1) end of Part 1, 41
(1) forms of death opposed in,
158
(1) Henry as "cold," 210
(1) *Henry IV* (2) compared to, 83
(1) Henry's insult to Hotspur,
153–156
(1) opening scenes of, 32–33
(1) prose and, 32
(2) Falstaff reason for, 40

(2) Gaultree episode, 24, 40–42,
61–62, 210–211
(2) literary sequence of, 68–69
(2) prescience deflated, 59–60
(2) trickery in, 41–42
(1&2) as "dylogy," 200
(1&2) formalism absent from,
211–212
(1&2) sources for, 37
Bloom on, 1–8
See also Falstaff, Sir John (*Henry
IV 1&2*); Henry Bolingbroke;
Henry IV (1), act 2, scene 3;
Prince Hal
Henry V
act 1, scene 2 of, 203–204
act 2, scene 4 of, 204
compositional order of, 209
Falstaff excluded from, 2
Falstaff's death, 200
Henry disguised as soldier, 108,
206–210
Henry VI (1) and, 84–87
Henry's marriage proposal to
French princess, 200
Henry's popularity, 206–210
Hotspur and wheel of fortune,
37–38
opening scene of, 100–101
Henry VI trilogy
(1) act 1, scene 3, 183
(1) compositional order of, 209
(1) *Henry V* and, 84–87
(1) literary sequence of, 69
(1) opening scene of, 130
(1) rose-picking scene in, 184, 186
(1) Talbot's heroism in, 74, 124–
125, 132
(1) Wars of the Roses and, 181
(2) death dominates end of, 134
(2) deaths of Glaucester and
Suffolk, 124
(2) *Henry IV (2)* compared to, 83
(2) Jack Cade and, 133–134
(2) lessons taught by, 73–74

(3) Constance of Brittany and, 93
(3) death scenes of, 134–135
(3) murder of Edward, 83
(3) predictions on Richard III, 51
(3) publication of, 123
(3) Towton allegory and, 137
tragedy as well as history, 123–124, 138
writing of, 130
See also death of John Talbot; Henry (*Henry VI* trilogy)
honor, gift exchange and, 143–146
Hotspur (*Henry IV (1)*)
Actaeonic futility expressed by, 153, 177–178
aggression of, 55
Bolingbroke and, 110
conciliatory tone of, 154–155
death of, 41, 162–163
end of scene 1 and, 153–154
evasive response to wife by, 176–177
fatalism of, 58
Glendower and, 158–159, 162
guns and, 157–158, 160
Henry's insult to, 153–156
leadership of, 33
Mortimer and, 156–157, 161–162, 163–164
persona of, 34–35
on pursuit of honor, 169–170, 205–206
"theme of honor's tongue . . . ," 146–147
tragic fate of, 74
underdog role of, 168–169
See also Henry IV (1), act 2, scene 3
Hotspur (*Henry V*), wheel of fortune and, 37–38
Howard, Henry, 53
Hubert (*King John*), 95, 98–100
hypocrite and person, 24, 29

imagery
Cain, 24–25, 26

gardens, 112
mirror, 29–30, 110, 116–117, 192
night/day imagery, 111
wheel of fortune, 25–26, 37–38
intermarriage of English royalty, *16t*, 17–19
introduction, 1–15

Jack Cade (*Henry VI (2)*), 133–134
Jerusalem, significance of, 57–58, 60
Jew of Malta (Marlowe), 23
John of Gaunt (*Richard II*)
on absolutism, 189
character of, 21
deathbed speech of, 27–28, 107, 109, 111, 122, 186–187
father of Bolingbroke, 18, 169, 184
property seized by Richard, 22
Richard's complicity in Gloucester murder told by, 182–183
theme of crusade and, 23
John Talbot *(Henry VI (1))*. *See* death of John Talbot
Johnson, Samuel, 3, 14
Jorgensen, Paul A., 147–149, 154
Justice Shallow (*Henry IV (1&2)*), 40–41

Kantorowicz, E.H., 27, 193
King John
anti-Catholic issues in, 93, 101
background of, 93
conclusion of, 101
confusion surrounding, 93, 101
dating of, 94
death of John, 98
See also specific names of characters
King's Two Bodies, The (Kantorowicz), 13, 27, 193
kingship, conceptions of, 187–188, 190–191

Lady Anne (*Richard III*), predictions of, 45, 46

Lady Blanch (*King John*), 95
Lady Percy (*Henry IV (1)*), 166
Lambarde, William, 190
Lancastrian house of royal family,
    18, 184
leadership, nature of, 23
Lewis (*King John*), 94, 95
Life and Death of King John, The, 4
    See also King John
Lives (Plutarch), 75
Lygate, John, 105

Machiavellianism, 23, 59, 197–199,
    205, 209, 211
Marlowe, Christopher, 14–15, 23,
    107, 192
masks in ancient times, 24, 29
Merchant of Venice, The, 211
Merry Wives of Windsor, The, Falstaff
    and, 4, 152
Midsummer Night's Dream, A, 152,
    181, 202
Mirror for Magistrates, A, 105–106,
    185
mirror imagery, 29–30, 110, 192
Mistress Quickly (*Henry IV 1&2*),
    40
Mobray (*Richard II*), 23, 24–25, 183
Mortimer (*Henry IV (1)*), 156–157,
    161–162, 163–165, 168

Neville, William
    cloak of invisibility and, 44, 63n2
    predictions of, 43–45
    wizards and, 43–44, 52–53
New Mimesis, A, (Nuttall), 11–12,
    200
Northumberland (*Henry IV (1)*), 166
Northumberland (*Richard II*), 115–
    116, 117, 169
nothing, double meaning of, 31
Nuttall, A.D., 11–12, 200

Obedience of a Christian Man
    (Tyndale), 188

Oldcastle. *See* Falstaff, Sir John
Outline of a Theory of Practice
    (Bourdieu), 143
Owen Glendower (*Henry IV 1&2*),
    34, 55, 64n10, 158–160

Pandulph (*King John*), 94
Peasants' Revolt, 22, 108
philosophy, medieval, 202–203
Pistol (*Henry IV (1&2)*), 40
Plutarch, 75
poetry of Richard II, 12–14, 28,
    184–185, 188, 193–195
Prince, The (Machiavelli), 23
Prince Hal (*Henry IV 1&2*)
    in act 2, scene 4, 39
    aloofness and, 26
    atonement speech of, 56
    central character, 33
    confidence expressed by, 37
    early soliloquy of, 197–199
    father's crown and, 41
    Hotspur and, 33
    humbling of self to father, 56–57
    linked with Iago, 197
    pledge fulfilled from *Part 1*, 57,
        63
    prophetic behavior of, 58–59
    rise of, 196–197, 199–200, 203
    self-validating prophecy of, 53–55
    style of, 196
    See also Falstaff, Sir John
Prince Henry. *See* Prince Hal
Prince John (*Henry IV (2)*), 40, 41,
    61, 210–211
prophecy in Shakespeare, 47–49
prophetic behavior in histories,
    43–66
    Henry IV, 56, 59–60, 61
    Henry V, 53–56
    Henry VI, 50–51
    Henry VIII, 48
    Lady Anne and, 45, 46
    naturalness of, 45, 64n6
    Neville and, 43–44

Prince Hal and, 33, 59
Richard III, 45–50, 51, 53, 59
understanding use of prophecies,
    61–63

Richard *(Richard II)*
    abdication scene, 29
    as God's anointed, 188–189
    central character, 29
    character of, 11–15, 21–22, 27,
        185–186, 190–191, 195
    death of, 25, 122, 193–195
    detachment of, 185
    introversion of, 28, 110–111
    John of Gaunt and, 27–28,
        186–187
    Marlowe and, 15
    marriages of, 111–112
    mirror scene, 30, 110, 116–117,
        192
    poetry of, 12–14, 28, 184–185,
        188, 193–195
    prison speech of, 30–32
    self-pitying monologues by,
        109–110
Richard "Crookback" *(Richard III)*
    archetype of arch villain, 104
    as hero-villain, 10–11
    "bad king," 69–70
    career of, 60
    destiny coerced by, 49–50
    dying assault on "Richmonds,"
        49–50, 51
    Iago and, 9
    prophecies and, 47, 51–53
    self-hate of, 50, 193
Richard II
    abdication scene, 20, 113–116
    Bloom on, 11–15
    Bolingbroke versus Mowbray and,
        182–184
    central theme of, 21
    conclusion of, 117–118
    criticisms of, 119–120, 195
    crusade theme and, 23, 32

    dating of, 94
    deposition scene of, 106–107
    Elizabeth I and, 189–190, 213n9
    Falstaff and anarchy, 73
    garden metaphor and, 112
    Henry VI compared to, 70–71
    Johnson on, 14
    lessons taught by, 73–74
    Marlowe and, 15, 111
    moral masochism and, 12
    night/day imagery in, 111
    opening scene of, 19, 108
    performances of, 120–121
    politics of Elizabethan era and,
        105
    revival in 1601, 113
    Richard III compared to, 77–80
    theme of beggar and king, 30
    tragedy as well as history, 15, 77,
        113
    in verse, 26, 32
    writing of, 19–20, 119
Richard II contrasted to Richard III,
    103–104
Richard III
    Bloom on, 8–11
    defeat of, 18
    Hastings and, 58–59
    Henry VI and, 70–71
    isolation of, 181
    opening scene of, 8–9, 51
    prophecy as self-revealing,
        45–46
    prophecy in face of death, 45
    Richard II compared to, 77–80
    tragedy as well as history, 69, 77
Richard III contrasted to Richard II,
    103–104
Richard the Lion-Hearted *(King
    John)*, 93
Richardson, Ralph, 4
Richmond *(Richard III)*
    "ordain'd" to kill king, 50–52
    predictions of kingship, 47, 48
    triumphant benediction of, 53, 63

sacredness of royal persons, 20–21,
  50–51
Shakespeare, William
  ambiguities exploited by, 62
  auditory appeal of, 148–149
  classical sources of political
    thought, 72
  demystification of history by, 63
  division of plays by, 123–124
  drama versus history, 23
  Machiavelli and, 23
  mastery of structural form by,
    89, 90
  prophetic behavior and, 63
  sources used by, 75
  tetralogies planned by, 74–76, 87
Shakespeare's History Plays (Tillyard),
  190
Shakespeare's Military World
  (Jorgensen), 147–149
Shaw, George Bernard, on Falstaff, 3
sources, classic, 37, 72, 75
structural pattern in histories, 67–92
  antithetical patterning of
    tetralogies, 83–84
  chiasmic patterning in two
    tetralogies, 77–78t
  comparison between usurpers,
    79–80
  compositional order and
    tetralogical form, 69–70
  dual myths and, 70–72
  Henry V and VI compared,
    80–83
  Henry VI versus *Henry V*, 84–87
  hereditary monarchy as setting,
    72
  incompleteness of, 87
  lessons taught, 73–74
  limited range of events produces
    repetition, 87–89
  models for second tetralogy,
    76–77
  overview, 67–69

planning of second tetralogy,
    74–76, 91n12
  Shakespeare's mastery of
    structural form, 89–90
  upward progress of second
    tetralogy, 73

Taming of the Shrew, The, 181
tetralogies, two. *See* dual myths of
  two tetralogies; structural pattern
  in histories
Thomas Mowbray (*Richard II*)
  analysis of speech to throne,
    141–143
  banishment of, 183
  Bolingbroke and, 24–25
Thomas of Woodstock (anon.), 19, 107,
  182, 183
Thomas of Woodstock (*Richard II*),
  24
Tillyard, E.M.W., 67, 68, 87, 121,
  190
time, role in Shakespeare, 38, 63
Titus Andronicus, 75, 91n16, 138–
  139
tragedies of Middle Ages, 105
Tragedy of Richard the Third, The, 9
  See also Richard III
*Troublesome Raigne of John King of
  England, The*, 94–95
Tudor myth of absolutism, 68, 69,
  87, 189–190
Two Gentlemen of Verona, The, 181
Tyndale, William, 188

Wars of the Roses, 18, 181, 183,
  184, 195
wheel of fortune, 25–26, 37–38
Woodstock, Thomas, 108
words, food for, 141–178
  See also Falstaff, Sir John (*Henry
    IV 1&2*); Hotspur

Yorkist line of royalty, 18